The Essential Talmud

THE ESSENTIAL TALMUD

Adin Steinsaltz

TRANSLATED FROM THE HEBREW BY

Chaya Galai

Weidenfeld and Nicolson

LONDON

Library of Congress Cataloging in Publication Data

Steinsalz, Adin.
    The essential Talmud.

    1. Talmud—Introductions.   I. Title.
BM503.5.S8   296.1'206'6   75-36384
ISBN 0-465-02060-7

Contents

[v]

Contents

PART THREE

Method

APPENDIX

PART ONE

History

1

What Is the Talmud?

IF THE BIBLE is the cornerstone of Judaism, then the Talmud is the central pillar, soaring up from the foundations and supporting the entire spiritual and intellectual edifice. In many ways the Talmud is the most important book in Jewish culture, the backbone of creativity and of national life. No other work has had a comparable influence on the theory and practice of Jewish life, shaping spiritual content and serving as a guide to conduct. The Jewish people have always been keenly aware that their continued survival and development depend on study of the Talmud, and those hostile to Judaism have also been cognizant of this fact. The book was reviled, slandered, and consigned to the flames countless times in the Middle Ages and has been subjected to similar indignities in the recent past as well. At times, talmudic study has been prohibited because it was abundantly clear that a Jewish society that ceased to study this work had no real hope of survival.

The formal definition of the Talmud is the summary of oral law that evolved after centuries of scholarly effort by sages who lived in Palestine and Babylonia until the beginning of the Middle Ages. It has two main components: the Mishnah, a book of *halakhah* (law) written in Hebrew; and the commentary on the Mishnah, known as the Talmud (or Gemarah), in the limited sense of the word, a summary of discussion and elucidations of the Mishnah written in Aramaic-Hebrew jargon.

This explanation, however, though formally correct, is misleading and imprecise. The Talmud is the repository of thousands of years of Jewish wisdom, and the oral law, which is as ancient and significant as the written law (the Torah), finds expression therein. It is a conglomerate of law, legend, and philosophy, a blend of unique logic and shrewd pragmatism, of history and science, anecdotes and humor. It is a collection of paradoxes: its framework is orderly and logical, every word and term subjected to meticulous editing, completed centuries after the actual work of composition came to an end; yet it is still based on free association, on a harnessing together of diverse ideas reminiscent of the modern stream-of-consciousness novel. Although its main objective is to interpret and comment on a book of law, it is, simultaneously, a work of art that goes beyond legislation and its practical application. And although the Talmud is, to this day, the primary source of Jewish law, it cannot be cited as an authority for purposes of ruling.

The Talmud treats abstract and totally unrealistic problems in the same manner in which it refers to the most prosaic facts of everyday life, yet succeeds in avoiding abstract terminology. Though based on the principles of tradition and the transmission of authority from generation to generation, it is unparalleled in its eagerness to question and reexamine convention and accepted views and to root out underlying causes. The talmudic method of discussion and demonstration tries to approximate mathematical precision, but without having recourse to mathematical or logical symbols.

The Talmud is best understood through analysis of the basic objectives of its authors and compilers. What were they aiming at, those thousands of sages who spent their lives in debate and

What Is the Talmud?

discussion in hundreds of large and small centers of learning? The key is to be found in the name of the work: Talmud (that is, study, learning). The Talmud is the embodiment of the great concept of *mitzvat talmud Torah*—the positive religious duty of studying Torah, of acquiring learning and wisdom, study which is its own end and reward. A certain talmudic sage who has left us nothing but his name and this one dictum had this to say on the subject: "Turn it and turn it again, for everything is contained in the Torah. Regard it and grow old in it and never abandon it, for there is no greater virtue."

Study of Torah undoubtedly serves numerous practical purposes, but these are not the crucial objectives. Study is not geared to the degree of importance or the practical potential of the problems discussed. Its main aim is learning itself. Likewise, knowledge of Torah is not an aid to observance of law but an end in itself. This does not mean that the Talmud is not concerned with the values contained in the material studied. On the contrary, it is stated emphatically that he who studies Torah and does not observe what he studies would better never have been born. A true scholar serves as a living example by his way of life and conduct. But this is part of the general outlook of the Talmud; for the student poring over the text, study has no other end but knowledge. Every subject pertaining to Torah, or to life as related to Torah, is worthy of consideration and analysis, and an attempt is always made to delve into the heart of the matter. In the course of study, the question of whether these analyses are of practical use is never raised. We often encounter in the Talmud protracted and vehement debates on various problems that try to examine the structure of the method and to elucidate the conclusions deriving from it. The scholars invested all this effort despite the fact that they knew the source itself had been rejected and was of no legislative significance. This approach also explains why we find debates on problems that were relevant in the distant past and were unlikely ever to arise again.

It sometimes occurs, of course, that problems or debates once thought impractical or irrelevant gain practical significance in some later age. This is a familiar phenomenon in the sphere of pure science. But this development is of little consequence to the talmudic student, as, from the outset, his sole objective has been to solve theoretical problems and to seek the truth.

The Talmud is ostensibly constructed along the lines of a legal tract, and many people commit the error of thinking that it is legal in essence. It treats the subjects with which it deals—basic *halakhah*, biblical verses, or traditions handed down by sages—as natural phenomena, components of objective reality. When a man has dealings with nature, he cannot claim that the subject does not appeal to him or is unworthy of perusal. There are, of course, varying degrees of importance to issues, but all are alike in that they *are*—they exist and note must be paid to them. When the talmudic sage examined an ancient tradition, he perceived it, above all, as a reality in itself, and whether binding on him or not, it was part of his world and could not be dismissed. When the scholars discuss a rejected idea or source, their attitude resembles that of the scientist contemplating an organism that has become extinct because of its inability to adapt itself to changing conditions. This organism has, in a manner of speaking, "failed" and died out, but this fact does not detract from its interest for the scientist as a subject of study.

One of the greatest historical controversies was that between the methods of the "houses" (schools) of Shammai and Hillel, which lasted for more than a century. It was eventually resolved in the famous dictum: "Both are the words of the living God, and the decision is in accordance with the House of Hillel." The fact that one method is preferred does not mean that the other is based on a misconception. It, too, is an expression of creativity and of "the words of the living God." When one of the sages ventured to say a certain theory was not to his liking, he was scolded by his colleagues, who informed him that it was wrong to say of Torah, "This is good and this is not." Such a view is analogous to the case of the scientist who is not permitted to say that a certain creature

What Is the Talmud?

seems to him "unappealing." This does not mean to imply that evaluations (even of appeal) should never be made; they should, however, be based on consciousness of the fact that no man has the right to judge or to determine that a certain object lacks beauty from the purely objective point of view.

This analogy between the natural world and Torah is ancient and was developed at length by the sages. One of its earliest expressions is the theory that just as an architect builds a house according to a blueprint, so the Holy One, Blessed be He, scanned his Torah in creating the world. According to this viewpoint, it follows that there must be a certain correlation between the world and Torah, the latter forming part of the essence of the natural world and not merely constituting external speculation on it. This way of thinking also engendered the view that no subject is too strange, remote, or bizarre to be studied.

The Talmud reflects so wide a range of interests because it is not a homogeneous work composed by a single author. When several people collaborate on a book, they have in mind a certain specific aim which lends the work character and direction. But the Talmud is the end result of the editing of the thoughts and sayings of many scholars over a long period, none of whom envisaged a final written work at the time. Their remarks were inspired by life, growing out of the problems submitted to them and the exchange of views between the various sages and their disciples. This is why we cannot discern a clear trend or a specific objective in the Talmud. Each debate is, to a large extent, independent of others and unique, and each subject is the focus of interest at the time it is being discussed. At the same time, the Talmud has an unmistakable and striking character of its own, which does not bear the imprint of an individual, or of the editors, but is collective, reflecting the quality of the Jewish people over a given period. Not only where the thousands of anonymous views are concerned, but also in cases where the identity of the author or proponent is known, the differences between individuals are blurred and the general spirit prevails. However violently two sages may differ, their shared traits and likemindedness must eventually become evident to the reader, who then discerns the overall unity that overcomes all differences.

Since the Talmud is concerned with subjects, ideas, and problems, there evolved over the centuries the custom of quoting various views in the present tense: "Abbaye says, Rabba says." This stylistic habit reflects the belief that the work is not merely a record of the opinions of the scholars of past ages, and it should not be judged by historical criteria. The talmudic sages themselves distinguished between personalities and periods (clarification of such questions is, in fact, an integral part of study), but the distinctions are only cited when strictly relevant and are not employed for evaluation and discussion. For these scholars time is not an ever-flowing stream in which the present always obliterates the past; it is understood organically as a living and developing essence, present and future being founded on the living past. Within this wide-ranging process, certain elements take on more stable form, while others, pertaining to the present, are flexible and much more changeable; the process as such, however, is based on faith in the vitality of each element, ancient as it may be, and the importance of its role in the never-ending, self-renewing work of creation.

This process of renewal is closely connected to the centrality of the query in the talmudic debate. To a certain extent, the entire Talmud is framed by questions and answers, and even when not explicitly formulated, questions constitute the background to every statement and interpretation. One of the most ancient methods of studying the Talmud attempted to reconstruct the question on the basis of the statement that served as a response. It is no coincidence that the Talmud contains so many words denoting questions, ranging from queries aimed at satisfying curiosity to questions that attempt to undermine the validity of the debated issue. The Talmud also differentiates between a fundamental query and a less basic inquiry, a question of principle and a marginal query. Voicing doubts is not only legitimate in the

What Is the Talmud?

Talmud, it is essential to study. To a certain degree, the rule is that any type of query is permissible and even desirable; the more the merrier. No inquiry is regarded as unfair or incorrect as long as it pertains to the issue and can cast light on some aspect of it. This is true not only of the Talmud itself but also of the way in which it is studied and perused. After absorbing the basic material, the student is expected to pose questions to himself and to others and to voice doubts and reservations. From this point of view, the Talmud is perhaps the only sacred book in all of world culture that permits and even encourages the student to question it.

This characteristic leads us to another aspect of the composition and study of the Talmud. It is impossible to arrive at external knowledge of this work. Any description of its subject matter or study methods must, inevitably, be superficial because of the Talmud's unique nature. True knowledge can only be attained through spiritual communion, and the student must participate intellectually and emotionally in the talmudic debate, himself becoming, to a certain degree, a creator.

2

The Oral Law—
The First Generations

SINCE ANCIENT TIMES the Jewish people have lived in accordance with the laws of the Mosaic code. For a number of generations, particularly in the days of the Judges and in the First Temple era (*ca.* 950–586 B.C.E.), these laws were not always strictly observed, but violation never reached such proportions that it implied rejection of this code in favor of some other legislative system. Though the people sometimes transgressed and were reproached by the prophets for their misdemeanors and sins, they continued to regard themselves as bound by insoluble ties to the body of law bestowed on them by divine revelation. This explains why Torah was studied and observed even in the most troubled and tragic eras. And almost from the first, the oral law, *Torah she-be-al-peh*, accompanied the written law, *Torah she-bi-khtav*.

We know very little of the origins and early development of the oral law, since information on cultural and spiritual life in the

The Oral Law—The First Generations

First Temple era is generally sparse. But from various hints in the Bible, we can ascertain how the oral law evolved to interpret and complement written legislation. It is clear, in principle, that every written code of law must be accompanied by an oral tradition. In the first place, the oral tradition is inherent in the very act of transmitting the use of words, in the very preservation and study of a language. Every idea, every word in the written law must be handed down from generation to generation and explained to the young. Where simple, everyday words are concerned, this occurs automatically, as part of the normal transmission of the living language, but there are always rarer words that call for special elucidation. Furthermore, even in the most conservative society, language evolves and changes and the written documents of one era may be unclear to the next generation. As long as the Jewish people spoke and wrote biblical Hebrew, the transmission was carried out with ease, but even then, a tradition, an "oral law," was needed to preserve the meaning of words. The basic, simple vocabulary was preserved over the centuries and never aroused controversy or misunderstandings. But less common words, for example, nouns denoting objects, plants, animals, and so forth were not always decipherable without the backing of an oral tradition.

Jewish scholars were obliged to admit relatively early that certain words in the Torah (Pentateuch)—the names of animals, for example—were unknown to them and that they were unable to identify them. In cases where words were not explained to the student by an elder who actually indicated the object and named it, their meaning could not be preserved for long. The basic task of the oral law, therefore, was to transmit the meaning of words. Some of these were easily understood, others were less clear. When the text of the Torah refers to "the boughs of thick trees" (Leviticus 23:40), for example, the term could be applied, linguistically speaking, to a number of botanical species. Thus, it was necessary for the parent or teacher to explain to the student that the reference was to the myrtle tree. Again, when the text speaks of *totafot* (phylacteries), the teachers of ancient times were obliged to explain that these were the same objects later known as *tefilin*. These elucidations, conveyed from one generation to the next, constituted a stage in the oral law that was crucial to understanding and, hence, to survival.

Other needs cropped up beyond this first stage, and one of these was definition of words and concepts recorded in the Torah. Values and customs inevitably changed and new problems arose, so that it became essential to define the precise meaning of certain words. For example, it is stated in the Ten Commandments that "the seventh day is the Sabbath of the Lord thy God; in it thou shalt do no labor" (Exodus 20:10). In every age this has immediately aroused a very practical question: how is labor to be defined? what does the definition encompass and what does it exclude? The Torah explicitly names certain labors that are prohibited on the Sabbath, such as plowing and harvesting, lighting a fire, and cooking and baking. But every generation posed its own queries on activities unfamiliar to previous generations. Again, if the text states: "Ye shall dwell in booths seven days" (Leviticus 23:42), the student must immediately ask himself how to define "booth." There are periods when the meaning of terms is common knowledge, because life is static and each generation emulates its predecessor, but queries on marginal cases and innovations arise in every age. Precise definition need not entail explicit legislation, but is derived from the ways in which people learn what should be done and how they should behave in various eventualities. The sages of each generation tried to give these traditions shape through a certain degree of generalization and abstraction.

Yet another important task of the oral law that went hand in hand with written law relates to laws based on popular customs or generally known facts that are not detailed in the biblical text and can only be learned through the oral tradition. When the Torah speaks of the slaughter of animals, for example, it says: "Thou shalt kill of thy herd and of thy flock . . . as I have commanded thee" (Deuteronomy 12:21), and the commandment referred to is related to this same oral tradition. If the text determines that a man divorcing his wife must write her a *sefer kritut* (bill of divorcement), the tacit assumption is that there are various ways in which a divorce may be written out and that such a bill of divorcement is a common phenomenon. All these facts belong within the domain of the "oral law," which must be handed down and memorized in order to help the community observe the precepts of the written law.

The need for formal transmission obviously increased as time went by. In the first generations after the divine revelation on Mount Sinai, the entire community knew the meaning and intention of each statement, and it would have been superfluous to engage in deliberate dissemination of such knowledge. In due course, the natural tendency of fathers to instruct their sons no longer sufficed, and education became a matter of deliberate and formal study. The young learned from their elders and teachers both the basic facts and their interpretation and elaboration, as well as how to turn theory into practice.

Thus we see that the Mosaic code, like any other body of law, required frameworks within which problems could be tackled, a living tradition that scholars erudite in both written and oral law were authorized and qualified to transmit to others. The Torah itself notes that there was a possibility that there would arise problems that could not be solved by mere perusal of the text and called for more expert knowledge. ". . . If there arise a matter too hard for thee in judgment between blood and blood, between plea and plea and between stroke and stroke, being matters of controversy within thy gates: then shalt thou arise and get thee up into the place which the Lord thy God shall choose. And thou shalt come unto the priests and the Levites and unto the judge that shall be in those days, and enquire; and they shall show thee the sentence of judgment" (Deuteronomy 17:8–9).

In the First Temple era we already find mention of *tofsei Torah* (those learned in Torah), people who engaged in study and interpretation of the law. At the beginning of the Second Temple era, when Ezra the Scribe read aloud to the people from the Torah (445 B.C.E), a group of Levites would stand at his side in order to expound the full significance of the text.

Ezra, who was a priest and scribe, is the first sage, of all those who studied and interpreted Torah and taught the people, to be identified by name. It was said of him that he was "a ready scribe in the law of Moses which the Lord God of Israel had given" (Ezekiel 7:6), and the task he undertook became the mission of all the teachers who came after him. "For Ezra had prepared his heart to seek the law of the Lord and to do it and to teach in Israel statutes and judgment" (Ezra 7:10). He was, therefore, the precursor of the age of the anonymous scribes, the period known in Jewish history as the era of the *Knesset Gedolah* (the Great Assembly).

This era, which corresponds approximately to the period of Persian rule over Palestine (*ca.* 539–332 B.C.E.), was not well chronicled. The exact nature of the Great Assembly is unclear; it may have been a permanent institution with legislative and executive powers, or merely the generic name for all the scholars of a given period. In fact, with few exceptions, the names of the sages and outstanding personalities of this age are unknown. The same cloud of obscurity envelops the activities of the members of the Great Assembly, and nothing is known of their conduct or methods. But, culturally and spiritually speaking, this period was a decisive one in the annals of the Jewish people. It gave Judaism its unique and well-defined spiritual framework, which has survived, despite changes and modifications, throughout the centuries in the Holy Land and the Diaspora. The work of the Great Assembly is linked to the activities of the sages of the time, who were known by the general appellation of *sofrim* (scribes) and, the Talmud says, were so called "because they counted all the letters in the Torah" (the world *sofer* in Hebrew means both "writer" and "counter"). This statement should not be understood in the narrow, literal sense. The members of the Great Assembly actually

The Oral Law—The First Generations

collected holy writings, decided which books would be canonized in the Bible, which chapters of each book should be selected, and gave the Bible its definitive form and style. The completion of the Bible, one of the greatest projects of the Great Assembly, also marked the beginning of the reign of the oral law.

Once the work of canonizing the Bible was completed, and it was accepted that the Bible was the central authority on which Jewish life was to be founded, the scribes were faced with the task of establishing order in the oral law. The tremendous body of material accumulated over the centuries was multiform and diversified and not always arranged in a manner that facilitated study. The scribes started out by studying those oral traditions which included interpretations, customs, and legal precedents, and their main achievement was the linking of these traditions to the written law. It was these scribes who evolved the basic methods of *midrash halakhah* (halakhic exegesis), that is, methods of learning and deriving *halakhah* from the biblical texts themselves, reconciling apparent textual contradictions, interpreting enigmatic statements, and analyzing and solving problems through perusal of the text. They also tried to find ways of introducing order into the mass of material so as to facilitate systematic transmission.

The Great Assembly also occupied itself with creating numerous new ordinances as the need arose. It should be recalled that the Jewish community in Judea at the beginning of the Second Temple period, which consisted of the group of returning Babylonian exiles and attendant remnants of the indigenous population, differed greatly in composition and structure from the community of the First Temple era. Although traces of ancient tribal divisions remained, they were no longer of great significance. Estates were no longer divided as they had been in the past, nor could the priests and Levites settle in all those cities that had once belonged to them. Even the Temple was not constructed exactly in accordance with the First Temple plan, and it lacked numerous items (the most striking omission being the Ark of the Covenant). The regime as a whole had changed; whereas in the First Temple era the monarchic system had prevailed, the focus of power was now gradually shifting from the nobles of royal descent to the High Priest and the Council of Sages, which later developed into the Sanhedrin. All these developments called for hundreds of new ordinances and enactments to regulate cultural and religious life.

The new way of life that took form adhered to the Mosaic code while taking change and advancement into consideration. The Great Covenant (see Nehemiah 9)—which can be viewed as the world's first constitution—was not merely a ceremonial proclamation of the people's obligation to observe all the laws of the Torah but also denoted acceptance of many other ordinances and customs. The members of the Great Assembly now faced the task of providing fixed patterns of behavior in many spheres that had formerly been left to the discretion of the individual. Thus they created a regular liturgy; the *Shemoneh Esreh* (eighteen benedictions), the central prayer of the Jewish liturgy to this day, was essentially formulated by the Great Assembly, as were other benedictions and various customs.

The scribes also turned their attention to problems of faith. It may be assumed that in ancient times, and even in the First Temple period, there were no precise formulations of such matters, and they were transmitted from one age to another as part of the general tradition without being particularly emphasized. At the same time the prophets and the schools of prophesy, or "sons of the prophets," as they are called in the Bible, were apparently centers of study and speculation in these spheres. But prophesy died out in the era of the Great Assembly, and this institution was faced with the additional task of handing down the spiritual heritage of the prophets to the younger generation. Parts of this heritage were contained in the liturgy and the benedictions instituted by the scribes. Some aspects were reflected in the commentaries on the written law. Others—of mystical nature—were taught as separate units with a certain degree of secrecy and were later included in the subject matter of *Ma'aseh Bereshit* (Act of

[16]

Creation) and *Ma'aseh Merkavah* (Divine Chariot), which formed the latter part of the Kabbalah.

The Second Temple period was, therefore, the era in which the foundations of Jewish law were laid and the spiritual image of the Jewish people was molded for centuries to come. The anonymity of the sages of this period suggests that they generally worked in unison, their aim being to arrive at generally acceptable conclusions with the approval of the supreme spiritual authority (the Great Assembly itself or the Sanhedrin, also known as the Council of Seventy Elders). Although this age had its share of problems, it was a generally tranquil period in which gradual and well-founded development took place, preparing the Jewish world for the upheavals to come.

3

The Oral Law—
The Era of the *Zugot* (Pairs)

THE ERA of the *zugot* (pairs) corresponds, to a large extent, to the period of Greek rule in Palestine (332–140 B.C.E.) and the subsequent era of the Hasmonean dynasty (140–37 B.C.E.). Culturally speaking, this was a time of conflict—against the Seleucid Greeks (whose decrees were an attack on the Jewish religion), against Hellenistic influences, and against the various heretical sects that were established during the period. The early days of this period were dominated by the great and legendary figure of the High Priest Simeon Ha-Tzadik (the Righteous). There is considerable lack of clarity about Simeon's historical role and exact dating, and it is very possible that the vagueness arises because two different people (grandfather and grandson) bore the same name and appellation. It may also be that the name was used to denote the collective activities of several High Priests in this period of transition between Persian rule and the commencement of Seleucid oppression.

The Jews were overjoyed at having rid themselves of their Persian rulers, and for a while they lived in harmony with the new Hellenistic rulers, particularly the House of Ptolemy in Egypt. Simeon is lavishly praised in the concluding section of the *Book of Ben Sira*, written in this period, where he is described in all the splendor of his priesthood as a leader of the people and a saint. In the talmudic sources he is defined as one of the "remnants of the Great Assembly." Many legends were woven around his personality, all of which hint at his awareness of the fact that an epoch in Jewish history was coming to a close. At the same time he ushered in a new era in which sages are known to us by name and are identified on the basis of their dicta and rulings. The anonymous scribe now yields to a small group of leaders, some of whose wise sayings and innovations have survived to the present day.

Although Greek influence was evident in the East many years before Alexander the Great conquered the Persian Empire, it was not deeply rooted in Palestinian life and culture. Even when Alexandria became a powerful center of Hellenistic culture, it was mainly the Jews of Egypt who felt its impact, while the Palestinian Jews generally encountered another aspect of Greek culture—external Hellenism, an ancient variation of levantinism that succeeded in combining the external trappings of Greek culture with various aspects of Near Eastern culture. This Hellenism blended easily with the Persian and Syrian cultures and religions, but because of the nature of the faith of the members of the Great Assembly, it could not arrive at a synthesis with the Jewish religion. At that time, and for many generations to come, this irreconcilability was not recognized as a confrontation between Greek philosophy and the spirit of Judaism. To the extent that contact was established between the two worlds—which differed so greatly in outlook—there was a high degree of mutual admiration. The external manifestations of Greek civilization attracted many Jews, and there was constant official pressure aimed at assimilating the people of Judea into the greater Hellenistic kingdom. In particular, it was members of the more prosperous strata in Judea who tended to favor religious syncretism.

This trend was counterbalanced by the emergence of religious sects referred to in Judeo-Greek sources as Hassidim (literally the pious). The spiritual leaders of this minority were the scholarly disciples and heirs of the members of the Great Assembly. The Seleucid rulers exerted increasing political pressure that reached its height in the enactment of the first coercive decrees in Jewish history directed against the very existence of the Jewish religion. As a result, a twofold process began within the Jewish people. The brutal persecution was countered by adamant refusal to transgress against the Torah on the basis of the concept of *yehareg ve-al ya'avor* (let him die rather than sin). This readiness to suffer and even die rather than betray the true faith is reflected in the talmudic sources and in the Books of the Maccabees. Simultaneously, the Jewish authorities introduced their own decrees aimed at discouraging fraternization between Jews and non-Jews. Not all these stringent regulations were readily accepted by the people, but in due course they became part of *halakhah* and of the Jewish cultural tradition.

These bitter times also called for creative activity and legislative endeavor aimed at formulating reasonable restrictions on the readiness of ardent believers to sacrifice themselves for the sake of their religion. The ordinance permitting defensive warfare on the Sabbath is attributed, at least by the Book of Maccabees, to Mattathias, father of the Hasmonean dynasty and first of the rebels against the Seleucids. It eventually developed into the ruling, supported by the biblical text, that in times of war and crisis it is permissible to violate the Sabbath. Similar definitions and enactments were added over the centuries, as the need arose, in turbulent times.

The triumph of the Hasmonean rebellion, which began as a popular religious uprising headed by the Hassidim, led to de facto liberation of Judea and Palestine from the foreign yoke. For a time it seemed that the Hasmonean rulers (who, as members of a priestly family, automatically became High Priests) would wield executive and political power, while the sages and their law court

The Oral Law—The Era of the *Zugot* (Pairs)

(*bet din*, which may be the *Hever ha-Yehudim* cited on the Hasmonean coins) would control internal affairs in accordance with established patterns. But this state of affairs did not endure, since the Hasmonean rulers, for political and other reasons, began to favor the *Tzedokim* (Sadducees), and the country was once again torn by strife.

We know very little of the origins of the Sadducees. They were few in number but exerted extensive social influence as many priests and rich men were included among them. Formally speaking, the Sadducees advocated religious conservatism, rejecting the oral law, its traditions and rulings, and calling for a return to observance of the written law alone. In fact, like the Karaites many generations later, they were obliged to create their own oral tradition in order to observe the written law satisfactorily. But their main concern was to confine the authority of the Mosaic code to the sphere of practical action, in the most restricted sense, in order to facilitate close emulation of Greek civilization. The Sadducees also rejected several tenets of faith accepted by the Jewish people at the time—belief in the immortality of the soul, in heavenly reward, and in the resurrection of the dead.

Although the Sadducees proclaimed the need to return to the old beliefs and patterns of conduct, they were actually an innovative sect. The bulk of the population, including those who had no particular sympathy for the Hassidim, continued along their well-trodden path, guided by the Pharisees (*Perushim*, meaning separatists, though apparently thus denoted only by others). The Hasmonean rulers, who awarded themselves the title of monarch—despite the resentment of the Pharisee heads of the Sanhedrin—and became increasingly involved in political activity, were attracted to the Sadducean way of thinking. Consequently, the relations between the monarch and the heads of the Sanhedrin were exacerbated, and in the days of Alexander Yannai the situation deteriorated into open warfare between the Hassidim and Alexander's mercenaries, with foreign factors intervening.

Information on the leaders of this age is sparse. The supreme

[21]

spiritual institution, the Sanhedrin, was headed by *zugot* (pairs of sages), one of whom served as *nasi* (president) while the other, his deputy, was the *av bet din* (head of the law court). There is no way of ascertaining the exact significance of these pairs, who apparently represented two schools of legislative thought, but the various methods they advocated still had so much in common that, with the exception of several maxims and general rulings, we have no information on most of them. The only personality known to us from this period is the *nasi* Simeon Ben Shetah, who lived during the reign of Alexander Yannai.

Simeon was the brother of Alexander's wife and therefore enjoyed eminent status and a certain immunity from the actions of the king. As one of the most vociferous opponents of the Sadducees, he was constantly at loggerheads with Alexander. His daring attempt to force the monarch to accept the authority of the Sanhedrin failed and contributed to the heightening of tension among the people. After Alexander's death, however, his widow, Salome (Shlomzion) ruled in his stead, and her reign is described in the Talmud as a brief "golden age." Salome restored the conditions that had prevailed at the beginning of the Hasmonean era, when internal religious affairs were controlled by the Sanhedrin, and her brother Simeon exploited his authority in order to introduce far-reaching changes. In various ways, mainly through heated ideological discourses, he succeeded in ejecting the heads of the Sadducees and their supporters from the Sanhedrin, and from then on this institution was exclusively Pharisaic in character. He eradicated the last traces of idolatry and sorcery, employing severe measures to this end, and succeeded in gaining acceptance for the principle of "the rule of Torah," that is, the assumption that the law of Torah and the will of God should determine the behavior of the entire nation. His insistence on observance of the strict letter of the law involved him in a personal tragedy when he was forced to agree to the execution of his own son on a trumped-up charge in order to maintain the principles of formal jurisdiction, thus creating a precedent valid for many generations to come. Simeon Ben Shetah also introduced many ordinances, the most renowned of which altered the text of the *ketubah* (standard marriage contract) in order to extend the rights of women and increase the stability of family life.

The activities of the "pairs" and the systematic dissemination of the oral law transformed the great scholars into leaders of the people, even when actual political authority and the high priesthood were in other hands. Shemaya and Avtalyon, who led the Sanhedrin in the generation after Simeon Ben Shetah, were from a family of proselytes and hence, apparently, of humble social origins. The people nevertheless regarded them as their true leaders, preferring them to the High Priest even at the height of the latter's popularity. The talmudic statement that the wisdom of the Torah is "more precious than pearls," than the High Priest who enters into the most holy places, was accepted by the entire nation.

4

The *Tannaim*

THE PERIOD of the *tannaim* may be strictly defined as beginning with Hillel and Shammai in the early days of Herod's rule. The name *tanna* means one who studies, repeating and handing down what he has learned from his teachers. In this period the general tradition of the oral law developed into a network of precisely formulated laws arranged by subject or mnemonic association. The scholars of the age were overmodest in adopting this title, since in fact this was an epoch of vital independent creativity in many spheres and of innovation of form and content. It was also a time of external and internal tension and crises: the destruction of the Temple by the Romans in 70 C.E. had made the reconstruction of the entire fabric of religious life an urgent necessity, while the *minim* (heretics, especially Gnostics) and Christian sects posed a grave threat to internal religious unity and the people suffered persecution at the hands of foreign oppressors. Yet, in the midst of these crises, Jewish culture blossomed.

The period was distinguished by new methods of study and, from the point of view of modern scholars, it marks the transition to a more thoroughly chronicled era. Whereas pre-tannaitic scholarship was collective and anonymous, with only a few names surfacing from the mass consensus, we now make the acquaintance of individual scholars. Their characters are multidimensional and most vividly drawn; they are distinguishable not only by their methods of study and teaching, but also by reason of traits and even outward appearance. Yohanan Ben Zakkai, one of the greatest figures of the age, tried to give a thumbnail sketch of each of his outstanding disciples: "R. Eliezer Ben Hyrcanus is a cemented cistern that never loses a drop; R. Joshua Ben Hananiah—blessed is she who bore him; R. Yosse Ha-Cohen is a *hassid* (pious man); R. Simeon Ben Nathanel is sin fearing; R. Eliezer Ben Erekh is an inexhaustible spring." Numerous stories and ancedotes about the *tannaim* illustrate their qualities and idiosyncrasies and bring them to life for us. It was in this period of individualization that the title of rabbi was created for those scholars who received official appointments, while others who did not receive *semikhah* (ordination) continued to be known by their names alone. This innovation led to an increase in the number of scholars and to the elevation of their status.

Hillel and Shammai were responsible for a new phenomenon in Jewish life—the evolvement of the two schools that bore their names (*Bet Hillel* and *Bet Shammai*). Despite all the controversies that raged between them, both schools fell within the traditionally accepted framework of Judaism. The halakhic disputes between them continued for many generations until the views of the House of Hillel finally prevailed. To a certain extent, the two schools reflected the personalities of their founders. Hillel, the *nasi* of the Sanhedrin, was born into a prosperous family in Babylonia, but went to Jerusalem to study under conditions of great penury, refusing to accept financial help from his relatives. He became *nasi* as the result of unexpected developments and, despite his high position, he never lost the common touch, retaining his modest and simple manner. His short and pithy maxims reflect his generosity, piousness, and love of mankind. Shammai, on the other hand, was an engineer, known for his probity and his consistency to the point of extremity in everything he did. In contrast to the congenial Hillel, Shammai was irascible and judged himself and others by stringent standards. His pupils resembled him to a large extent, being sharp witted, acerbic in their responses, and tending toward severity in judgment. Although a minority, they were evenly matched against the more liberal school of Hillel, and the clashes between the groups were often extremely heated and sometimes even violent. A well-known legend tells of a heathen who approached Hillel and insisted that he wished to learn the entire Torah while standing on one foot. It was then that Hillel, in order to define Jewish law in one sentence, coined his most famous dictum: "Do not unto others that which you would not have them do unto you. That is the entire Torah; the rest is commentary. Now go and study."

Hillel's disciples, though "lenient and modest," won the hearts of the sages, and the office of *nasi* was held by scions of the Hillelite family for over 400 years until the Sanhedrin ceased to exist. With the exception of several brief intervals, Hillel's descendants, who were awarded the honorary title of *rabban* (our teacher), led the scholars and were often the true leaders of the nation, acknowledged by both the people and the civil authorities.

One of the intervals in the consecutive rule of the House of Hillel is associated with the name of one of the greatest of the *tannaim*, and possibly one of the greatest scholars the Jewish people has ever produced, Rabban Yohanan Ben Zakkai. One of the youngest of Hillel's pupils, he lived to a very old age (according to tradition, 120), and to him fell the task of reconstructing the fabric of Jewish life after the destruction of the Second Temple in 70 C.E. Rabban Yohanan was opposed to the revolt against the Romans since he sensed that it was doomed to fail and that dire consequences would follow. Before the fall of Jerusalem, he slipped away from the city and succeeded in obtaining the permission of Vespasian (later to become emperor) to establish a spiritual center at Yavneh and to continue the Hillelite succession.

The *Tannaim*

After the destruction of the Temple, he faced the challenge of establishing a new center for the people and helping them adjust to the new circumstances whereby religious ardor had to be diverted to another focal point now that the Temple had ceased to exist. Yohanan Ben Zakkai issued ten important and urgently needed ordinances in order to adapt Jewish life and *halakhah* to the new reality and perpetuate the memory of the Temple until such time as it could be rebuilt. The very fact that Jews were able to nurture and develop their national and cultural life in the 2,000 years that followed attests to the success of his endeavors.

The next generation was dominated by three scholars, each an outstanding personality in his own right. The Sanhedrin was headed by Rabban Gamaliel (known as Rabban Gamaliel of Yavneh, to distinguish him from his grandfather), who reorganized that institution with great forcefulness and drive in order to transform it into the supreme legislative and judicial anthority of the Jewish people. Although his erudition was conceded, his severity and assertiveness, however great and worthy the cause, aroused the resentment of his colleagues, and he was even deposed from the presidency for a time. His brother-in-law, R. Eliezer Ben Hyrcanus, was known as Rabbi Eliezer the Great. He was the son of a very rich family and began to study at a relatively advanced age, but his outstanding abilities, phenomenal memory, and charismatic personality soon advanced him to the first rank of scholars. His own teacher said of him that if all the sages of Israel were in one scale of a balance and R. Eliezer in the other, he would outweigh them all. Although his official mentor was Rabban Yohanan Ben Zakkai, he leaned toward the House of Shammai and tended to conservatism in his halakhic rulings. On one occasion, when he refused to accept the majority ruling, the sages were forced to excommunicate him after a dramatic struggle, in the course of which he is depicted as calling on the forces of Nature and on the Almighty for aid. His friend and rival R. Joshua then made the famous statement that Torah no longer resided in Heaven but was entrusted to the judgment of the majority of sages on earth.

[27]

Despite these confrontations, R. Eliezer was revered by his contemporaries, and his rulings are among the cornerstones of mishnaic oral law.

R. Joshua Ben Hananiah was a totally different personality. A poor man who earned his living as a blacksmith, he was nevertheless undoubtedly the preeminent scholar of his day. He is described as an ugly man whose wisdom enchanted all those who met him, whether scholars or laymen, Jews or members of the ruling families of Rome, whom he met when visiting Rome as the representative of his people. He was a witty and congenial man and was universally loved and admired.

These three sages headed the large group of scholars at the "Yavneh vineyard." Their scholarly achievements and the halakhic debates held in their *yeshivot* (academies) constitute one of the important foundations of mishnaic literature. The evidence cited by various sages and the summaries of their rulings during the one or more days of a special session were recorded, almost without editing, in a special tractate of the Mishnah, *Eduyot* (Testimonies). The group included several elders who had been active before the destruction of the Temple and younger men whose impact would only be felt a generation later. Among the junior pupils we find the names of several scholars who were to become prominent around the time of the completion of the Mishnah. The wide range of personalities included the venerable sage R. Dossa Ben Harkinas; the outstandingly brilliant young R. Elazar Ben Azaria, who was appointed *nasi*—as the compromise candidate—at the age of eighteen; the logical and moderate R. Ishmael Ben Elisha; and R. Tarfon, the eccentric priest, a generous and modest man with his own distinctive brand of humor, usually directed against himself. We also find among this group Rabbi Akiva, taking his first steps toward the leadership of the next generation.

R. Akiva Ben Yosef, "whose name resounds throughout the length and breadth of the world," was a great and romantic figure who overshadowed all his contemporaries. He was born into a common family, and his father (or possibly grandfather) was a proselyte. Akiva himself was a shepherd, extremely pious but illiterate, one of the *ammei ha-aretz* (unlearned people). Rachel, the daughter of one of Jerusalem's richest men, fell in love with him and was determined to marry him despite his poverty and lack of education, since she discerned his outstanding qualities. Refused the support of her father, the young couple lived in dire poverty, and at the age of forty Akiva first began to learn to read. Because he came to scholarship at a relatively advanced age, he was endowed with profound and original insight and approached each problem from a fresh point of view. He was absent from home for many years, on the advice of his wife and with her encouragement, and studied under the greatest of scholars, R. Joshua and R. Eliezer. During this time, Rachel was so poor that she had to shear her hair and sell it to buy food. When R. Akiva returned to his home, accompanied by many of his pupils, his shabby and careworn wife came timidly to greet him. He turned to his disciples and said: "My learning and yours is hers by right." He also told them that the definition of a rich man was "he who has a wife whose deeds are worthy."

Although Akiva started out as a disciple of the Yavneh sages, they soon acknowledged his erudition and magnetic personality, and he was invited to join their ranks as an equal colleague, taking part in several political deputations to Rome. Since he lived to a ripe old age (tradition speaks of 120), he became the leader of the following generation of sages as well. When Bar-Kokhba's rebellion against Rome began in 132 C.E., R. Akiva, unlike most of the sages of his time, not only supported the uprising fervently but even declared Bar-Kokhba to be the Messiah. It was apparently Akiva who gave the rebel leader his appellation (Bar-Kokhba means "son of a star," recalling the verse, "There shall come a star out of Jacob" [Numbers 24:17]). Before the rebellion, R. Akiva apparently made many journeys throughout the Jewish world— from Babylonia to Egypt, through North Africa and Gaul—in order to recruit funds and rally political support, and possibly even to coordinate a similar uprising in Rome. On his return to Palestine, he placed his thousands of disciples at Bar-Kokhba's disposal.

The Roman legions were hard put to crush the rebellion, and a bitter struggle was conducted following the lines of a "scorched-earth policy" that devastated Judea. This war claimed close to a million victims, including an entire generation of Akiva's disciples. After the Romans crushed the uprising, Emperor Hadrian promulgated a number of cruelly oppressive decrees, including a ban on Torah study. Akiva, who believed that study was the source of Jewish life, continued to teach publicly, despite the risks involved. When a friend warned him of the dangers, he replied with his famous parable: "The fox saw the fish fleeing the nets in the water and proposed to them that they come and live on dry land. They said to him: 'Fox, you are not the wisest of animals, but a fool. If we live in fear in the water which is our habitat, how much more will we fear on dry land, where we will find our death.' " Rabbi Akiva succeeded in training a new group of young disciples, who became the leaders of the next generation, before he was apprehended by the Roman authorities. He died a martyr's death after being tortured, and he expired with the *Shema Yisrael* prayer on his lips. His didactic methods and halakhic system were carried on by his various disciples and became the basis for the perpetuation of the oral law, just as his approach to mysticism became the basis for study of this subject in centuries to come.

We know more of Akiva's disciples than of any other generation of *tannaim*. In this generation we find R. Judah Ben Ilai, a moderate who advocated compromise with the Roman authorities and a faithful disciple who edited a commentary on the book of Leviticus, *Torat Kohanim*, based on his rabbi's method. R. Meir, a gifted man whose sudden flashes of brilliance amazed his contemporaries, "who could not grasp his meaning," came from a family of proselytes related to the Roman emperors. He was a clerk by occupation, and his life with his famous wife, Berurya, was marked by a series of personal tragedies. A fascinating expounder and an extremely gifted writer, he laid the foundations for the writing of the Mishnah. His contemporary, R. Simeon Bar Yohai, was a charismatic, gloomy, mysterious figure who emulated Akiva in his consistent opposition to the Roman rulers and was therefore forced to hide for many years in a cave with his son, R. Elazar. Like Akiva, he followed his own path in commentary on the Bible. It was from Simeon's academy that the *midrashim* on Exodus (*Mekhilta*) and on Numbers and Deuteronomy (*Sifrei*) emerged; later generations also attributed to him composition of the basic kabbalistic work, the *Book of Zohar*, whose chief protagonist he was. R. Yossi Bar Halafta was a taciturn, moderate man who was universally liked, and whose halakhic method is regarded as the most reliable because of its consistent logic. The hereditary *nasi* of the Sanhedrin was Rabban Simeon Ben Gamaliel the Second, of the House of Hillel, who regarded himself as inferior to his colleagues, "a fox among lions," but nevertheless endeavored to rebuild a way of life and discipline for the people. Posterity was more appreciative of his value as a legislator and accepted his rulings in almost every case.

Rabban Simeon Ben Gamaliel was succeeded as *nasi* by his son, R. Judah Ha-Nasi, the greatest scholar of his day, revered by his disciples and by posterity. In his lifetime he was known as *rabbenu ha-kadosh* (our sainted rabbi) and in due course came to be known simply as Rabbi. R. Judah combined two rare qualities, "Torah and greatness in one setting"; he was both an outstanding scholar and the foremost political figure of his time. Although ascetic by nature, he adopted an outward appearance of great splendor and lived, an ailing and abstemious man, in a luxurious palace. His special status was bolstered by his large personal fortune and his close ties with the Roman rulers. There are many tales of his friendship with the Roman Emperor Antoninus, who may have been Marcus Aurelius or Alexander Severus.

Although he lived in a peaceful era and was on excellent terms with the authorities, R. Judah sensed that the tranquillity could not endure for long and should be exploited for the implementation of a project that could provide the leverage for continued study of the Torah. Because of his apprehension lest the Torah be forgotten by the people over the years, he decided to violate the accepted prohibition against recording oral law and to compose a work comprising its main points. In fact, he succeeded in bringing this idea to fruition, creating a work second in importance and sanctity only to the Torah—the Mishnah.

5

The Compilation
of the Mishnah

AS THE ORAL LAW was transmitted from teacher to disciple
over the centuries through oral instruction, the need for some
form of arrangement and editing of the material became evident.
The reasons were mostly mnemonic, since the vast quantity of
oral material could no longer be committed to memory through
repetition and intensive study alone. In earlier generations, when
the oral law adhered closely to the written law, the latter served,
inter alia, as an instrument for reminding the student of the *halakhah* derived from each verse. This use of the biblical text not
only as the legal and logical basis for oral law but also as a mnemonic aid was carried over to talmudic literature and Jewish literature in general. It created the concept of *asmakhta* (support),
that is, citing a biblical text that is not the direct source of
the *halakhah* but that is combined, by some exegetic method, with
a known *halakhah* to serve as a mnemonic aid. Use of this method
was so widespread that sometimes it is almost impossible to dis-

tinguish between the authentic commentary and that which serves merely as an *asmakhta*. But this use of the text was only appropriate to those subjects on which there were numerous texts and a smaller number of commentaries and *halakhot*.

Many areas of oral law, however, developed far beyond the isolated verses that served as their substantiation. In these spheres it was deemed necessary to classify numerous details into more general categories. Initially this was apparently done by simple means and was meant to facilitate memorization and study. Certain subjects were classified and arranged by numerical series, and thus we find lists of "four main causes of injury," "thirty-nine principal labors prohibited on the Sabbath," and so forth. Great superstructures of *halakhah* were erected around these definitions in greater detail. Simultaneously, the scholars were obliged to seek rules and generalizations that would further both understanding and absorption of the numerous details. These basic rules are not fundamental legal concepts or theories, but rather summaries, that is, attempts to organize the detailed material in a certain way and to find the common denominator for a number of isolated *halakhot*. In fact, many laws, some extremely ancient, were formulated in this fashion. This approach was sometimes stated explicitly, as in the "important rule for Sabbath" or the "important rule for the tithe," as an attempt to generalize details. Other such generalizations are not named as such; for example, "women are exempt from all of the positive precepts related to time." Sometimes the principle is phrased as a basic example from which other things are inferred, rather than in the form of a rule.

These and other methods apparently served only as aids to study and proved their worth in periods when life and culture were, to a large extent, static. But as time passed, many changes occurred and new subjects emerged and required analysis, augmenting the basic study material. It was sometimes imperative to reformulate or modify rulings. The disputes with the Sadducees led Pharisee sages to emphasize certain aspects of *halakhah*. The fact that increasing numbers of foreigners were becoming active in various spheres of life in the Jewish community also aroused the need for new enactments. Political and religious relations with the Samaritans were unstable, and as a consequence the halakhic attitude to this sect underwent a change.

The vast amount of material accumulated over several generations began to constitute a problem at -a time when Jewish religious and judicial institutions maintained a certain hierarchy and employed uniform methods of legislative ruling, all matters in dispute being submitted to the Great Sanhedrin in the Temple for unequivocal judgment. But breaches began to appear in the wall of uniformity in the Hasmonean era, and open controversy erupted in the days of Hillel and Shammai, when the existence of two different schools of thought was officially recognized.

The expansion of elementary education and its reorganization on a nationwide basis by the High Priest Joshua Ben Gamala, together with Hillel's opening of the academies to a wider range of the population, created both a large influx of students and a corresponding increase in the number of teachers who organized their own large or small academies. This tendency was even more marked after the destruction of the Temple, when central authority was undermined in many ways. As long as all the sages were gathered together and the main work of scholarship was carried out by one group of men, the uniformity of tradition was preserved. But the proliferation of teachers and the establishment of separate schools created, however unintentionally, a plethora of forms and methods of expression. Each teacher had his own method and phrased his oral rulings in his own singular fashion. Sometimes the differences were merely external, but there were also vitally significant divergences, both deliberate and unconscious. When the sages met, they could no longer rely on a single limited and uniform tradition; they were now obliged to compare a number of traditions—those of their own teachers and of other scholars. It was no longer sufficient to be acquainted with the teachings of one's own mentor, and the student was obliged to acquaint himself with the work of other scholars on the same subject, or with relevant traditions. Thus students were forced to memorize vast quantities of material because of the "explosion of knowledge."

These developments, which were manifest for several generations in the Second Temple period, apparently inspired the scholars to create the frameworks according to which the Talmud was compiled. Laws were classified and represented by short and easily memorized phrases. This very brevity sometimes detracted from clarity, since the formulations could not encompass each and every detail; but they served as the focal point for various subjects and issues that had been clearly legislated. It is known that such laws were already in existence in the Second Temple era, and possibly dated from the beginning of the Hasmonean period. Certain isolated laws undoubtedly date from an even earlier age. There are certain *halakhot* which the Talmud itself attributes to the period of Nehemiah, that is, the beginning of the Second Temple era.

The systematic organization of *halakhah* as a whole into clearly defined units was apparently carried out by Rabbi Akiva. His contemporaries compared his activity to the work of a laborer who goes out into the field and heaps into his basket whatever he finds at random, then returns home and arranges each species separately. Akiva had studied numerous disorganized subjects and classified them into distinct categories. His disciples seem to have carried on his method according to the general guidelines Akiva had established. R. Meir proved the most gifted at this task, and his system served as the groundwork for R. Judah Ha-Nasi's codification work.

R. Judah started by classifying most of the subjects of *halakhah* in the widest possible sense into six categories, the "Six Orders of the Mishnah," each dealing with a range of related subjects. In several of these *sedarim* (orders) there is great homogeneity of subject matter, while in others slightly divergent material was included to encompass the entire spectrum of relevant issues. The

The Compilation of the Mishnah

orders were then divided into smaller books dealing with more limited subjects: "Benedictions," "Sabbath," and so forth. Each such book was called a *masekhet* (tractate), apparently from the word *masekha* (the loom on which cloth is woven). The tractates are divided into chapters and the chapters into smaller units known as *mishnayot* (singular: *mishnah*) dealing with a specific *halakhah* or several related *halakhot*.

The general work of classification had apparently been going on for some time, and R. Judah's main achievement was to summarize the oral law and contain it within a precisely formulated and more restricted framework. He took advantage of the fact that his academy was attended by most of the outstanding scholars of the time and by disciples from all the schools of study. He started by collecting universally accepted material and clarifying its formulation. Since his aim was to create a book that could serve as the basic text for generations to come, it was vital to expend effort on precise phrasing, in order to encompass a whole world in each phrase. The text had to be extremely concise, since R. Judah assumed, with justification, that there would be no immediate revolution in methods of study and that the Mishnah itself would be taught orally as the basis for all further study. Thus each sentence or phrase was actually a summary arrived at after discussion and debate in his academy.

Many ancient *halakhot* and *mishnayot* were introduced into the new compilation in their original form, sometimes accompanied by a later explanation and sometimes unchanged, with the ancient dialect preserved intact. (In the talmudic era it was commented that certain *mishnayot* reflected not only the method but also the special mode of expression of the inhabitants of Jerusalem or Judea). Generally accepted *halakhot* were recorded in a way that preserved their essence, but it was also necessary to summarize the methods and disputes of numerous generations of sages. R. Judah, as noted, based his work on R. Meir's compilations, but they underwent editorial changes, such as amendments, summarizing, the citing of variant methods, or rejection of the statements of one school in favor of those of another. Thus many sources were weeded out, especially old disputes that had already been settled by subsequent generations. The Mishnah, however, retained several controversial methods that had not been accepted as *halakhah* because of their importance for comprehending the issue and their value as comparative sources.

R. Judah tried, insofar as possible, to create formulas reflecting the general consensus on most issues. Where he believed that he was expressing the main intention of the *halakhah* he did not denote the source, marking it as *stam mishnah* (plain *mishnah*) without naming the author or formulator. Most of the *mishnayot* contain such formulations, but in many cases the scholars did not reach final conclusions on the intent, and then R. Judah identified the main methods used in exploring the *mishnah* by naming their most important proponents. Sometimes a list of the various conflicting opinions is given, and sometimes R. Judah declares a certain method to be the basic one and notes it anonymously, appending the qualifications and views of other sages. It goes without saying that there is a high degree of consent regarding ancient controversies that were eventually resolved, while the number of disputes in the Mishnah increases as we approach the era of R. Judah himself. The Mishnah is a large body of material pertaining to the opinions of the sages of the generation immediately preceding Rabbi Judah's, but there is also a detailed record of the disputes of his own generation, and his own view is sometimes noted as an isolated opinion opposed to the general consensus.

According to the sources, R. Judah not only edited the Mishnah but also utilized it in practice in the course of his studies with his contemporaries. He sometimes changed his opinion on certain issues and consequently introduced amendments into the *mishnayot*. At times he was unable to introduce certain of his new formulations or theories into the work, since a previous ruling had already been accepted, and sometimes additions contradicting his own previous decisions were made. Similarly, a new formulation occasionally rendered previous *mishnayot* superfluous, but since it was the rule that "a *mishnah* does not move from its place," both statements were retained.

These facts attest to the uniformity and stability of the Mishnah in R. Judah's lifetime. After his death only minor modifications and additions were made, and his project remained basically unchanged. He succeeded in completing the Mishnah and endowing it with its permanent form and character, thus rounding off the period of the *tannaim*. Posterity was liberated from the burden of studying vast numbers of *halakhot* from hundreds of various sources in order to learn the oral law. A clearly fashioned work that served as the source for all new study was now available. There is still no clear evidence as to whether the Mishnah was recorded in writing and was widely distributed (as one school of thought claims) or was formulated orally (as many others believe), but in any case it was now a complete and sacred work, second only to the Bible in its sanctity.

6

The *Amoraim* in Babylonia

THE CODIFICATION of the Mishnah and the death of R. Judah marked the beginning of a new era, the period of the *amoraim* (from the verb *amar*, to speak or interpret), interpreters of the Mishnah. Members of the generation that bridged the gap between the *tannaim* and the *amoraim* were still living in R. Judah's later years and for about a generation after his death. These sages, R. Judah's young colleagues and disciples, regarded it as their obligation not only to engage in study and interpretation of the Mishnah, but also to continue his compiling and editing of the source material of previous generations, since R. Judah had collated only a very small part of the vast treasury of wisdom taught in the various academies. Although it was generally agreed that his codification work was the most important, it was thought worthwhile to preserve the extraneous material as an aid to study and for comparative purposes.

R. Hiya and R. Oshaya, his outstanding disciples, compiled several additional collections of oral law, of which the work known as *Tosefta* (literally addition) has survived as an independent book. It, too, is a summarized version of the oral law, but it is based on the method of a different academy, that of R. Nehemiah, who was one of Akiva's disciples. The *midrashei halakhah* (halakhic exegeses), which elucidated and emphasized the ties between the written and oral laws, were compiled and edited mostly in these years. Other scholars continued to draw up compilations of tannaitic material, but only traces of these have remained. The abundance of this material is illustrated by an allegorical interpretation of a verse from the Song of Songs: "Threescore queens—these are the sixty tractates [of the Mishnah]; fourscore concubines—the *toseftot;* virgins without number—the *halakhot.*" The isolated *halakhot* and compilations of tannaitic material outside the Mishnah are known as *baraitot* (outside teaching), that is, extraneous material.

The work of preserving and codifying the vast body of oral law went on for several generations, but its importance waned as the main focus of Torah scholarship shifted elsewhere. Those scholars who engaged in memorization of the vast number of *baraitot* were still known as *tannaim,* but the term took on new significance. *Tannaim* were no longer creators of the oral law but individuals gifted with phenomenal memories who did not always comprehend the full significance of what they were memorizing. They were to be found for many generations in the larger academies, serving as living archives utilized by the sages in order to clarify and elucidate various problems that cropped up in the course of the study of the Mishnah.

For the next few hundred years (*ca.* 200–*ca.* 500 C.E.), the sages were known as *amoraim.* At first the title referred to a certain task that evolved in the period of the *tannaim.* The great scholars would address the general public on matters of *halakhah* and *aggadah* (legend), and by tradition the sage would address his audience from the rostrum in Hebrew, while his disciples repeated his remarks in Aramaic (the *lingua franca* of the period) for the benefit of those ignorant of Hebrew. Such translators were also active during the reading of the Torah in public, immediately rendering each verse into Aramaic so that its content could be understood by all. Thus the *amoraim* were essentially translators and some-times popularizers of the basic halakhic teachings of the scholars. After the mishnaic period, the sages regarded themselves as *amoraim* of the Mishnah. Their task was to explain and expound the text to the people, rather than to create independent *halakhah*. In due course the *amoraim* became the mentors of the people and introduced their own halakhic innovations, but out of humility they continued to call themselves by this title.

The period of the completion of the Mishnah was of historical significance for yet another reason—the emergence of the in-dependent and important center of learning in Babylonia. Al-though there had been scholars in Babylonia in every generation, including several of the greatest *tannaim*, such as Hillel, Jewish life in Babylonia had been regarded as an offshoot of Palestinian culture, rather than self-sufficient in spiritual matters. When no one appeared qualified to succeed Rabbi Judah as spiritual and political leader of the people, however, the authority of the Pales-tinian center weakened. In addition, after Rabbi Judah's death, political and economic conditions in Palestine deteriorated, and subsequent emigration to other countries brought about the strengthening of centers of learning in the Diaspora.

As the importance of the Palestinian center diminished, the great *amora* R. Abba Ben Ibo (known as Abba Arikha—Abba the tall one) was confronted with the task of establishing a spiritual center in Babylonia (it eventually overshadowed the center in Pal-estine). In his youth R. Abba travelled from Babylonia to Palestine with his uncle and teacher, R. Hiya, a disciple and colleague of R. Judah. R. Abba himself had completed most of his education under Rabbi Judah and was one of the members of the Sanhe-drin. He lived in Palestine for many years, though apparently he returned to Babylonia on occasion, and in the end he went back to the country of his birth for personal reasons. There he found a number of eminent scholars but discovered that scholarship was only imperfectly organized and standards were lower than in Pal-estine. R. Abba was acknowledged to be one of the outstanding

The *Amoraim* in Babylonia

Palestinian scholars, ordained by R. Judah himself, a compiler of *mishnayot* and an expert on the traditions of both Palestine and Babylonia. To avoid offending the existing communal leadership of Babylonia, he settled in the small town of Sura, rather than in one of the main centers of scholarship, and established an academy there. Babylonian scholars were soon attracted to the new center and thousands of disciples flocked to study there. R. Abba exerted such strong influence over the Babylonian community that he began to be referred to simply as Rav, the name he is known by to this day. The authority of the Sura center over most of Jewish Babylonia was recognized, and the Sura academy survived in various forms for 700 years.

Renowned as a pious and noble man, Rav succeeded by his own personal example, aid, and encouragement, in raising Babylonian standards of scholarship. One of his younger contemporaries, the Babylonian sage Samuel, established a second center in the town of Nehardea. Although this academy later moved, it remained the partner and friendly rival of Sura as long as Babylonia flourished as a Torah center.

Rav and Samuel together constituted the first generation of Babylonian *amoraim* who cast the mold of Torah scholarship in that country for generations to come. They were close personal friends, although completely unalike in character. Rav's family traced its lineage back to the House of David, and he was connected by marriage with the *resh galut* (exilarch, or hereditary leader of Babylonian Jewry). He was well versed in the Palestinian tradition of study and edited several collections of *mishnayot*. It was in his academy that the definitive commentary on the Book of Leviticus (known as *Sifra Debei Rav*) was composed, and several of the main New Year prayers are attributed to him. Samuel was a totally different personality, not only in outward appearance but also by occupation. Whereas Rav engaged in trade on an international scale, Samuel was one of the outstanding physicians of his day, a great astronomer, and head of the court of the exilarch.

[43]

The method of study that evolved in the two academies concentrated on elucidation of the Mishnah by citing corresponding
sources from extraneous *mishnayot* in an attempt to arrive at an
analysis of the Mishnah from all possible angles. Because, according to the *halakhah*, there was no way of officially ordaining
scholars outside Palestine, the Babylonian sages could not be
known by the title of rabbi and were therefore denoted *rav*, a title
attesting to their scholarship without according them official halakhic status. Since, for the same reason, no Sanhedrin-like body
could develop in Babylonia, the aim of learning in many spheres
was not necessarily to reach clear halakhic decisions. This restriction intensified the natural tendency of all the *amoraim*, including
those in Palestine, to concentrate on the theoretical and elemental
aspects of study.

The two great academies differed greatly in their approach to
study and analysis of the Mishnah. As a result, study in that and
subsequent generations was based on the controversies between
Rav and Samuel. It was later determined that on questions of civil
law, Samuel's rulings prevailed, while in other spheres Rav's
decisions were accepted. This did not, of course, prevent their
disciples from continuing to peruse both methods.

In the following generations many Babylonian sages made their
way to Palestine and became prominent there, but the Babylonian academies were already so large and important that they
evolved their own independent methods of study and schools of
thought. Rav was succeeded at Sura by his disciple R. Huna,
while Samuel's heir was R. Judah, who had also studied under
Rav and who transferred the academy from Nehardea to Pumbedita, where it remained. The scholars of this period include R.
Hisda, who lived to a ripe old age; the blind R. Sheshet, one of
the most erudite men of his age, who had a sharp tongue and very
definite views, "a man harder than iron"; and R. Nahman, the
son-in-law of the exilarch, who was a scintillating judge in the
tradition of Samuel.

The third generation of Babylonian *amoraim* boasted two outstanding personalities: Rabba (short for R. Abba), a brilliant man ("uprooter of mountains," according to his contemporaries) who became an academy head at a very early age; and R. Yosef, the great expert on the Torah. R. Yosef went blind in his old age but maintained his congeniality and his warm relationships with his disciples, eventually replacing his friend Rabba as academy head. The debates between these two men became part of the regular curriculum of the academies. There were scholars who brought summaries of Palestinian scholarship to Babylonia, and this renewed contact inspired two sages who are regarded as the central pillars of Babylonian learning, Abbaye and Rava. Abbaye was the nickname that Rabba gave his nephew, Nahmani Ben Kaylil (the word apparently means "little father," since he was named after Rabba's father, Nahmani). An orphan, he was brought up by his uncle and lived, like him, in penury, farming for a living and studying by night and during the slack agricultural season. He was a favorite disciple but also a sharp critic of R. Yosef, and he learned from both mentors, becoming academy head after R. Yosef. Rava, whose full name was Abba Ben Rav Hamma, was the follower of another school, that of R. Nahman and R. Hisda. A very rich merchant who was on close terms with the Persian royal house, he lived in the important and prosperous commercial center of Mehoza. Rava was apparently younger than Abbaye, but they were friends from youth despite their conflicting opinions. Hundreds of debates between them are quoted in the Babylonian Talmud, and the discussions which they and their disciples held are classic examples of the methods of the Babylonian Talmud. Both had incisive minds, but Abbaye tended somewhat to formalism, while his colleague generally represented a more realistic outlook. Abbaye was more moderate in his conclusions and preferred simple solutions, while Rava's decisions were clearer, although his halakhic method was more complex. In numerous areas they were in accord, and many important halakhic elements are the fruit of their joint efforts.

Their intellectual output was so great in quantity and so profound in quality that the scholars of the next generation—R. Papa, R. Nahman Bar Isaac, and R. Huna Ben Rav Joshua—engaged, to a large extent, in elaborating the theories of these sages and deriving conclusions from them. It was later recognized that the age of Abbaye and Rava constituted a turning point in Torah scholarship. Until their time, traditions handed down from teacher to disciple had played a central role in study, while from then on, critical analysis, individual research, and the development of new methods became increasingly important. Consequently, the conclusions of later generations, arrived at after examination and elimination, were of greater significance from the halakhic point of view.

In the sixth generation of Babylonian *amoraim*, there emerged another striking personality, R. Ashi, the head of the Sura academy, who created one great center for Torah study. Despite the decisive influence of his activities, we know little of his origins and family background, but it is known that he was an extremely rich man who maintained close ties with the Persian authorities and was the political leader of the Babylonian Jewish community, wielding greater authority than the exilarch himself. Furthermore, R. Ashi was universally acknowledged as the greatest scholar of his age. It was this combination of "Torah and greatness in one place" that characterized him, as it had R. Judah Ha-Nasi. R. Ashi was impelled to undertake the task of redacting the Babylonian Talmud, fearing that, disorganized as it was, the vast bulk of oral material was in danger of sinking into oblivion over the years. During the many years (close to sixty) that he served as academy head, he dedicated himself to the project of constructing a framework for the Babylonian Talmud. This was a gigantic task, greater in scope than the compilation of the Mishnah and calling for entirely new methods of organization and editing. R. Ashi himself is not mentioned in the Talmud as often as are other sages, but the large quantity of material cited anonymously bears his individual hallmark.

His task could not be completed in one generation, and after he had finished the groundwork, the work was continued by his successor, disciple, and colleague, Ravina. These two scholars are regarded as the "last of the teachers," rounding off the amoraite period. R. Ashi's disciples and their pupils after them continued the task of redacting the Babylonian Talmud, and the final work contains the names of several sages who lived a century after R. Ashi. But their contribution was more in the nature of supplementation and final editing, the main work having been carried out by the two great scholars.

For almost 200 years afterward, scholars studied the Talmud, introducing minor amendments and additions. This group, known as the *savoraim* (expositors), gave the work its final shape. In most cases, only their names are recorded and very little is known of their personalities or achievements. No single scholar is named as having officially completed the writing and editing of the Talmud (as is the case with the Mishnah), hence the significant saying: "The Talmud was never completed." There was never a time when intellectual activity founded on the Talmud came to a standstill, and it continued to take on new forms for many generations to come.

7

The *Amoraim* in Palestine

ALTHOUGH the death of R. Judah Ha-Nasi marked the end of the mishnaic period, mishnaic scholarship continued for a further generation, bridging the gap between the *tannaim* and the *amoraim*, both historically and intellectually speaking. The scholars of this generation, who engaged in study and interpretation of the Mishnah, were also editors of compilations of various extraneous *mishnayot*. Most probably, one of the main reasons for this activity was the absence of a leader capable of replacing R. Judah.

R. Judah had named as his successor to the presidency his eldest son, Rabban Gamaliel Ben Rabbi, who was renowned for his moral qualities but was certainly not regarded as the preeminent scholar of the age. One of R. Judah's favorite disciples, R. Haninah, was appointed head of the academy. From this time on, the presidency of the Sanhedrin, though a prestigious post and of great political significance, was generally regarded as unimportant from the point of view of scholarship. Simultaneously, the academy heads no longer wielded the political and social authority that had characterized the office of *nasi* during the Hillelite dynasty. The problem was a complex one because Rabbi Judah's disciples included such great scholars as R. Hiya and R. Oshaya, R. Yannai, and R. Levi, who were obliged to found their own academies and compile their own *baraitot*.

It was only in the second generation that truly amoraitic activity began, although some of R. Judah's disciples were still alive, including the two sons of R. Hiya, Judah and Hezekiah, and R. Joshua Ben Levi, who was renowned for his saintliness. The residence of the *nasi* and location of the Sanhedrin, Tiberias—known then as *Beit Vaad Gadol* (the Great Meeting Place)—was not the sole important center; various scholars continued to establish their own centers in other towns: Lydda in Judea, Caesarea on the border of Lower Galilee, and Zippori in Galilee, the traditional rival of Tiberias.

The period of the blossoming of the Talmud in Palestine is associated with the name of one man, the embodiment of Palestinian learning, R. Yohanan (also known as Bar-Naphka—son of the blacksmith). R. Yohanan, who lived to a venerable age, knew R. Judah Ha-Nasi in his youth and was one of the youngest of his disciples, but he had studied mostly under R. Yannai and R. Hezekiah. His private life was marked by tragedy, considerable sacrifice, and great perseverance for the sake of his studies. He was born into a prosperous family, but because of his preoccupation with the Torah, he was gradually forced to sell all his property. He outlived his ten sons (although, according to legend, one survived him, went to Babylonia, and became one of the greatest scholars of the fourth generation there). The most glorious epoch of Palestinian learning began with R. Yohanan's appointment as head of the Tiberias academy. The *nasi* at that time was R. Judah's grandson, also called R. Judah, and known as *nesia* (Aramaic for president), to distinguish him from his grandfather. In some sources he too is referred to as Rabbi, since he was likewise a great scholar. An admirer and supporter of R. Yohanan, he had served for many years as academy head and developed uniquely Palestinian methods of study.

Although R. Yohanan himself had studied under Babylonian sages and revered Rav and Samuel (in his letters, he addressed them as "our teachers in Babylonia"), he developed a method that was uniquely his own. The method used by scholars in Palestine to clarify problems was generally simpler than the approach prevalent in Babylonia. The Palestinian scholars were confident in the knowledge that they were authorized to determine basic *halakhah* without endeavoring to interpret the Mishnah in complicated and casuistric ways. R. Yohanan's basic tenets for halakhic rulings were unambiguous, and he tried to find a uniform method of interpreting the various *mishnayot*. He was tremendously erudite in mishnaic literature and traditions and was blessed with great analytical ability. Because of his powerful personality and his methods of study, his authority was also accepted by the great scholars of Babylonia, who saw in him the mentor of their generation. Many of the important *amoraim* in Babylonia decided to move to Palestine in order to study under him. The brothers of the great Babylonian *amora* Rabba wrote to him: "You have a teacher in Palestine, R. Yohanan," implying that even he could learn from this great scholar. In fact, many of R. Yohana's most prominent disciples were Babylonian scholars who settled in Palestine and became ardent admirers of the country's methods of scholarship.

These Babylonians included Rav's brilliant pupil R. Kahana, who was both his disciple and his friend; R. Elazar Ben Pedat, the disciple of Rav and Samuel, who became R. Yohanan's favorite student; the important priests R. Ami and R. Assi; the enthusiastic R. Zira, who was renowned not only as a scholar but also as the most righteous and pious man of his generation; R. Abba, the *dayan;* and R. Hiya Bar Abba, the devoted disciple who became the greatest authority on his rabbi's teachings, as well as many others. All Palestinian scholars naturally regarded themselves as R. Yohanan's pupils. The most prominent among them was the aristocratic R. Yossi Bar Haninah of Caesarea, a learned and humorous man who was thought to be the model for the talmudic

The *Amoraim* in Palestine

phrase: "This was laughed at in Palestine." There was also R. Abahu, a learned man of noble qualities who was famed for his handsome appearance. He was an extremely rich international trader who was on close terms with the official representatives in Caesarea and was very active among non-Jews and the various heretic sects.

Closest of all to R. Yohanan was his brother-in-law, Resh Lakish, R. Simeon Ben Lakish, his colleague and partner in debates. Resh Lakish had studied in his youth but was forced by poverty to sell himself as a gladiator, an ordeal he survived because of his tremendous physical prowess. A dramatic encounter with R. Yohanan changed his life. It is related that R. Yohanan was bathing in the Jordan when he spied Resh Lakish diving into the water and said to him admiringly: "Your strength should be dedicated to Torah." Resh Lakish, in turn, was impressed by R. Yohanan's great physical beauty and answered in the same spirit: "Your beauty should be dedicated to women." Then R. Yohanan promised Resh Lakish that if he changed his ways and returned to his studies, he would give him his sister, who was Resh Lakish's match in beauty, in marriage. In fact, Resh Lakish resumed his studies and became one of the greatest scholars of his day, revered even by his brother-in-law. At this later stage in his life, Resh Lakish became an ascetic who never laughed and never spoke in public to those whose character was in any way questionable; (it was said that those to whom Resh Lakish spoke in the marketplace could obtain loans without guarantors). Hundreds of intellectual discourses between R. Yohanan and Resh Lakish are cited in the sources. R. Yohanan regarded such debates as the perfect way to further knowledge, and compared himself, in the absence of Resh Lakish, to a man trying to applaud with one hand. Resh Lakish died before R. Yohanan, and the latter, who blamed himself for his brother-in-law's death, was inconsolable and died shortly afterward.

In R. Yohanan's lifetime the Tiberias academy became the world's greatest center for study of the oral law, and its head, who was an authority on both *halakhah* and *aggadah* (legend) was universally revered. Although he was given to outbursts of anger, R. Yohanan treated his disciples like sons. The Talmud describes him thus: "If one takes a cup of pure silver, drops into it seeds of the red pomegranate, decorates the cup with roses and places it between sun and shadow, its beauty is comparable with that of R. Yohanan." The Palestinian center became even more prestigious in his day, and many Babylonian disputes were resolved by "a letter from Palestine." R. Yohanan's teaching was held in such great esteem that his rulings were often accepted, even when they conflicted with the opinions of both Rav and Samuel.

The position of the *nehutei* (those who go down) was created in order to stabilize and regulate contacts between the Palestinian school and Babylonia. The *nehutei* were scholars who went from Palestine to Babylonia to convey the innovations of the Tiberias academy. Several of them were merchants who were obliged to make the journey in the course of their business, but most were emissaries of the Palestinian academy sent for this specific purpose, or, occasionally, to obtain financial support for an institution of study that the Palestinian community was incapable of maintaining. The most important emissaries were the scholar Ulla (known in Palestine as Ulla Bar Ishmael) and Raba Bar Bar Hanna (a traveller renowned for his imaginative tales, which were often political and religious allegories), both contemporary with the third generation of Babylonian sages; and Rav Dimi and Rabin, emissaries to the fourth Babylonian generation. The Babylonian Talmud contains a substantial amount of material originating in Palestine, thus illustrating the fact that Palestinian learning was transmitted to the Babylonian academies and was analyzed and developed there.

R. Yohanan lived to a ripe old age and enjoyed such prestige and status that generations later it was said that he alone had created and edited Palestinian scholarship. This, of course, would have been an impossibility, but it is true that the bulk of the work was carried out by him together with his disciples.

The *Amoraim* in Palestine

The Palestinian academy continued to flourish in the next generation. Since R. Yohanan's disciples were all great scholars and had been encouraged to engage in independent creative activity, there was no sudden crisis after his death. They continued their scholarly work, although the Tiberias academy was no longer the lodestar for scholars, and students continued to arrive from Babylonia. The most famous was the Babylonian sage, R. Jeremiah, whose unique method of questioning, aimed at clarifying the marginal problems of *halakhah*, sometimes angered his Palestinian teachers, unaccustomed as they were to this kind of discussion. Yet R. Jeremiah regarded himself as a Palestinian, and once taunted the Babylonian scholars, calling them "foolish Babylonians, who, since they reside in an obscure country, pronounce obscure sayings." The Babylonians took this criticism in good turn and agreed that "one of them [Palestinians] is worth two of us [Babylonians]."

In the fourth century newly emergent political processes began to exert increasing pressure on Palestinian Jewry, eventually causing material and spiritual impoverishment. The central authority of Rome was undermined after the fall of the last Severan rulers, and the wars between the various pretenders to the throne engendered considerable tension, increased the tax burden, and subsequently weakened the economic foundations of the entire empire. The Jewish community of Palestine, which had already suffered as the result of various revolts, was particularly vulnerable, since most of the Jews were farmers and hence unable to conceal their income from the authorities. Christianity, until then a persecuted minority faith, was beginning to gain strength, and at the beginning of the fourth century it became, for all practical purposes, the official religion of the state. The persecution of Jews that ensued severely affected the Palestinian community, and a wave of emigration resulted. Jews moved to Rome, European countries, or Babylonia, the Palestinian academies were forced to reduce their dimensions, and the number of students shrank. In the fourth generation of *amoraim*, it was noted that, as

[53]

a result of persecution and the economic situation, the public was less interested in study of *halakhah* and preferred *aggadah*, which was more easily understood and offered solace to the oppressed.

The situation was so grave that the Palestinian scholars were forced to expedite the work of editing and codifying the oral law. They created a work, corresponding to the Babylonian Talmud, known as the Jerusalem Talmud. It was not composed in Jerusalem (which, at that time, was a pagan city known as Aelia Capitolina, to which Jews were forbidden access), but over the years the name of Jerusalem had become a synonym for Palestine as a whole. The work was apparently completed in Tiberias and also, in part, in Caesarea.

Although the basic source material was the Mishnah, and the scholarly methods were essentially identical, there are considerable differences between the two Talmuds. The Jerusalem Talmud discusses at length several subjects that are almost completely ignored in the Babylonian work, namely *halakhah* relating to Palestine and its agriculture. On the other hand, the Jerusalem Talmud contains very little legend. This is the paradoxical outcome of the intense preoccupation with *aggadah* in Palestine. Since the Palestinian sages devoted great attention to *aggadah* and, particularly in later generations, to the composition of prayers and liturgical poetry, they did not deem it necessary to edit aggadic literature; this material was collated much later in the works known as *midrashei aggadah* (aggadic exegeses).

In addition to these dissimilarities in the organization of material and intellectual and scholarly methods, the works differ in the quality of the editing. The redaction of the Babylonian Talmud was carried out with great restraint and punctiliousness, and generation after generation corrected numerous details, whereas the Jerusalem Talmud was never properly edited. The material was compiled imprecisely and in haste, one of the reasons it was regarded for so long as a kind of appendix, a stepbrother to the Babylonian Talmud. Then again, the Babylonian Talmud received its final form in a later period and was therefore regarded as a more authoritative summary of the problems of the oral law. Furthermore, the scholarly methods of the Babylonian Talmud, with its great scope and keen intellectual analysis, left more room for intellectual development. Attention focused on the Babylonian work for centuries, and only in the past few hundred years has interest been reawakened in the Jerusalem Talmud, though always as a source of secondary importance. The Palestinian body of learning was studied mainly through its reflection in the Babylonian Talmud or in the various *midrashei aggadah*.

8

The Redaction of the
Babylonian Talmud

THE METHOD of redaction of the Talmud reflects its nature
and the ways in which it differs from the Mishnah. The latter is
basically a book of law, mostly consisting of rulings in all the
spheres of oral legislation. Differences of opinion between sages
appear in abbreviated form, and only rarely are the original disputes quoted or other areas, such as the *midrash* on *halakhah* and
aggadah, explored. The Talmud, however, is not a complete work
in itself and should be regarded as a kind of summarized sketch of
the debates of the sages. Its main significance lies not in its halakhic conclusions but in the methods of research and analysis by
which the conclusions are drawn. Despite the editing and summarizing, the Talmud reflects the methods of study of the Babylonian academies, and should be seen as a slice of life, as the essence of the intellectual experience of generations.

R. Ashi's work of editing did not consist of the summarizing
of the discussions of each generation; he created a complex struc-

The Redaction of the Babylonian Talmud

ture and the end result was a kind of symposium of views on halakhic problems, spanning all the generations. A large part of the lure of the Talmud, as well as its indecipherable and enigmatic qualities, results from its unique form, the fact that it records discourses and debates and contains not only definitive conclusions but also the alternative solutions proposed and rejected.

It would, of course, have been impossible as well as unnecessary to include all the words of wisdom expounded over the centuries in dozens of centers of learning. The editors aimed at extracting the most important and representative rulings and dicta from the hundreds of thousands recorded and tried to weave them together into a complete fabric.

Although the structure of the Babylonian academies changed somewhat over the generations, the basic format remained more or less unaltered. We can therefore cite later descriptions in order to reconstruct scholarly methods of redaction and teaching. Study and teaching of the oral law were not carried out within a single framework, but rather in various forms. The Talmud reflects mainly the methods of instruction of the academy in its busiest periods of study, but it also records other methods. The most popular method of instruction was by public exposition in the course of *pirka* (holiday sermons) by the great scholars who lectured on halakhic matters to an audience not necessarily composed of students. Under the supervision and guidance of the greatest scholars (the academy heads), these public addresses were sometimes delivered by sages who were closely connected with the exilarch or related to him by blood. More important in scope and number were the sermons delivered in synagogues, generally on the Sabbath. On these occasions the sage would discuss a specific halakhic problem of topical interest, and in order to hold the attention of his audience (which, incidentally, included many women), he would introduce aggadic elements into his lecture. This method of combining *halakhah* and legend in Sabbath sermons was preserved in part in the Talmud. The *mi-*

drashei aggadah contain a large number of these sermons (*Tanhuma* and *Psikta*), and halakhic works from the gaonic period were also written in this fashion. (This method is still employed in the synagogues of Iraqi communities.) The audience did not play a passive part on these occasions: they asked questions and the scholars among them would sometimes enter into debate with the speaker. But the custom was that such arguments were low-keyed, and sharp criticism was reserved for the private debates held in seclusion.

Although many halakhic innovations were first expounded at public lectures, study itself was confined to the academy. The study procedure had been established in ancient times—according to the talmudic sages themselves—in the period of the prophets, if not earlier. The need for regular procedure arose from the fact that there was no stratum of professional students, and scholars were obliged to engage in trade or commerce in order to support themselves, studying in their spare time. Only the *nasi* or the heads of the great academies were maintained by public funds, since they devoted all their time to study, though they sometimes engaged in other occupations if this were possible. Most of the scholars, like the overwhelming majority of people at that time, were apparently farmers. Some were artisans (we know of sages who were builders, blacksmiths, shoemakers, tanners, and clerks, as well as physicians), and some were merchants or peddlers. However, young scholars, who were supported by their families and could study without interruption for several years, and rich men, who lived off the income of their estates, constituted the main nucleus of the academy student body, attending all the classes taught by the academy head. Sometimes the academy head was himself a rich man or received large public grants for maintenance of the academy, in which case he himself would subsidize the students. The large and permanent academies also had buildings donated to them or land on which permanent buildings were constructed. The students usually lived in lodgings or in small hostels throughout the course of their studies.

The Redaction of the Babylonian Talmud

But even at the best of times, full-time students constituted only a small percentage of those attending the academies. For the wider student body there existed the *yarbei kalla,* the two months of the year (in Babylonia, Adar and Ellul, slack farming seasons) when students came to the academies to study. Each month was devoted to one tractate of the Mishnah, and the tractate for the next study session would be announced and its general outlines explained. Thus the scholars could peruse the tractate in their own homes, clarify the problems for themselves, collect material pertaining to the subject, and arrive at the next study session equipped with questions and answers.

The academy head presided, seated on a chair or on special mats. In the front rows opposite him sat the important scholars, including his colleagues or outstanding pupils, and behind them all the other scholars. When the academies were larger, particularly in Palestine, the order of seating was based on a precisely defined hierarchy. In the first row sat the great scholars, in the second row the less important sages, and so on. A student who displayed particular brilliance or outstanding erudition was advanced to a row nearer the front, while those whose performance proved disappointing were demoted. This custom dated back to the Sanhedrin, where those seated in the front row of scholars were candidates for the *bet din* (court of law) when another judge was needed or when a seat fell vacant.

The head of the academy opened the discussion and noted the innovations or commentaries on the *mishnah* discussed that day. This task was sometimes entrusted to the scholars in the front rows. Sometimes excerpts from the *mishnah* were read and one of the *tannaim* (those scholars of phenomenal memory who served as living archives) was asked to recite one of the *baraitot* pertaining to the subject, and then the *baraita* and its relations to the *mishnah* were discussed.

With regard to each *mishnah,* there were a number of fixed questions to be clarified. Who is the *tanna* whose method is reflected in this *mishnah* (*man tanna*)? What is the textual source (*mnalan*) and the exact situation to which this *mishnah* refers (*hikhi dami*)? There were also numerous exegetic and textual questions aimed at establishing the definitive version of the *mishnah:* the names of the sages, or the order or exact spelling of words; deciphering the meaning of certain words or incomplete sentences; uncovering the basic principles underlying the *halakhah;* explaining anomalies and contradictions between the *mishnah* and other mishnaic material; and drawing wider halakhic and theoretical conclusions from the narrow issue discussed in the *mishnah.*

The academy head, or the sage delivering the lecture, would give his own interpretation of problems. The scholars in the audience would often bombard him with questions on the basis of other sources, the views of other commentators, or their own logical conclusions. Sometimes the debate was very brief and restricted to an unequivocal and conclusive response to a given question. In other cases other scholars would offer alternative solutions and a large-scale debate would ensue, the academy head serving as chairman, summing up or casting his vote in favor of a certain viewpoint. The issues clarified at a particular session were then transmitted to other academies (there were two central academies in Babylonia in most generations) and were perused by scholars throughout the country. They studied the material during the year, and when the problem surfaced again the new material—proposals, comments, and reservations—was appended to the existing rulings.

Discussion at the academies was free and open, often skipping from subject to subject. Debates on specific questions were often expanded into basic examinations of several issues, or else deviated from the subject in hand to analysis of a totally different question. Sometimes the academy head himself would combine several dicta related by association rather than by subject matter. Occasionally, particularly during discussions of ethical or social questions, the debate would touch on legend or mysticism.

Since study was extremely intensive and consisted mainly of the exchange of views between important scholars, the students

The Redaction of the Babylonian Talmud

could not, as a rule, follow and memorize all that was said. Therefore, after the regular study periods, repetitive sessions were held. They were not conducted by the academy head himself but by a special teacher (or, in the large academies, several such teachers) known as *resh kalla* or *rosh bnei kalla*, who would explain and expand the material and examine its significance together with the students. The *rashei kalla* were regarded as second in importance only to the academy heads (several of them rose to this position), but they were in fact in closer contact with the student body than with their superiors and were particularly well liked. There is a theory that one particular Aramaic blessing (*yekum purkan*) included in the Ashkenazi prayerbook is based on the farewell benediction which the students proclaimed to the *resh kalla*.

R. Ashi's editing of the Talmud was based on the minutes of the discussions at his academy, which, as the central and most important institution of learning, attracted great scholars who had attended several other academies and studied under the most prominent teachers of the previous generation. His academy was familiar with a large body of material taught elsewhere, some of which was known to all the students and cited anonymously without the author's name. Many other subjects cited anonymously in the Babylonian Talmud are actually quotations from the discussions held in R. Ashi's academy or in institutions headed by his disciples, who continued his work. Talmudic texts should not be regarded as verbatim protocols of study sessions, but they do constitute a kind of précis of the typical debates of the talmudic sages.

In the following generations, the work of redaction and compilation did not diverge greatly from the basic rules, and both the debate format and the arrangement by association were retained. Moreover, since it was necessary to encompass a vast quantity of material and to edit it in accordance with the order of the Mishnah, if often transpired that a certain *mishnah* served as the starting point for a long series of discussions of varied subjects only remotely related to it. This is why the Talmud is arranged according to the very general and vague classification used in the mishnaic order; many questions which, logically speaking, should appear in a tractate dealing with a certain given subject appear elsewhere because of the associative connection. This is strikingly evident in the case of matters to which no special tractate is devoted in the Talmud itself and which were appended to certain tractates because of the logical connection or a combination of circumstances. Thus mourning laws are to be found in the *Moed Katan* tractate, which deals mainly with *halakhah* for the intermediate days of festivals; rules for the writing of Torah scrolls, *tefilin*, *mezuzot*, and so forth appear in the tractate that discusses Temple sacrifices; there are other examples of such classification.

Often aggadic material was appended to tractates for various associative reasons, sometimes by subject, sometimes because a discussion wandered away from the issue in hand and touched on other matters.

That the Talmud is a kind of record of discussions in the academies is attested to by the fact that in those tractates containing a large number of chapters, most of the study material appears in the first few chapters. This was both because there was more time available for study of these chapters, and because the students were then more alert. In the later chapters, discussions are briefer, reflecting procedure in the academies.

The incomplete indexing and arrangement of material do not result from a dearth of editorial talent but rather derive from a certain type of approach. In Jewish literature as a whole, there are very few works with clear schematic frameworks because the assumption is that Torah, as a reflection of life itself, cannot be artificially compartmentalized, but must develop naturally from subject to subject.

On the other hand, the Talmud scrupulously respects detail and takes great pains to convey statements accurately. The sources are punctiliously cited and any doubts as to authenticity or traditions are faithfully reported. What is more, talmudic re-

The Redaction of the Babylonian Talmud

daction created a precise terminology for classification of quotations and debates. There is a special annotation for *mishnayot*, *baraitot*, or for the maxims of an *amora*. There are also classifications for different types of questions and differentiation between the nuances of queries. The Talmud distinguishes, for example, between conjectures and assumptions which are refuted at the end of the discussion and those which are accepted and between contradictions which cannot be reconciled and problems to which solutions exist. The order in which various matters are presented is also significant, indicating the relative weight to be attributed to the solutions. It is because of this precision, the outcome of generations of endeavor, that the Talmud, which at first glance appears inconsistent and disorganized, is revealed to be, in fact, a most consistent work with its own fixed methods of analysis. Because of the quality of the editing, it serves as a halakhic source of outstanding importance, though this was not the original aim. And because of the profound stability of its method and ways of thinking, its mode of expression and writing, it was possible for talmudic creation to be continued for many centuries.

9

Talmudic Exegesis

EVEN BEFORE the Talmud was completed, it was evident that this work was to become the basic text and primary source for Jewish law. It is actually the last book of source material in Jewish literature, since the works that followed were to a large extent based on it, derived their authority from it, and consulted it whenever necessary for elucidation of theoretical and practical problems.

Copies of the Talmud or of isolated tractates reached all the Jewish communities, including the remotest settlements in Asia, Africa, and Europe. But from the first it was a difficult subject of study even for the most gifted of scholars. Because of the Talmud's nonsystematic editing, each section demanded a certain degree of prior knowledge, and the background or basis of concepts was not always clearly explained. The material therein, reflecting as it did a specific way of life and the content of the debates held in the Babylonian academies, sometimes appeared to students in other countries or other ages to be disjointed or incomplete. The language also created problems; the Aramaic-Hebrew jargon in which the Talmud was written remained the

Talmudic Exegesis

dialect of Babylonian Jewry for many generations, but in other countries the Jews spoke indigenous dialects. Even in Babylonia, Aramaic eventually yielded to Arabic, brought in by the Moslem conquerors in the mid-seventh century.

Thus scholars in the various Diaspora communities encountered problems in the course of the studies and found it necessary to consult the commentaries on the Talmud. The natural authorities best equipped to clarify problems were the heads of the great Babylonian academies of Sura and Pumbedita. These scholars, known by the title of *gaon* (which initially meant head of a great academy, but changed in meaning after several hundred years of imprecise use), were the heirs of the *amoraim* and thus a primary source for explanation of the Talmud. The *geonim* continued to teach the Talmud in accordance with amoraite tradition. At the height of their achievement, disciples flocked to hear them from all over the Diaspora. But for the Jewish world as a whole, their influence was embodied in the *responsa*, of which only remnants have survived. The communities posed questions relating mostly to practical *halakhah*, but also of theoretical interest. In their letters of response, the *geonim* would explain difficult words and terms and elucidate entire subjects (*sugiyot*). These letters were the first commentaries on the Talmud, neither systematic nor complete but composed in response to need. It was only the last of the *geonim* who began to compose commentaries on whole tractates, and these, too, consisted mainly of interpretations of difficult words or phrases. Gaonic literature was mostly concerned with halakhic rulings and with the practical conclusions to be drawn from the talmudic text.

The need for more comprehensive interpretation of the Talmud was greatly intensified when the ties with the *geonim* were weakened for various political reasons. The great Moslem Empire disintegrated into a number of rival kingdoms which were not always easily accessible to one another. The center of the caliphate, Baghdad (where the large academies were located), also waned in importance, and various upheavals eventually led to the closing down of these institutions, bringing to an end the period of the *geonim*. Certain Jewish communities, in Europe for example, were never able to maintain regular contact with the *geonim* and were obliged to become culturally and spiritually self-sufficient.

By the time the Babylonian center began to decline, in the eleventh century, two important Jewish centers had developed elsewhere. One of these was in the Maghreb (North Africa and Spain) and the other in Europe (Italy, France, and Germany). They constituted the nucleus of the development of the two traditions—Sephardi and Ashkenazi, respectively—that differed in many ways from the outset. The African-Iberian center continued the tradition of Babylonian Jewry: it too was under the rule of the Moslem Empire; its language was Arabic; it was exposed to the same cultural influences; and it maintained consecutive and close ties with the *geonim*. Thousands of *responsa*, letters, and books were sent from Babylonia to the North African countries to guide the Jews there. West European Jewry, on the other hand, was connected (through Greece and Italy) for the most part with Palestine, and a large part of the liturgy, as well as the basic tenets of faith, were derived from Palestine. The Jews of the Moslem countries were strongly influenced by Arab philosophy, science, poetry, and language, which were then in full flower. In contrast, Europe was then steeped in the ignorance and gloom of the Dark Ages, and the Jews there had nothing to learn from the culture of their host countries; they were obliged to create their own spiritual life almost entirely without the aid of the great and distant institutions of Jewish learning. It is not surprising, therefore, that two parallel schools of talmudic exegesis—Sephardi and Ashkenazi—emerged.

The scholars of Spain and North Africa, like the *geonim*, tended toward a systematic approach to Jewish studies. Their main achievements were in the spheres of *halakhah* and halakhic ruling, and they took a comprehensive view of matters without dwelling excessively on minutiae. The first important commentary on the Talmud produced by this school was that of R. Hananel Ben Hushiel of Kirouan, in North Africa. It is characterized by outstanding brevity and avoidance of detail and attempts to summarize each *sugiya* and record its gist, adding explanations of words or terms only when absolutely necessary. Sometimes Rabbenu Hananel omits the explanation of a certain section and contents himself with writing "and this is simple," meaning that it needs no explanation. A similar method is employed by his contemporary and fellow-countryman R. Nissim Gaon in his work *Mafteah Manulei Ha-Talmud* ("A Key to the Locks of the Talmud"), which is more disjointed than Rabbi Hananel's work and deals only with elucidation of selected *sugiyot*. Both works are repositories of the teachings and commentaries of the *geonim*. Sephardi exegetic literature continued along this same path in later generations. Although it emulated the example of Ashkenazi literature in some ways, and commentaries became both more detailed and easier to study, there was still a tendency to seek halakhic conclusions, clarify *sugiyot* as units of meaning, and seek to arrive at a synthesis of talmudic material. These traits characterize the commentaries, known as *shitot* (commentaries), of the Spanish sages— Maimonides' commentary on the Mishnah, written in the twelfth century; the works of R. Meir Abulafia and Rabbenu Moshe Ben Nahman (Ramban), written in the thirteenth century; and those of R. Shlomo Ben Adret (Rashba), written in the fourteenth century.

The exegesis of the European communities developed differently. Great scholars emerged in Europe from the gaonic period onward. The most famous was Rabbenu Gershom of Mainz—known, because of his great influence and the important enactments he introduced, as Maor Ha-Golah (Light of the Diaspora)—who composed a brief commentary on various talmudic tractates. But the greatest commentator was undoubtedly R. Shlomo Yitzhaki of Troyes, known as Rashi, who studied under R. Gershom's disciples. Rashi, who lived in the eleventh century, studied at German and French academies, was active in many spheres, and wrote a number of wide-ranging works on halakhic ruling. He wrote *responsa* to halakhic queries and composed a number of liturgical poems, several of which appear in modern prayerbooks. But his greatest achievements were his great commentaries on the Bible and his monumental work on the Babylonian Talmud, in which he introduced exegetic methods that are valid to this day. The latter can serve as the model for all exegesis; it is written in pure Hebrew and with great clarity. When his Hebrew failed him, Rashi avoided lengthy explanations and simply used the appropriate foreign word. The commentary is written succinctly, giving rise to the popular saying: "In Rashi's time each drop of ink cost one golden coin." At the same time it dwells on almost every sentence in the Talmud, explaining difficult terminology and elucidating each matter in context by adding the words needed to complete an idea and background information whenever necessary. Rashi avoided summing up issues or involving himself in questions of halakhic ruling, and he did not usually attempt to expound at length on the correctness of his theories.

Centuries of scholars nurtured on Rashi's commentary were able to decipher his unique expressions and to demonstrate how he arrived at the solution implicit in the text by introducing a few words or by changing the word order in a sentence. In fact, this commentary possesses the rare quality of being easily comprehensible to both scholars and laymen. Rashi succeeded in interpreting most of the Babylonian Talmud and, incidentally, carried out the important task of determining the basic text and establishing a definitive version for study purposes which is accepted to the present day. He wrote several editions of exegetic works on some of the tractates, bringing them up to date as he went along on the basis of experience with his numerous disciples. Although over the centuries many scholars have levelled criticism at various details and offered their own interpretations,

Talmudic Exegesis

it has been universally agreed that Rashi's work remains the basic and principal commentary on the Talmud.

Many copies of the work were disseminated in Rashi's lifetime, sometimes as *kuntresim* (separate pamphlets) rather than in book form, and this is why his commentary is referred to as the *perush ha-kuntres* (pamphlet commentary). His commentaries on several sections of the Talmud were still incomplete upon his death and were completed by his disciples. Although he had no sons of his own, his three sons-in-law, his grandsons, and great-grandsons constituted one of the most impressive dynasties in Jewish history, all taking part in the task of compiling additions and appendices to the talmudic exegetic work. These were known as *tosafot* (additions) because the *baalei tosafot* (authors of *tosafot*) felt that they were merely adding to an already completed work.

The following anecdote was related to illustrate the methodology of the *baalei tosafot* and the enormous erudition and intellectual effort invested in their work; although it lacks historical substantiation, it nonetheless provides a vivid picture of their methods. It was said that sixty of the greatest scholars of the age decided that each would study one of the tractates of the Talmud until he was perfectly acquainted with all its details. When each had completed his studies, they assembled and began to study the Talmud in unison, from the beginning, and whenever they arrived at any point directly or indirectly related to another tractate, the scholar who had studied that particular tractate would comment on the issue or cite the other source. Then all the sages discussed the subject and pooled their knowledge. Thus the modest project that commenced with notes on Rashi's commentary developed into a much more extensive work. To a certain extent, the *tosafot* belong within the framework of talmudic commentary and contain many exegetic comments, quotations from the first commentators, discussions of various phrases and versions, and so on. But they should also be seen as a further step, a continuation of the Talmud that utilizes its intellectual methods. Just as the talmudic sages studied the Mishnah and clarified its various facets, so the authors of the *tosafot* engaged in perusal of the Talmud itself, and their work may be regarded as the "Talmud on the Talmud."

In their present form the *tosafot* are not single works by separate authors but a collective project created by the scholars of France and Germany during the twelfth and thirteenth centuries. Some of the commentaries, questions, and elucidations were rendered in the name of their authors; others were recorded anonymously, as the end product of discussions in various academies or the outcome of editorial summarization. There are at least two basic versions of the *tosafot:* one named after the town where it was completed, *Tosafot Sens;* and the main version, included in most printed editions of the Talmud, *Tosafot Touques.* Other versions remained in manuscript until very recently or have survived as remnants in quotations or in the work of other scholars.

The *baalei tosafot* include R. Samuel Ben Meir, also known as Rashbam, the grandson of Rashi. He too wrote a commentary on the Torah, much more rationalistic in spirit than that of his grandfather. Renowned for his great piety and fanatic observance of religious precepts, the Rashbam completed several sections of Rashi's commentary on the Talmud. Even more celebrated was his younger brother, Jacob Ben Meir, known as Rabbenu Tam. A merchant by occupation, he sometimes wrote on Hebrew grammar or poetry in both the Ashkenazi and the Sephardi style, and he composed important works of halakhic rulings. But his main importance lies in his work as the greatest of the *baalei tosafot.* Almost every page of the Talmud includes comments by Rabbenu Tam. He displayed such amazing knowledge of the talmudic text that he was regarded by other sages as one of the greatest talmudic scholars of all times, surpassing even Maimonides. His intellectual brilliance was so great that one scholar commented that he was hesitant to pass judgment on the basis of Rabbenu Tam's opinions since "he had the heart of a lion, and one cannot know whether he really intended to interpret in this way or merely wanted to display his brilliance, and we cannot refute his state-

Talmudic Exegesis

ments." Rabbenu Tam found a worthy critic in his nephew, R. Isaac Ben Samuel, known as Rey, who sometimes defended Rashi or other accepted works of exegesis against Rabbenu Tam's queries—although he himself developed other critical methods. One of the most important of the later authors of the *tosafot* was R. Meir of Rothenburg, who was also an important codifier and may be regarded as one of those who rounded off the period of the *tosafists;* he tended to summarize halakhic problems.

Although the *baalei tosafot* did not deal exclusively in talmudic exegesis, it is no longer possible to study the Talmud without taking their commentaries into account. Through their widely variegated analytical work, distinguished by its extraordinary critical perception, they blazed the trail for all other methods of talmudic interpretation. Even the most modern research on the Talmud, with its scientific, systematic approach, is merely an expansion and development of ideas which the *tosafists* first tackled.

In the important Jewish center in southern France, there developed an intermediary system which may be classified half way between the Sephardi and Ashkenazi methods of exegesis. This center was situated midway between the other two, both spiritually and geographically speaking, a fact reflected in its work. Its crowning achievement was the work *Bet Ha-Behira*, by R. Shlomo Ben Menahem, known as Ha-Meiri, who combined the textual and linguistic exegesis of Ashkenazi scholars with the halakhic summaries of Sephardi scholarship. The expulsion of Jews from France in the twelfth century destroyed this center, and its like never emerged again.

For centuries no new commentaries were composed, although new methods of study and research developed. It was only in the sixteenth century that comprehensive exegesis was again undertaken, this time in the great Jewish center in Poland. The work by R. Meir of Lublin is a classic example of the commentaries written by academy heads in that country. It is, to a large extent, an elucidation of difficult subjects in the Talmud and, even more, in the *tosafot*. His method is simple and his commentary is considered easily understood, although, as the fruit of study in a certain academy, it shows the effect of the normal fluctuations of study periods and the varying degree of interest displayed by scholars at different times.

A totally different method was evolved by R. Solomon (Shlomo) Luria, known as Maharshal. His commentaries are usually extremely brief, and he discusses many types of problems, offering decisive rulings. He was preoccupied mainly with the task of establishing the correct version of the talmudic text, and his work contains thousands of proposals for amendment of the text, many of which appear in later printings of the Talmud without comment. His corrections and notes were perused and discussed for generations.

The most important and influential of the later commentaries on the Talmud is *Hidushei Aggadot Ve-Halakhot* ("Novellae on *Aggadah* and *Halakhah*"), by R. Samuel Eliezer Edels, known as Maharsha. Unlike many other commentators, who ignored the aggadic element in the Talmud, the Maharsha continued the tradition of the first commentators, providing a wider interpretation of talmudic exegesis and a broader interpretation of talmudic legend through synthesis. He combined elucidation through the talmudic *peshat* (literal) method of exposition, philosophical hints in the style of the medieval sages, and commentaries based, to some extent, on the Kabbalah. His explanation of the halakhic section of the Talmud is devoted to the talmudic text itself and also dwells extensively on Rashi and the *tosafot*. He utilized various methods, although he preferred a simple approach and often rejected the Maharshal's proposals for textual amendment as insufficiently substantiated. On the other hand, he developed various new aspects of analysis and discourse. Characteristically, he rounded off several of his commentaries with the phrase *vadok* (look into it), which implies that there is room for further development of the theme in order to arrive at more convincing proof. The Maharsha's commentary became extremely popular, and for many generations study of the Talmud was based on perusal of

Talmudic Exegesis

the source itself, of Rashi and the *tosafot*, and of R. Samuel's commentary.

After the invention of the printing press, talmudic exegesis expanded at a tremendous rate. Thousands of works were composed to elucidate various talmudic tractates, specific issues or certain types of problems. But to the present day no new commentary has been written on the Talmud as a whole. The standard method of study consists of utilizing the great classic exegetic works, the commentaries on them, and the exegesis on the commentaries themselves (known as the "arms bearers" by later generations).

10

The Printing of the Talmud

AFTER the final redaction of the Talmud, the need arose for copies of the completed work for study purposes. At that time books were copied out by hand, and the weightier the work the more expensive and laborious the task. The few precious exemplars were jealously guarded by their owners, who were not always willing to loan them, even for copying purposes. Several of the books written in the Middle Ages contain words of praise for those loaning and copying books, services that were regarded as an important aspect of scholarship. One has only to recall that the Talmud contains approximately two and a half million words to understand why copies were few and far between, even at times when there were no stringent restrictions on its distribution or when the economic situation of the Jews permitted widespread copying of texts. Many copies of the Talmud were apparently written out by the students themselves from the books available in the academies and were not earmarked for public use, as they were often filled with written comments. In the period of the *geonim*, the great Babylonian academies were often asked to supply copies of the Talmud, and the first copies in Spain were

The Printing of the Talmud

apparently made from a version that a visiting *gaon* dictated from memory. It was the custom for scholars to memorize large quantities of material from the oral law. Certain individual tractates were widely disseminated because they contained frequently taught material of practical importance or were regarded as part of the basic curriculum, but complete editions of the Talmud were rare. Rashi's teacher, for example, never studied the *Avodah Zarah* tractate, simply because he never succeeded in obtaining a copy of it. Similar conditions apparently prevailed in many Jewish communities throughout the world.

Although the shortage of copies could be attributed to technical difficulties alone, the problem was exacerbated by persecution. The Talmud was banned several times during the Middle Ages, a fate it has also suffered on occasion in modern times. Many volumes were lost or mislaid in the course of the wanderings resulting from frequent decrees of expulsion, and some books were confiscated by order of the authorities. Particularly destructive in its impact was the interdict against taking books out of the country during the expulsion from Spain, when many volumes were buried.

It is not surprising, therefore, that Jews took a great interest in the printing press from the outset. It was necessary for them to study the techniques of printing and to produce the letters themselves, from the design stage to the casting of the lead molds. The first printed Jewish books apparently date from the 1470s. After these first successful printing efforts, the printing of the Talmud as a whole was undertaken. The technical difficulties were many, and the project entailed an enormous amount of work, from compiling and proofreading the manuscripts to the actual printing. The first known printed edition appeared in Guadalajara, Spain, in 1482. We do not know whether the entire Talmud was printed there, as only remnants have survived. During the expulsion of the Jews from Spain ten years later, and from Portugal several years after that, all Jewish books were confiscated. The existence of this particular edition was unknown until very recently. A better known edition—apparently never completed—was printed in the towns of Soncino and Pisarro, and other editions appeared elsewhere.

Throughout this period the Jews were fearful of engaging in printing the Talmud because of the negative attitude of the Catholic Church, but in 1520 Pope Leo X gave permission for publication, and printing of the first complete edition of the Talmud commenced in Venice. The work was carried out by the Christian printer Daniel Bomberg, who had moved to Venice from Antwerp. Bomberg played a very important part in the annals of Hebrew printing. Many basic works were first printed at his press and received their accepted format there, and his was the definitive edition of the Babylonian Talmud. The basic format of the pages, the number of sheets, and the location of the main commentaries on the page were determined in that first edition, and almost all editions since have copied this format. Here and there we find exceptions to the rule, but they generally refer in some way (through special markings or divisions) to the original text. The talmudic text is printed in the center of the page, with the Rashi commentary on one side and the *tosafot* on the other. In order to differentiate between the text and the commentaries, the former was printed in square letters—a simpler form of the script in which Torah scrolls are written—while the latter appear in cursive script. Since the Jews of Western Europe were unfamiliar with the square letters, which are of Sephardi origin, they called them "Rashi's script" (that is, the letters in which Rashi's commentary was printed). The Bomberg press was not the first to utilize them, but it helped bolster the tradition, and exegetic and rabbinical literature was printed in these letters for hundreds of years afterward. The order of the pages and sheets was of great practical importance. The appearance of this edition made it possible to introduce an accurate method of denoting quotations by name of tractate and number of page and sheet—the sheet is the double page, each side being numbered. The printing of the *tosafot* by the side of the text was of more theoretical significance. In the seventeenth century, the Maharal of Prague complained about the study methods of his day and pinned part of the blame on the fact that the *tosafot* were printed adjacent to the talmudic text, so that a tendency developed to accept specific formulae based on the views of the *baalei tosafot*.

This first edition was far from perfect and suffered from various flaws, errors, and a large number of omissions, which were corrected in due course. Other editions—particularly that of another Christian printer, Justinian of Venice, which also served as a model—generally tried to improve on previous versions. Subsequent editions were proofread with great precision and included more detailed indices for biblical verses and halakhic rulings and appended commentaries by contemporary scholars. This process has continued to the present.

Pope Julius III intervened in the process of printing and disseminating the Talmud shortly after this period by prohibiting publication of the work and ordering the burning of existing copies (1553–54). Thus the Talmud could not be printed in Italy, and other European countries were indirectly affected. In many countries the Talmud could only be printed after official permission was obtained, and often only Christian printers succeeded in obtaining the necessary permit. Censorship of Jewish sacred literature in general, and the Talmud in particular, became more stringent. The Basel edition (1578 onward) is an extremely truncated version that omitted an entire tractate, *Avodah Zarah;* unfortunately, other editions were based on this incomplete one. Several editions were printed in Poland before that country came under the influence of the Jesuits, and a number were printed in Amsterdam (which, as part of the tolerant Netherlands, permitted the publication of almost any Hebrew book) and in Protestant Germany.

Two important editions whose impact is felt to the present day appeared in Slavuta and Vilna. The Russian authorities, for reasons of their own, decided to confine the publication of Jewish books to as few centers as possible, and requests for printing permits encountered enormous obstacles. The two above-mentioned printings were carried out under license, and the work went into a number of editions.

From the mid-eighteenth century it became the custom to print in editions of the Talmud rabbinical warnings against the printing of any new edition for a specific period of time. The demand for books was apparently limited, and since printing costs were extremely high, the publishers were afraid that some other printer might produce a new edition, thus competing with them and causing them financial loss. These warnings constituted the first copyright rules and served to encourage printers to continue their work. But since there was no central religious authority for the entire Jewish world, it often occurred that, because of lack of information on events in other communities, or for other reasons, *haskamot* (literally agreements, that is, authorizations) were granted for the production of several editions of the Talmud almost simultaneously. This led to disputes among the publishers and sometimes among the rabbis who had signed the different *haskamot*. Thus, certain editions—some of high quality—could not appear in full because of competition among printers. Sometimes the project was divided up among different towns.

The important Slavuta and Vilna editions were also the subject of controversy. The Slavuta printers produced a beautiful edition of the Talmud, which was rapidly sold out, and the Vilna printers then decided to issue their own edition within the period of the printing ban. As the status of the Slavuta edition was not sufficiently clear, the latter also decided to obtain an impressive number of *haskamot* from rabbis in their region. A large-scale feud ensued when the facts came to light; almost all the rabbis in Poland and Galicia sided with the Slavuta printers, while the Lithuanian rabbis supported the Vilna printing press. This controversy had political implications as well, since the Slavuta printers were Hassidim, and their rivals were Mitnagdim (opponents of the hassidic movement), who were closely connected with the Enlightenment movement. The dispute ended in trag-

The Printing of the Talmud

edy when, as the result of the activities of informers, the Slavuta printers were sentenced to heavy prison terms and their press was closed down. In fact, they were punished as a direct consequence of their ties with the Hassidim and not because of their printing activities.

Although the work of the Slavuta press was continued to some extent at Zhitomir in the Ukraine, initiative was now in the hands of the Vilna press. It was owned by members of the Rom family, who produced a large number of editions of the Talmud, several of which are still regarded as exemplary. In some places, particularly among Polish Hassidim, there was categorical refusal to use these editions, one of the main reasons being the appending of commentaries by scholars who were not universally approved. In general, the Vilna editions are considered works of art, with higher standards of proofreading than other editions; hyperbolic stories were told about the editions' great accuracy.

These last editions of the Talmud, published at the end of the nineteenth and beginning of the twentieth centuries, contained new material in the form of a number of ancient commentaries copied from manuscript, which expanded the horizons of scholarship by enabling students to engage in comparative analysis. The proliferation of students, amelioration of the economic conditions of Jews in certain countries, and lowering of the cost of books have led to the publication of a large number of editions of the Talmud in our century. The introduction of modern printing methods has made printing both easier and cheaper.

The second half of the twentieth century has produced an abundance of photographed editions of the Talmud (based mostly on the Vilna editions) in various sizes and forms, and the number of complete and partial editions must now run into the hundreds. At the same time the invention of offset printing hindered progress in that the talmudic text itself is no longer subjected to the close scrutiny, examination, and amendment once customary, and errors (including printing mistakes) are perpetuated from edition to edition. It should be noted, however, that in some countries, particularly Israel, attempts are being made to arrive at improved versions, to add punctuation, vowelling, and various illustrations; this marks the beginning of a new kind of development in publication of the Talmud.

The Jerusalem Talmud has always been regarded as inferior to the work produced in Babylonia. Fewer manuscripts of the former were produced, and it was disregarded by the great commentators. The first printed edition of the Jerusalem Talmud was produced by Bomberg in Venice in 1524 from a single manuscript (the Leyden manuscript, now in a library in that city). Several editions were printed from this source, which is still regarded as the basic edition. Another important edition was published in Amsterdam, apparently on the basis of several different manuscripts; in the nineteenth century editions were produced in Zhitomir and Vilna (by the Rom family), but, generally speaking, few editions of the Jerusalem Talmud appeared because it was studied by fewer scholars and because of the problems involved. Only about thirty editions have been produced to the present day, and they cannot compare in precision and in the quality of the commentary to the Babylonian Talmud. The Jerusalem Talmud still awaits its redeemer.

11

The Persecution and Banning of the Talmud

THE SAGES believed that it was the oral law—the Mishnah and the Talmud—that rendered the Jewish people unique. It was said in one of the *midrashim* that at some time in the future all the nations would claim that they too were Jewish: "Then the Holy One, Blessed be He, will say: he who holds my mystery in his hand, he is truly Israel. And what is this mystery—it is the Mishnah." In this, and many similar stories, the sages emphasized the importance of the oral law as proof of Israel's singularity, as the definition of true Judaism. The view that the oral law was the bulwark of Judaism was prevalent in the non-Jewish world as well, particularly among Christians. Attempts were made as early as the seventh and eighth centuries to prohibit study of the Talmud, but they failed. For generations Western Europe was unaware of the internal problems of the Jewish people and the importance of its direct and indirect spiritual influences, but when the Catholic Church adopted a more severe attitude toward ene-

mies within its own ranks, it also began to examine Jewish literature and, to a large extent, the Talmud.

Much of the responsibility for this attitude rests with various
Jewish converts to Christianity who tried to engage in public
debate with Jewish scholars. They were well aware of the value
of the Talmud for Jews and directed their hostility against it.
Some converts tried vainly to exploit talmudic texts in order to
demonstrate the truth of Christianity. R. Moshe Ben Nahman,
who was permitted on one occasion to speak freely in the course
of such a debate, commented ironically that if his opponent's
claims were correct, then the talmudic sages themselves should
have converted to Christianity; the fact that they had remained
Jewish was sufficient proof of the degree of veracity of the converts' "evidence." At the same time, several European rulers and
Church dignitaries were convinced that the Talmud contained
anti-Christian material and, on the basis of informers' charges,
they ordered that all anti-Christian statements and libel against
Christ be erased from the books. This anti-talmudic campaign and
the various decrees of the popes reached their height when, as the
result of internal disputes in the Jewish community and at the urg-
ing of certain converts, Pope Gregory IX ordered the burning of
copies of the Talmud in Paris in 1240. Similar decrees were issued several times in the course of the thirteenth century, on one
occasion by Pope Clement IV in 1264, and thousands of copies
were consigned to the flames. The Jews regarded the destruction
of the Talmud as an almost unparalleled national catastrophe. R.
Meir of Rothenburg was inspired to compose a lament that has
survived among the laments of the Ninth of Av. The decrees did
not encompass all of Europe; in the Iberian Peninsula, for example, the Talmud was not burned but merely censored by statements considered derogatory to Christianity being removed.

Church leaders were not unanimous in their views on the subject. A Church synod in Basel in 1431 reaffirmed the stringent
ban on the Talmud, but there were other opinions as well. In 1509
a convert named Johannes Pfefferkorn tried to incite church leaders

The Persecution and Banning of the Talmud

to burn the Talmud in all countries under the rule of Charles V. A champion appeared, however, in the form of a Christian, Reuchlin, who pleaded the cause of the Talmud. Although the controversy was not settled at once, and copies of the Talmud were burned in several towns by the bishops, Reuchlin's arguments appear to have had some effect. In 1520 Pope Leo X permitted the printing of the Talmud, and several editions appeared in the next few decades. But this situation did not endure, and as the result of the intensification of the Counter-Reformation, and due to the efforts of several converts, Pope Julius III ordered the work burned again in 1553. This decree, carried out in the various Italian states, apparently resulted in the destruction of tens of thousands of copies of the Talmud. The harshness of the decree was alleviated by Pope Pius IV's announcement at the church synod at Trent in 1564 that the Talmud could be distributed on condition that those sections which affronted the Christian religion were erased. As the direct result of this decision, an edition was printed in Basel under the supervision and censorship of Catholic monks. It was cruelly truncated and censored, but still did not satisfy the Church and, in a papal bull issued in 1592, Clement II finally prohibited study of the Talmud in any version or edition. The ban did not apply to the whole of the Christian world, since large parts of Europe (the Protestant countries and those under Russian and Turkish rule) did not accept the authority of the Catholic Church, but it was put into operation in most parts of Italy. The Jews of Italy tried to evade the ban in various ways, the commonest being study of the book *Ein Yaakov* (after it too was banned, they changed its name to *Ein Israel*), which contained the aggadic text of the Talmud, and study of R. Isaac Alfasi's *Sefer Halakhah*, which contained much of the talmudic *halakhah*. But the anti-Talmud decree had a decisive impact on the cultural life of Italian Jewry, which never regained its former splendor. This was a vivid historical illustration of the fact that a Jewish community which did not study the Talmud was condemned to attrition.

[83]

No similar decree was issued in any other European country, but there was a widespread tendency to censor the Talmud. In later times printers gradually and clandestinely restored those sections which had been censored, but despite these efforts the best editions of the Talmud are mutilated because of the changes and "corrections" introduced by the censors.

The censored Basel edition was the archetype of such editions, as the censor erased or amended all those parts of the text he regarded as insulting to Christianity or various peoples, or as reflections of superstitious views. The Basel censor, Father Marco Marino, first erased the forbidden word *Talmud*, replacing it by other terms, such as *Gemarah* or *Shas*, initials of Hebrew words for Six Orders. Wherever the text used the word *min* (heretic, originally applied to Gnostic sects and only rarely to Christians), he changed it to read Sadducee or Epicurean. All mention of Rome, even where reference was undoubtedly to the pagan Roman kingdom, was altered to read *Aram* (Mesopotamia) or *Paras* (Persia). The words *meshumad* or *mumar* (convert) were also forbidden and amended. A grave problem for all the censors was the word *goy* (gentile), which they always changed (sometimes puzzling scholars, who were unaware that the censor was responsible). For a time the word *goy* was changed to *akum* (initials of "worshippers of stars"), but a convert informed the authorities that this term too constituted an affront to Christianity, since *akum* also denoted the initials of "worshipper of Christ and Mary." It was therefore necessary to find substitutes, and the most common was the insertion of the word *kuti* (Samaritan) for *goy*. In the Basel edition the censor ordered that the word *kushi* (African, Kushite) be inserted in place of *goy*.

Wherever the Talmud makes derogatory reference to Jesus or to Christianity in general, the comment was completely erased, and the name of Christ was systematically removed, even when the reference was not negative. The Basel censor also decided to erase what he considered examples of personification of the Deity, as well as enigmatic legends. In certain cases he added his own comments in the margin. For example, where the text states that man comes into the world without sin, he added "According to the Christian belief, all men are born tainted with the sin of the first man." Sections which he regarded as offending modesty were also eradicated, and other changes were made as well, as in the talmudic saying: "A man who has no wife cannot be called a man," which offended his sensibilities as a celibate monk. He changed it to read "A Jew who has no wife . . . ." The *Avodah Zarah* tractate was not printed at all, since it deals with the holy days of non-Jews and relations with them.

Although the omissions and erasures were partially restored in other editions, there were always new censors in other countries who introduced new distortions and changes. The Russian authorities, for example, decided that Greece could not be mentioned in the Talmud, since Russian culture was supposedly inspired by that of Greece, and the word was therefore altered wherever it appeared. Some Russian censors declared that the phrase "Greek language" was offensive and changed it to read "language of *akum*." The ignorance of many censors led to the misspelling of names, and many of the errors were perpetuated from edition to edition. Some changes resulted from short-lived political calculations, such as the instruction of the Russian censor at the time of the Russo-Turkish War that the word *goy* be replaced by Ishmael, a change which engendered a whole series of absurd errors.

The Talmud was not the sole work affected by the heavy hand of the censor, but because of its scope and range and the thousands of changes introduced over the centuries, it was impossible to correct all the mutilations even in editions published in countries free of censorship. Offset printing perpetuated many of the mistakes and omissions, and only in the most recent editions have attempts been made to restore the original format of the text.

PART TWO

Structure and

Content

12

The Structure of
the Talmud

BOTH the Babylonian and the Jerusalem versions of the Talmud are arranged according to the order of the Mishnah, which they expound and elaborate. The Mishnah is divided into six basic sections or *sedarim* (orders). The orders, known by their Hebrew initials as the *shass*, have become synonymous with the Talmud, particularly since the Christian censors decided that the word Talmud was taboo. Each order deals with a specific category of problems.

Seder Zeraim (the Seeds order) is devoted to *halakhah* relating to agriculture and Palestinian crops, leaving offerings to the priests and Levites, and gifts to the poor. The order of the tractates is not identical in all editions, but they are usually arranged by size or, to be more exact, by number of chapters. Each tractate usually deals with one specific subject, such as the *Shevi'it* tractate, dealing with the laws of *shemitah* (the seventh year when the land lies fallow) or *Bikurin* (on the offering of first fruits), but related problems are sometimes appended. The seventy-four chapters of this order are divided into eleven tractates, only the first of which, *Berakhot*, is slightly out of the ordinary, since it deals not with agricultural laws but with benedictions and prayers. In other versions this tractate was transferred to the *Moed* order. Since *Seder Zeraim* was also known as *Seder Emunah* (Faith order: it was said that "a man believes in the eternal life and therefore sows seed"), the *Berakhot* tractate is appropriately located at the beginning of the order.

The second order is *Seder Moed* (Holidays). Its twelve tractates deal mainly with the festivals throughout the year and its subject matter ranges from Sabbath laws (to which two tractates are devoted) to laws for fast days. The *Shekalim* tractate is the exception in that it deals with the half-shekel tax that covered the maintenance of the Temple, and ways of collecting and distributing it. Since this tax was collected at regular intervals, the tractate was included in *Seder Moed*.

Seder Nashim (Women) is the third order and deals mainly with laws pertaining to marriage, from the ceremony itself to laws of incest, divorce, and property. Five tractates are devoted to these subjects and two more are appendices—*Nedarim* (Vows), dealing to some extent with the relations between man and wife, and *Nazir*, which discusses laws relating to the *nazirite* (ascetic who takes special vows). The *Sotah* tractate, containing *halakhah* on women suspected of adultery, also covers more remote subjects, which are included only because of associative links.

The fourth order, *Nezikin* (Damages), is also known as *Yeshuot* (Rescues), since a considerable part of it deals with saving the victim from his persecutor. Originally it opened with a tractate also known as *Nezikin*, which discussed civil jurisprudence. But since it was a very long tractate of thirty chapters, it was divided into three parts, known as gates, which are now entitled *Baba Kama* (first gate), *Baba Metzia* (middle gate), and *Baba Batra* (last gate). In general this order deals with civil and penal law, the procedure of law courts, vows, punishments, and so forth. A section of the religious criminal code was devoted to the prohibition of pagan worship in any form whatsoever, and a special tractate (*Avodah Zarah*) was devoted to this subject. Another tractate, *Horayot* (Decisions), deals with the crucial problem of what to do in the case of erroneous Sanhedrin decisions that plunge the entire nation into error. The *Eduyot* (Testimonies) tractate is a compilation of testimonies on ancient *halakhah* that was in danger of falling into oblivion and on unusual aspects of *halakhah*, apparently amassed at a special session of the Yavneh court. Another tractate, which is out of place in this order and differs from most of the other tractates, is *Avot* (Fathers), which deals not with *halakhah* but with ethics and philosophy; it contains the sayings and aphorisms of mishnaic sages. Because of its unique content, this tractate was included in many prayerbooks and was translated into other languages.

The order of *Kodashim* (Holy Things) is devoted mainly to laws pertaining to the Temple and to sacrifices. Of the eleven tractates in this order, ten deal in detail with Temple procedure and with types of sacrifice. The eleventh tractate, *Hulin* (Common Things), also known in ancient times as *Shehitat Hulin* (Common Slaughter), is the only one which does not deal with sacrifices; it contains the laws of ritual slaughter and details on kosher and nonkosher foods, as well as various scattered laws that were not numerous enough to deserve a separate tractate.

The sixth order, *Toharot* (Purity), deals with the most complex and involved halakhic subject—the laws of ritual purity and impurity. These laws, which were observed mainly in the period of the Temple (and for several subsequent generations in Palestine), consist of minute and extremely involved details based on ancient traditions in which the logical connection is not always discernible. Only one tractate, *Nidah*, was of practical significance at that time, since it discusses laws on the periodic ritual uncleanliness of women. This order is considered the most difficult of all, and the greatest *amoraim* had difficulty in deciphering it.

According to the modern division, there are 517 chapters in all (with slight variations between versions), arranged in sixty-three tractates. The traditional number of tractates was sixty, and the present number is apparently the result of splitting several tractates, such as *Nezikin*, into independent sections. The various tractates already had names of their own in the talmudic period, generally reflecting the central theme, and these titles have remained almost unchanged. The chapters too have names, some of them dating from the talmudic era, based not on content but on the opening words. When several chapters commenced with identical words it was necessary at times to give them distinguishing titles, but no great emphasis was placed on these names. The order of chapters in each tractate is normally stable, although it may not always appear orderly and logical. Sometimes a tractate is organized systematically, from the general to the particular, but in several tractates the criterion is the order of the law under scrutiny, the material concerning the earlier part of a commandment coming first. Tractates that contain material in addition to their central subject are usually organized so that the central theme is discussed first, followed by marginal questions. There was also a tendency to begin various tractates with issues that aroused the interest or curiosity of the reader, though they were not necessarily of great importance.

The chapters of the Mishnah are divided into subsections called *mishnayot*, each of which usually discusses one law or several related ones. The subdivision of the *mishnayot* is not uniform, and there are differences between the traditions; but in all printed copies of the Mishnah the division is almost identical. This is why indices of the Mishnah quote the tractate, number of the chapter in the tractate, and number of the *mishnah* in the chapter. For example, the saying "All of Israel have a portion in the next world" appears in *Sanhedrin*, Chapter 10, *Mishnah* 1. In the Middle Ages only the number of the chapter was cited, in most cases without the name of the tractate, on the assumption that the latter would be generally known, and without denoting the *mishnah*, because there was, as yet, no permanent division into *mishnayot*.

The Structure of the Talmud

Although the *amoraim* studied all the orders of the Mishnah, they concentrated, in Babylonia at least, on the four that dealt with questions of everyday life; these essentially constitute the subject matter of the Babylonian Talmud. The *Zeraim* order, which deals with agricultural laws, was only tenuously related to life in Babylonia, since most of the *halakhah* pertained to Palestine in the Temple period. In this order only the *Berakhot* tractate deals with legislation for daily life, such as prayers and benedictions. Nor was the *Toharot* order of great practical use in Babylonia, and only the *Nidah* tractate was singled out for study, dealing as it does with female purification rituals. Most of the tractates in the other four orders were elucidated in the Babylonian Talmud, and thirty-six tractates are still extant. Recently several scholars have tried to extract from the Talmud material relating to the tractates that were not studied in depth and to create in this way a kind of "synthetic" Talmud.

The situation was slightly different in Palestine. Since agricultural laws were pertinent for everyday life there, the Jerusalem Talmud discusses all the tractates of the *Zeraim* order. In the Middle Ages there was a section of the Jerusalem Talmud devoted to the *Kodashim* order, but by the time the Talmud was first printed this section had been lost to scholarship. Almost a century ago, a scholar claimed to have discovered the manuscript of this order, but it is generally regarded as a modern forgery. Of the entire *Toharot* order, the Jerusalem Talmud singles out only a few chapters of the useful *Nidah* tractate for perusal, and in all it covers thirty-nine tractates.

The sixty tractates of the Mishnah and their elucidation in the Talmud constitute a single unit, but additions were introduced over the centuries, which are known by the general and imprecise term *masakhtot ketanot* (small tractates). These are not of a kind. Some are ancient and apparently formed part of ancient compilations of external *mishnayot;* most are summaries edited in a later period, mostly the gaonic period, although some of their sources are extremely ancient. These "small tractates" include a number that deal with ethics and conduct, and some scholars believe there may have been a seventh order of the Mishnah (even before the editing of the *mishnayot* by R. Judah Ha-Nasi), possibly known as *Seder Hokhmah* (Wisdom). We find among these works the *Avot of Rabbi Natan*, a much expanded version of the *Avot* tractate, the *Derekh Eretz* (Conduct) tractate, dealing with rules for correct behavior on all occasions, and others. There are also tractates dealing with laws that were not interpreted in the Talmud, such as the *Sofrim* (Scribes) tractate on the writing of scrolls, the *Semahot* tractate, which discusses mourning laws, and others. These tractates are not an integral part of the Talmud itself, although they were sometimes studied and are regarded as illuminating guides to conduct and to certain aspects of *halakhah*.

13

The Subject Matter of
the Talmud

THE LIST of tractate names suffices to give some impressions of the scope of the Talmud, but it does not exhaust the tremendous range of subjects. The purpose of the Talmud is *talmud Torah* (literally study of Torah) in the widest sense of the word, that is, acquisition of wisdom, understanding, and knowledge, since Torah is regarded as encompassing everything contained in the world. An allegory in the Talmud and the commentaries depicts the Torah as a kind of blueprint for construction of the world. Elsewhere, the Talmud calculated that the scope of Torah was several times that of the world. Thus all of life is of interest to scholars and constitutes fit subject matter for the Talmud, to be discussed in brief or at length. The concept of Torah is immeasurably wider than the concept of religious law, and while Jewish religious jurisprudence encompasses all spheres of life and overlooks almost nothing, the scope of Torah is even wider. Habits, customs, occupational hints, medical advice, examinations of human nature, linguistic questions, ethical problems—all these are Torah and as such are touched upon in the Talmud. And since all of life is permeated with Torah, the sages are not merely teachers, offering *ex cathedra* instruction; their very lives constitute Torah, and everything pertaining to them is worthy of perusal.

The sages themselves said, "Random conversations, jests, or casual statements of sages should be studied," and sometimes important *halakhah* is derived from chance remarks made without any educational intent. This being so, the actions of the sages are of even greater significance. Everything a sages does in every sphere of endeavor must be carried out in a spirit of truth and should be Torah itself. Disciples often studied closely the behavior of their rabbi in order to learn how to conduct themselves. An extreme example of this was the disciple who was reported to have concealed himself under the bed of his great teacher in order to discover how he behaved with his wife. When queried on his inquisitiveness, the young disciple replied: "It is Torah and deserves to be studied," an approach accepted by both rabbis and students as valid. Since certain matters pertain to Torah, there is no room for reticence or for exclusion of certain spheres of behavior from the general rule. It is extremely interesting to note that, although the talmudic sages were marked by their almost excessively modest approach to sexual life and the naked human body and were shocked by profanity, there was no taboo on study of the minutest details of these subjects. Discussions were based on euphemisms and used the most delicate terms; however, the scholars could dwell on both normal and deviant details as long as these were considered pertinent.

This wide range of interests is characteristic not only of *halakhah* in the limited sense of the word but of Torah in the fullest sense. An illuminating exchange of views has been preserved on this subject in the Talmud itself. One of the prominent scholars asks his son, also renowned for his learning, why he has discontinued his visits to the lectures of one of the academy heads. The

The Subject Matter of the Talmud

son replies resentfully: "Every time I come he gives me trivial subjects to study," and explains that the great rabbi had lectured on regulations of lavatory hygiene. "If so," says his father, "then you should renew and increase your visits, since he is dealing with important matters crucial for daily life." In light of this attitude, it is not surprising that the Talmud contains medical hints, remedies against disease, explanations of folk sayings, and many hundreds of anecdotes about various famous personalities. These matters do not form part of the regular curriculum of study, and although certain scholars adhered strictly to the subject at hand as long as they were inside the academy, this did not imply that they denied the values of other matters. R. Zira, the sage, who was famed for his piety and saintliness, went to Palestine against the advice of his rabbi. Before leaving he felt the need to see his teacher for the last time without being seen, so he concealed himself and listened while the rabbi instructed the bathhouse attendants in their duties. Later he noted that he was overjoyed at having learned something new from his beloved mentor.

At the same time, certain restrictions were applied to subject matter. However great the scope of Torah, the sages were never concerned with scientific speculation for its own sake and displayed no interest whatsoever in philosophy, whether in its Classic Greek, Hellenistic, or Roman versions. Talmudic study of subjects corresponding to general philosophy is constructed in a totally different fashion. Similarly, the sages were indifferent to science itself, whether astronomy, medicine, or mathematics. In these, as in other spheres of science and knowledge, they recognized only the boundaries of Torah and they studied these matters on only two planes, dealing with science only when it related directly to *halakhah* and with the natural sciences only when there were general ethical and ideological implications. Their attitude to medicine is characteristic of this approach. Since laws pertaining to ritual impurity call for considerable knowledge of animal anatomy and physiology, the sages developed this sphere of study and succeeded, through research efforts that were not based on prior knowledge of prevailing scientific theories, in arriving at amazingly accurate conclusions. In this, as in other areas, they anticipated modern science while endeavoring to employ an empirical approach without having recourse to theoretical structures that did not derive directly from tested facts. They never deviated from the domain of fact into pure scientific speculation, since this was of no concern to them.

The same is true of the study of human problems. In certain fields of anatomy it was necessary to arrive at precise conclusions, and in those cases the sages did not rely on the scientific knowledge of their day but conducted their own experiments. In laws of defilement, for example, it was important to determine the number of bones in the human body, and to this end, R. Ishmael's disciples examined the corpses of women sentenced to death and executed by the authorities. Their conclusions were remarkably accurate and are still valid. On the other hand, they did not deal with the medical or physiological problems of the human body. Their yardstick for deciding whether a certain medicine was efficacious or a quack remedy was scientific testing. As for astronomy, where precise factual data were required (the length of time between new moons, for example), they succeeded in obtaining the necessary information but took no interest whatsoever in theoretical astronomy. Their image of the world, as ascertained from several sources, is inconsistent and appears very primitive at first glance. When one studies their statements, however, it becomes clear that they were not engaging in real cosmological speculation but were contemplating an ideal spiritual world, although they avoided abstract expressions. When they wrote that the land rests on the mountains, the mountains on the sea, and the sea on a pillar named *tzaddik* (righteous one), it is evident that the description was not meant to be taken literally.

Those sages who were physicians by occupation were, of course, obliged to acquaint themselves with the medical lore of their time. Those who were professional surveyors studied geometry, and the mathematicians were well versed in their subject.

The Subject Matter of the Talmud

But these were professional studies and were not related to talmudic study except to the degree that they were needed for halakhic rulings or ethical opinions.

The restrictions on scientific studies applied mainly to method: the talmudic scholars respected facts and tried to limit their studies to tested factual themes. They were indifferent to scientific speculation, whether tested and proved or in the realm of philosophical conjecture, because they were preoccupied with their own unique ways of thinking.

Thus the spiritual world of the sages was not closed to external influence or knowledge. "If you are told that there is wisdom among the nations, believe it," they said. At the same time, however, they tried to confine themselves to what they regarded as important, and when they studied Torah they tried, as far as possible, to remain within its boundaries. Some of the mishnaic and talmudic sages were acquainted with Greek and classical literature, but this knowledge had almost no impact on their way of thinking where talmudic scholarship was concerned. In this they differed greatly from Egyptian Jewry, which tried to combine Greek culture with Judaism.

Since almost all of the talmudic scholars engaged in common occupations, they were involved in everyday life. Many knew several languages, and one of the qualifications for the appointment of members of the Sanhedrin was expertise in a number of sciences and in languages. Traces of their erudition are abundantly evident in the Talmud, each related subject itself becoming Torah.

The view of the Torah as all-embracing accounts for another trait of talmudic literature—the constant transition from issue to issue and sphere to sphere without specifying the differences between them. Talmudic debate, with its associative methods, is not limited to the *halakhah*. Any subject under the sun may be related to another matter by internal association. Sometimes, for example in a discussion of marriage laws, evidence will be cited from the sphere of criminal law or sacrificial law, and the two categories are not regarded as differing in essence. What is more, halakhic debate on an extremely prosaic subject will sometimes shift almost imperceptibly to the sphere of ethics, allegory, or metaphysics. Only in the Talmud can one read the following statement: "On this subject there were differences of opinion between two Palestinian sages, and there are those who say that it was a debate between two angels from Heaven" without finding the juxtaposition strange. After all, mundane affairs, abstract discussions of *halakhah*, and questions pertaining to the heavenly sphere are all concentrated together within the concept of Torah, and each interacts with the others.

14

Prayers and Benedictions

IN the First Temple era, prayer was entirely spontaneous; when a man felt the need to petition his God or thank Him, he prayed in his own words and on his own ground, and in times of trouble or particular stress he would come to the Temple to utter his prayers there. The formal regulation of prayer had already commenced; the first psalms had been composed and were sung by the Levites on special occasions in the Temple, so that the general public was aware of the existence of certain official prayer ceremonies that took place at fixed times.

The need for a recognized version of prayers became pressing at the beginning of the Second Temple era. Many of the returning Babylonian exiles had only sparse knowledge of the Hebrew language and of basic concepts of Judaism. When they wanted to pray, they lacked both language and content. The Great Assembly therefore decided to compose a standard prayer reflecting the wishes and aspirations of the entire people. It was composed of eighteen benedictions, each dealing in brief with one subject. This prayer, most of which has survived to the present day and still constitutes the basis of the synagogue service, consists of three opening benedictions, three closing benedictions, and twelve intermediary ones containing various requests and supplications. In the mishnaic era the first three benedictions were named *Avot* (Fathers), in praise of the faith of the fathers; *Gevurot* (Power), reflecting the power of the Almighty culminating in the resurrection of the dead; and *Kedushah*, extolling His holiness. The concluding prayers are known as *Avodah* (Worship), supplication for the restoration of worship in the Temple and the return of the spirit of God; *Hoda'ah*, thanksgiving for life and all that is good; and *Shalom*, a request for peace in the world. The twelve intermediary benedictions are various requests, both universal and particular, for knowledge, repentance, forgiveness, redemption, healing of the sick, success of crops, ingathering of the exiles, righteous judgment, punishment of the wicked, reward of the pious, rebuilding of Jerusalem, restoration of the rule of the House of David, and, finally, a request that all these supplications meet with response. The prayer as a whole is known as *Shemoneh Esreh* (the eighteen benedictions) or merely as *Tefilah* (prayer), and it has been the focal point of all Jewish prayerbooks since it was written.

Fixed times were determined for prayer, corresponding to the times of public sacrificial ceremonies in the Temple. One prayer was recited at dawn at the hour of *tamid shel shahar* (morning sacrifice), a second at the time of the *minhah* (evening sacrifice). The *ma'ariv* (evening prayer) was said in the evening or at night and was not directly connected with the time of sacrifice. The status of this third prayer was not clear, and hundreds of years later scholars were still arguing the question of whether it was binding, like the other two, or optional. This controversy over a point that does not appear vitally important led at one time to a "revolution" in the procedure of the Sanhedrin, when the strong-willed *nasi*, Rabban Gamaliel, clashed with the greatest scholar of the age, R. Joshua Ben Hananiah, and was eventually deposed.

Once the wording and timing of prayers were permanently fixed, it was the turn of another important institution—the syna-

Prayers and Benedictions

gogue. Since prayer was based on the needs of the community as a whole, it was decided that services should be conducted in public. The standardization of the prayer service did not, however, affect the private supplications that each individual directed at God in his own style and according to his own needs. The question of how many people constitute a "public" is an ancient one, and the answer too is so old that we do not know exactly when it was first given or whether it was accepted as part of the basic tradition of oral law. Be that as it may, it was determined that ten men made up a congregation for purposes of public worship—hence the term *minyan* (number), meaning the minimum of ten adult males permitted to conduct a public prayer service. The synagogue, therefore, was the place where the local congregation convened in villages, towns, or suburbs in order to pray, and it was also utilized as a place of assembly when necessary. Most synagogues also served as schools for local children and sometimes as *batei midrash* (religious academies) for adults. The synagogue was known poetically by the people as *mikdash me'at* (little temple) but could not actually substitute for the Temple itself, since the aims of the institution were different—community prayer, study, and assembly. In Jerusalem itself many synagogues existed while the Temple was still standing. Some served certain areas of the city or people of specific origin, such as the synagogue that served those Jews who had returned over the years from Babylonia and who maintained contact with one another. There were also synagogues whose congregations were composed of people of the same occupation or profession. One of the sages wrote of the relation between the synagogue and the Temple: "In the early morning hours people would come to the Temple to attend the morning sacrifice. From there they would go to the synagogue for the morning prayer service and would then return to the Temple for the additional sacrifice on holidays and the Sabbath, and then again to the synagogue for the *musaf* prayer." Thus the Temple was the place of ritual and sacrifice, where the individual could seclude himself in a corner and offer his own private supplication whenever he felt the urge. The synagogue, on the other hand, was the place for community prayer, where the individual was a participant rather than a spectator.

From the first, the links of the synagogue to the Temple were emphasized, and all synagogues were built facing Jerusalem, while those built in Jerusalem faced the Temple itself. In later generations, during and after the talmudic era, synagogue architecture emulated the structure of the Temple. The Holy Ark, corresponding to the Holy of Holies in the Temple, was located at the foremost end. The Torah was read in the central area, approximating the great altar in the Temple.

In the Second Temple period, the regular prayer service was augmented by the reciting of the *Shema Yisrael* prayer ("Hear, O Israel, the Lord our God, the Lord is One"). This prayer evokes the general obligation to study and memorize the teachings of the Torah at all times, an obligation observed by the individual to the extent that circumstances and time permitted. In order to give this precept fixed form, two excerpts were selected from the Torah that elucidate the basic tenets of Jewish faith and exhort Jews to commit them to memory (Deuteronomy 6:4–9; 11:13–21); these were recited in the early morning and in the evening. For many generations the Ten Commandments were also added, but this custom was suspended because certain heretical sects claimed that these verses contained the essence of Torah and that all the rest was marginal. In order to demonstrate that the sections recited daily did not epitomize Torah, the sages decided to omit the Ten Commandments. The *Shema Yisrael* recitation was usually linked to the public prayer service, and various ways of reciting it were established. Thus the basic format of prayer consisted of recitation of excerpts from the Torah, together with supplication and thanksgiving.

As the synagogues had existed for so long and the format of prayer was well established, no basic changes took place in the prayer procedure after the destruction of the Temple, though it was necessary to alter the phrasing of certain benedictions and to

Prayers and Benedictions

include prayers for the rebuilding of the Temple and restoration of worship. One of the alterations introduced into the service shortly after the destruction was not, however, connected to the Temple itself but to the problem of the heretic, Gnostic, and Christian sects. At that time the small sects were proliferating and advocated a syncretistic combination of religions. There were Judeo-Christians and Gnostics who reconciled their beliefs with continued Jewish worship. These sects, either in self-defense or for purposes of ideological harassment, often employed measures that Judaism had always roundly condemned—namely, informing on their brethren and denouncing them to the Roman authorities. Matters reached such a pass that the Sanhedrin sages at Yavneh decided to add to the *Shemoneh Esreh* an additional benediction (which is in fact a curse) on heretics and informers. The search for a suitable author for such a "benediction" led them to the scholar known as "Little Samuel," who was renowned for his great humility and even more for his tolerant attitude toward enemies. The text he composed was inserted in the prayer, which now consisted of nineteen sections, though it retained its traditional name.

Since written books were most precious in those times and there was a tendency to avoid recording matters pertaining to the oral law, the various prayers were not written down but rather memorized. Not everyone, of course, knew the prayers by heart. This was particularly true in the early days of the Second Temple era, when traditions, as well as reading and writing, were transmitted from father to son, as the Torah commanded. It was at this time that the post of *shliah tzibbur* (public emissary) was established. The emissary was well acquainted with the formula of the prayers; he recited them aloud so that the congregation could pray in unison. For a number of generations, and certainly in the mishnaic and talmudic periods, this task did not call for any kind of incantation or singing. The man chosen as *shliah tzibbur* was usually a respected member of the congregation, capable of leading others in prayer. It became customary (the custom is still prevalent, though no longer necessary) to repeat the prayers aloud, so that those who did not know the words could recite them after the *shliah*.

The basic format of public prayer could not retain its original simplicity for a number of reasons. First, the need arose to add prayers for special occasions throughout the year, Sabbath and holidays, fasts, droughts, or various calamities. The wording of prayers was amended and expanded, so that the simple *Shemoneh Esreh*, for example, took on different forms, and as time passed, the process was intensified. *Piyyutim* (liturgical poems) and supplications were appended; some have survived and others, including thousands of *piyyutim*, were relevant only to their time and place, and only remnants of them have remained in compilations or manuscripts. Certain practical questions also arose in each age regarding the rules for prayer: time and place, exact phrasing, amendment, and shortening. These queries were studied by the mishnaic sages, who expressed varying opinions. Because different customs had evolved in various communities, the sages were obliged to introduce uniformity and establish clear rules.

In addition to the brief and longer daily prayers, there were also various benedictions. The Torah had already hinted at the obligation to extol and thank God for food, and this concept was expanded in the Talmud thus: the whole world belongs to God and man has no right to enjoy it without asking his leave. The various benedictions (mainly *berakhot ha-nehenin*) recited by those enjoying some pleasure are in fact requests for such permission. The Talmud also states, more emphatically, that he who enjoys the blessings of this world without benediction is violating sanctity. Thus many benedictions were composed for recitation before partaking of various pleasures, mainly food and drink. Mishnaic and talmudic sages engaged in clarification of the wording of benedictions, composed new blessings for every type of foodstuff, and sought rules to define the hierarchy of benedictions, from the most general to the most specific.

In addition to these routine benedictions there were many

blessings for events. There is a special blessing to be recited when some event rejoices the heart and, in contrast, a benediction for occasions of sorrow and catastrophe. The mishnaic sages said that "a man must recite a benediction over evil as over good" and should endeavor to accept whatever occurred joyfully. This obligation to bless evil occurrences is not merely a minor detail within a general precept but reflects an outlook on life. Where other faiths believed in dualism or in two divinities, one creating only good and the other generating evil, Judaism always believed in one all-embracing entity. This viewpoint also found expression in the daily prayer and in the benedictions recited in the event of catastrophe, recalling the words of Isaiah that were also quoted in the prayer service: "I form the light and create darkness; I make peace and create evil, I the Lord do all these things" (45:7). The benedictions related not only to such generalized issues but also to various minutiae of everyday life and of nature, on the basis of the conviction that a man should relate his life and all that he saw around him to the all-encompassing faith. Thus there is a benediction to be recited upon seeing the ocean for the first time, upon seeing strange animals, upon seeing rare natural phenomena, and even for ostensibly prosaic occasions—upon seeing the first blossoms of spring, on the rain, and even on beautiful women. These subjects are discussed at length in the Talmud, mainly in the *Berakhot* tractate, which is devoted to benedictions.

15

The Sabbath

THE CONCEPT of the Sabbath is a fundamental part of Judaism, and its importance is stressed from the story of the Creation in the Book of Genesis to the explicit precept in the Ten Commandments to refrain from labor on the seventh day. The basic injunction "Thou shalt not labor on the Sabbath" is repeated several times in the Torah and reiterated again and again by the prophets.

The basic view of the Sabbath as a day of rest appears very simple but arouses a number of problems when put into practice. First and foremost, it is necessary to establish the definition of "labor." The term may be interpreted to mean any work that entails excessive effort or activity for which payment is rendered, or in many other ways. Each of these definitions lends a new dimension to the interdict and changes the way in which the Sabbath is observed. The oral tradition, which relies on detailed analysis of the biblical sources, arrives at another conclusion as to the nature of the labor forbidden on the Sabbath, based to a large extent on the concept of *imitatio Dei* suggested by the sources on this question in the Torah itself. The prohibition is not related to the defi-

The Sabbath

nition of labor or to the payment of money but to the injunction to refrain from acts of deliberate creation in the physical world. Just as God ceased from His labor—creation of the world—on the Sabbath, so the children of Israel are called upon to refrain from creative work on this day. This general abstract definition was not formulated thus in the Talmud, where generalized and abstract definitions are avoided. Furthermore, no single definition could cover all the complex problems likely to develop. Instead, the Talmud chose an elemental model for those actions prohibited on the Sabbath—the work of construction of the Tabernacle in the desert, explicitly prohibited by the Torah. A large part of the halakhic discussion in the Talmud on forbidden and permitted acts is an elaboration and expansion of this basic model and the derivation of practical conclusions from it.

First it was necessary to analyze the categories of basic activities carried out during the construction of the Tabernacle, and this analysis was summed up in a list of "thirty-nine basic labors," or acts of creation, that were undoubtedly carried out at that time and constitute *avodah*, that is, prototypes of the work forbidden and permitted on the Sabbath. The *mishnah* in which this list appears classifies the types of work by objective, from preparation and cultivation to processing of leather, metal, and fabrics. Each of these thirty-nine *avodah*, or basic categories of labor, has its offspring (*toladot*), a type of labor similar in essence, although differing in detail. The unique character of talmudic literature is discernible in the ways in which various subjects are related to one another. Milking cows, for example, comes under the category of "threshing." The classification appears meaningless at first glance, but the association becomes clear when the internal logical structure is analyzed: threshing is an action aimed at extracting the edible content from an object that is not itself earmarked at the time for consumption; milking fulfills the same function, although in a different sphere.

Typology is only one facet of the problem, however, and there is also a quantitative side to the discussion. To state that a certain task is forbidden on the Sabbath is to create a general prohibition, specifying what should not be done. It is still necessary to define what marks certain acts as trivial, from the practical point of view, as, for example, when a bad intention was present but was not implemented in an act of creation. Writing is forbidden on the Sabbath, but what are the significant limits of writing? In this case the sages decided that two letters constituted a significant unit so that the writing of more than one letter should be regarded as work in the fullest sense of the word. An act of creation calls for qualitative as well as quantitative definition. It is obvious that spoiling, defacing, and destroying are not labors unless they form part of a network of positive acts. He who destroys a building is not regarded as engaging in work unless the act of destruction is carried out for purposes of building a new structure that makes use of the destroyed object or replaces it.

Then there is the question of intention (*kavanah*). According to the Talmud *melekhet mahshevet* (intentional work) was prohibited by the Torah; this implies that work which does not call for mental effort is not creative. A man who carries out a certain action unthinkingly and later discovers that he has created something is not engaging in work, since his efforts lack the component of intention. This subject is not easily defined, since there will always be a question of the nature of the intention that transforms mere action into creative work. There were sages who restricted the concept of *kavanah*, claiming that intentional work is any labor that a man carries out with prior knowledge of its consequences. Other scholars held that intention has more precise significance and that anyone carrying out an activity that he did not originally intend to execute in this way could not be regarded as having worked on the Sabbath. An extreme example of this attitude is the view of the *tanna* R. Simeon Ben Yohai that a man who intended to pick a certain bunch of grapes and picked another bunch instead had not truly been working—even if, as far as he was concerned, there was no practical difference between them. The definitions and differences of opinion on this subject

The Sabbath

are often extremely subtle, fine distinctions being drawn between various aspects of intention, knowledge, and intentional and unpremeditated consequences.

Although the network of explicit interdicts contained in the Torah or deriving directly from it is wide ranging, it was extended even further in ancient times by the creation of various restrictions— *seyagim* (literally fences) aimed at preserving the framework of the Sabbath—although the restricted activities had not always been explicitly prohibited by the Torah. These restrictions are extremely ancient, and some undoubtedly date from the Torah era itself. The Talmud noted that some generations had taken a very stringent view of Sabbath prohibitions, both out of zealous regard for the sanctity of the day and because the need was felt to observe the strict letter of the law when the public was lax. In due course a tendency developed to belittle the importance of some of these restrictions, because it was felt that the people had accepted the idea of Sabbath observance and that the introduction of further restrictions was therefore superfluous. At the same time, attention was always paid to those restrictions that were given the name of *shevut* (rest) in the mishnaic period and were aimed at highlighting the image of the Sabbath as a day of rest. A classic example of such an ancient restriction is the ban on commerce on the Sabbath. Commerce as such does not belong within the general framework of creative work, since whatever it produces is not physically evident. Nevertheless, we know that this ban existed as far back as the days of the first prophets, and even when a large proportion of the population took up pagan worship all stores were closed on the Sabbath and it was unthinkable to trade on that day. In the beginning of the Second Temple period (in Nehemiah's day), the Jews refrained from trading even with non-Jews on the day of rest. The *shevut* prohibitions are wide ranging and are among the first examples of the introduction of additional restrictions in order to preserve the basic nucleus of precepts. The *shevut* rules encompassed many acts that were not prohibited in themselves but could, however unintentionally, bring about strictly forbidden actions. For example, the practice of medicine was forbidden on the Sabbath (unless a question of life and death were involved), as was the playing of musical instruments. It is interesting to note that the Temple was "extraterritorial" as far as *shevut* prohibitions were concerned. Most of them were not observed in the Temple on the assumption that the priests could be trusted to observe all precepts and that the needs of the Temple itself were sacred.

The ancient bans, which were the subject of protracted and inconclusive debate for centuries, included the ban on *muktzeh* (literally excluded or out of bounds). This was essentially a prohibition against the handling of certain objects and utensils that were related to work forbidden on the Sabbath. The assumption was that a man handling such objects on the Sabbath might—out of forgetfulness or habit—engage in work. According to talmudic tradition, the ban was strictly observed at the beginning of the Second Temple period, under the Great Assembly. In later generations it was reexamined, and scholars tried to classify the various interdicts in this sphere into those that should be observed strictly and those that were less stringently observed, on the basis of classification into objects unfit for Sabbath use and those used for permitted work. Here too there were scholars who tended to take a more liberal view, while others wanted to maintain the restriction almost in its original form, and extremely subtle distinctions were drawn between various kinds of actions and objects.

Yet the nature of the Sabbath is such that it cannot be associated only with prohibitions and negation. To a certain extent, its meaning (and this is what distinguishes it from imitations adopted by other peoples) lies in the fact that it is not a day of gloom, hedged in by strict prohibitions. The phrase "Call the Sabbath a delight" (Isaiah 58:13) inspired several customs included within the generic term *Oneg Shabbat* (Sabbath delight). They include, for example, the three Sabbath festive meals, the

The Sabbath

injunction to wear festive garments in honor of the Sabbath, and so on. The lighting of Sabbath candles was also originally part of the *Oneg Shabbat*, a way of insuring that the Sabbath meal would be eaten in the light. The Torah exhortation: "Remember the Sabbath day to sanctify it," which was originally a general injunction to mark the commencement of the Sabbath by word and deed, was also stylized, together with the benedictions and prayers. A Sabbath *kiddush* (sanctification), a special benediction recited over a glass of wine, was composed. The manifestations of *Oneg Shabbat* (it was even said that "sleep is a delight on the Sabbath") included spiritual aspects. The sages introduced the reading of a portion of the Torah—which came to be known as *parashat ha-shavua* (the portion of the week)—on Sabbath morning and during the *minhah* prayer. In the talmudic era, scholars preached on Sabbath afternoon. In short, the sages fashioned the image of this day as a time of "sanctity, rest, and delight."

Another aspect of the Sabbath laws was the construction of a whole network of fixed boundaries within which a man is permitted to act, to walk, and so on. The view that Sabbath rest entails remaining in one place was stated in the Torah: "Let no man go out of his place on the seventh day" (Exodus 16:29); this is the very first Sabbath precept, actually preceding the Ten Commandments. The injunction was taken literally by various sects, including the Karaites, who refrained from going out of doors on the Sabbath for any purpose whatsoever. The oral tradition is more liberal on this question but also much more complicated. The first elaboration of this theory is the "Sabbath boundary" (*tehum Shabbat*), the area in which a man is permitted to walk on the Sabbath. The boundaries were determined, to a certain extent, on the basis of the conditions prevailing when the Jews lived on their own land, and certain cities had 2,000 cubits of land adjacent to them on either side. But after the transition to unwalled settlements or irregularly constructed large cities, many problems arose, and it was necessary to determine more flexible rules for the Sabbath bounds. The ban on carrying objects on the Sabbath was more limited in scope, but wider in its theoretical significance and relation to the everyday world. This ancient ban was widely studied in the Second Temple period, and it was necessary to create a theoretical model in order to include all types of buildings, streets, and courtyards in one framework and thus further solution of numerous queries. Some interdicts were spelled out in the Torah, and in the Second Temple period the sages added new bans, as well as enactments aimed at making life easier.

Generally speaking, "four authorities" were established for the Sabbath, that is, four types of areas defined according to the way in which they were bordered and by practical usage. These range from *mekom petur* (exempt location), an unrestricted area where carrying burdens on the Sabbath is permitted; *karmelit*, semi-built-up areas, fields, and oceans, on which there are certain restrictions; *reshut ha-yahid*, the private domain, which is clearly demarcated; and *reshut ha-rabim*, the public domain. The precise demarcation of these areas and determination of the relationship between them is an involved subject in its own right, but becomes even more complicated with the introduction of the concept of *iruvin*. Attributed to King Solomon, *iruvin* is, in essence, the expansion of the concept of the fixed boundary. The establishment of permanent borders between various locations is undoubtedly important for defining the nature of these places, as regards Sabbath laws, property rights, and so forth. But here the concept of boundaries is extended to forms of demarcation that are not so evident to the eye, although, to a certain extent, they are no less real. In a way this denotes the transition from a concrete, simple approach to a more abstract and modern view of borderlines between objects (countries, public and private domains, etc.) that no longer depend on physical demarcation but are, rather, related to symbols and conceptual recognition. The *Iruvin* tractate of the Talmud, which deals with this whole range of subjects, contains

The Sabbath

practical and theoretical discussions of the essence of borders as such.

In the most general sense, the numerous Sabbath laws are an expanding network of minute details deriving from several basic concepts, which eventually create an almost Gothic structure made up of thousands upon thousands of tiny and meticulously fashioned details clustered around the original form.

16

The Festivals

MOST OF the tractates in the *Moed* order deal with holidays and special occasions throughout the year. The Jewish festivals may be divided into those explicitly mentioned in the Torah, and the special days of rejoicing or mourning established in later generations. All the festivals mentioned in the Torah, apart from the Day of Atonement, which is a unique festival and differs from all others, have a common denominator in that they are all *mikraei kodesh* (holy convocations) with special precepts attached to each. Most of the subjects pertaining to festival *halakhah* in general were included by the sages in a short tractate, originally known as the *Yom Tov* tractate and later known as the *Betza* tractate, after the opening word.

Like the Sabbath, the festival is a day of rest, but it differs from the seventh day in two ways. First, it is less strictly observed than the Sabbath, a fact which, paradoxically enough, led the sages to take a strict view of some of the festival legislation in order to prevent profanation of the day. Second, all labor was forbidden on the Sabbath, while the festival bans cover only *melekhet avodah* (that is, physical work), while work related directly to the preparation of food (lighting a fire, cooking, baking, etc.) was permitted. Some of the scholarly discussions of the sanctity of the festivals were aimed at elucidating the special aspects of holidays and conducting a comparison with the Sabbath laws.

A good deal of space is devoted in these discussions to the question of *yom tov sheni shel galuyot* (second day of festivals in the Diaspora). The fixing of this second day and the relevant discussions dramatize the history of the period. The Jewish festivals (and, in fact, most of the calendar) are based on the lunar calendar. *Rosh hodesh* (first day of the month) was fixed for the day when the new moon appeared. The sages of the mishnaic period had access to quite accurate information on the length of the average lunar month (within two seconds of the time now established by astronomers), but in principle did not rely on this data; on this issue, as on many others, they demanded empirical evidence of the appearance of the new moon. Testimony was taken from two independent witnesses who had seen the new moon with their own eyes. The witnesses appeared before the authorized court, and if after thorough investigation their testimony was found to be reliable, *rosh hodesh* was fixed on that day. The sole court authorized to discuss this subject and to determine the beginning of the new month, and hence the dates of the holidays, was the central *bet din* in Jerusalem; subsequently it was the Great Sanhedrin in its places of exile within Palestine. Only once, when Palestine was devastated by war and the court was unable to meet because of the decrees of the hostile authorities, did R. Akiva determine the dates of the festivals from the Diaspora. An attempt by one of the important sages, R. Hananiah, nephew of R. Joshua, to fix the dates in Babylonia encountered the violent opposition of the Palestinian sages, who sent special emissaries to foil this scheme and proclaimed dramatically that the fixing of the calendar from outside Palestine was a denial of the Torah and an attempt to establish a semi-idolatrous Temple in Babylonia. The leaders of Babylonian Jewry immediately abandoned this scheme, although the affair remained emblazoned in the collective memory of the sages for generations as "Hananiah's sin."

Since only the great *bet din* in Palestine was authorized to determine the dates of months and festivals, it was necessary to inform Jews outside Palestine of the dates within the first few days of the month (since the important festivals occur from the tenth of the month onward). As long as the important diasporas were located in countries close to Palestine (Egypt and Babylonia), a simple form of signalling was employed: special beacons were lit on high hilltops in Palestine and thus the news was transmitted within several hours to Babylonia. The first obstacle to this system was introduced by the Samaritans, who resided mainly in central Palestine and with whom relations had been strained since Yohanan Hyrcanus captured their region and destroyed their Temple on Mount Gerizim. The Samaritans began to sabotage this signalling system by lighting beacons at other times, and it was necessary to invent a new method—the dispatch of special emissaries to the Diaspora. But however fast these emissaries travelled—they were permitted to violate the Sabbath—they were not always able to arrive at their destinations in time, particularly as the Jewish communities were becoming increasingly dispersed. This was why the Jews of the Diaspora began to celebrate festivals for two consecutive days in order to settle doubts, since there can be only a one-day difference between a twenty-nine- or thirty-day month. This custom was observed for many generations, although the information often reached the Diaspora in good time. Meanwhile, the Palestinian emissaries were being harassed by the Roman authorities. The Romans realized that as long as the Jewish communities abroad were dependent on the *bet din* in Palestine they would remain subservient to the Palestine center and dependent on it. They therefore detained the emissaries, in some cases even imprisoning them.

In the end the *nasi* Hillel the Second decided, in the fourth century, that it was impossible to continue in this way, and a session of the Sanhedrin decided to draw up binding regulations to fix the dates of festivals and years, submit them to the great *bet din* for approval so as to give them legal sanction, and publicize them in the Diaspora. After the publication of the calendar, Jewish communities became independent of Palestine regarding the dating of festivals.

Then there arose the problem of how to celebrate the second day of a festival in the Diaspora when it was no longer essential. The Palestinian scholars who were questioned replied that although the central reason had disappeared, the Diaspora should continue to observe ancient customs. The second day of the festival, observed out of respect for tradition, came to be known as "the second festival day of the Diaspora." It closely resembled the first day of the holiday, with slight differences in the reading of the Torah and *haftarot* and, in later generations, in the liturgical poems; but it was considered necessary to define the relations between the two days and the actions permissible on the second day.

Externally speaking, the two days of the Rosh Hashanah (New Year) festival belong within this category, but in the Talmud the sages differentiated between the cases. The fact that the New Year is celebrated for two days is not connected with problems of communication with the Diaspora but rather to the procedural problems of taking evidence at the beginning of the month. In the Second Temple period it was sometimes necessary to extend the New Year to two days because the witnesses were tardy; after the destruction of the Temple only one day was celebrated for some time, until the old custom was restored in commemoration of the Temple. As to the other festival days, even when two days are celebrated because of doubts about timing, they remain "festivals of doubt," only one being the true festival. In contrast, the two days of Rosh Hashanah are regarded, from the point of view of *halakhah*, as one "long day" lasting forty-eight hours for celebration purposes.

A factor common to several festivals is *hol ha-moed* (the intermediate days of the festival). The two important festivals of Passover and Sukkot (the Feast of Tabernacles) last for seven days, but only the first and last days are festivals in the precise meaning of the term, while the days in between are called festive days but are not clearly defined by the Torah. The Talmud discussed them at length, and it was agreed that this was one of the cases in which the Torah did not supply unequivocal rules, the matter being left to the sages. Scholars laid down new rules for *hol ha-moed:* no work was then to be done which was connected with an occupation or trade unless failure to work could cause considerable loss, or unless the artisan was obliged to work in order to survive. Many details derive from this generalized definition, and a short tractate of the Talmud, *Moed Katan*, is devoted to them.

In addition to the general aspects of the festivals as a whole, there are specific detailed *halakhot* for many of them. Rosh Hashanah is distinguished by the precept of blowing the *shofar* (ram's horn), and this injunction, which appears simple, called for a lengthy elucidation of the meaning of the text: what exactly was meant by the term *shofar* in terms of the materials; what was the meaning of the word *tekiah* (blowing), and so forth. There were apparently various traditions on this subject in the mishnaic period, and scholars composed different combinations of musical tones in order to reconcile the theories. Their rulings are still the basis for customs, although certain modifications were introduced over the centuries, and different communities have evolved their own traditions of *shofar*-blowing.

Another subject of discussion was the actual dating of the beginning of the year. The Torah suggests two possible dates for the commencement of the year, one at the beginning of the autumn and the other in the month of Aviv (spring). According to tradition, a situation developed that corresponded closely to the general calendar: the counting of months by their ancient appellations (first month, second month, etc.) commenced with the month of Nissan, the date of the Exodus from Egypt, while for most other events the year commenced with the month of Tishri (September). Thus the Jewish calendar year begins in the seventh month and ends in the sixth, just as the general calendar ends in the tenth month according to the ancient count which started

The Festivals

with March. What is more, it transpires that there are at least four "new years." The normal count commences in Tishri and is the most important of the four; for various promissory notes, however, the count begins in Nissan; for purposes of dating plantations (important for various agricultural laws), the year begins on the fifteenth of Shevat. This corresponds to the situation in most parts of the world where the calendar year, the fiscal year, and the school year all commence in different months. The Rosh Hashanah prayers, which are unique in form, are discussed at length in the Talmud, since, despite the fact that the main prayers were composed in ancient times, it was necessary to determine a uniform version for the entire nation, and the sages were not always in accord. Here too we find divergence of custom, each community adding its own details as time went by.

Sukkot (the Feast of Tabernacles) is characterized by the injunction to dwell for seven days in tabernacles or booths and to take four species of plants for the special benediction ceremony. These are examples of precepts that appear to provide adequate details but could never have been observed without an extended oral tradition of additional definitions and practical ordinances. The question of how to define a tabernacle is fundamental and contains within it dozens of other queries. What is the area of the tabernacle? How should it be constructed? What distinguishes it from a house? What materials should be used? These problems are related to the questions of boundaries and demarcations. How is one to decide when the wall of a certain structure constitutes a real boundary and when it is a symbolic border? Then there was the question of whether the definition of a boundary fence that is valid for one set of laws (on Sabbath, for example) can also be applied to tabernacle *halakhah*. The sages have several ways of solving these and other problems. They rely first and foremost on ancient tradition and on those sections of the Torah that deal directly or indirectly with this question. They then analyze the issue in accordance with the fixed talmudic forms of debate and try to adapt the general definitions in this sphere to those employed in religious and civil law. They thus arrive at a general consensus as to the main points of the law, although there is always room for differences of opinion on details.

The problem of the *arba'ah minim* (four species) was also solved basically by tradition, since there is no way of identifying the species of plants mentioned in the Torah without consulting tradition. But on this subject as well there is room for development of wider and freer discussion, extending to other spheres. One of the most important rules relating to the precepts states that they should be observed in the spirit of the verse: "This is my God and I will glorify Him" (Exodus 15:2); in other words, a way that is redolent of beauty and grace. This rule is particularly applicable to the Sukkot precept that speaks of "the fruit of goodly trees" (*etz hadar*, Leviticus 23:40). There was room here for detailed discussion of the meaning of *hidur* (beauty) for each of the species.

Sukkot customs were closely linked to tradition. One such ancient custom, for example, was the ceremony of pouring water on the altar on festive days, which was connected with the prayers for the coming year and in particular with the supplication for rain in its season. The custom was enthusiastically sanctioned by the traditional leaders of the people and was indirectly responsible for a violent clash with the Hasmonean ruler, Alexander Yannai. According to what is related in the Talmud, and similarly in the writings of Josephus Flavius, Alexander Yannai, when High Priest, was accorded the honor of pouring water on the altar. But since he favored the Sadducee claim that the written law made no mention of this custom, he demonstratively poured the water on his own feet, and the people, in their resentment, spontaneously stoned him with *etrogim* (citrons). The king summoned his army of foreign mercenaries to his aid, and they conducted a slaughter among the people then assembled in the Temple. This was one of the immediate causes of the civil war between the king and his supporters and the leaders of the Sanhedrin.

Pesah (Passover) has its own particular precepts: the eating of *matzah* (unleavened bread) and the prohibition against the consumption of *hametz* (leaven) throughout the festival. These precepts were observed all the more strictly because of the grave warning in the Torah that any person consuming *hametz* during Passover "shall be cut off from Israel" (Exodus 12:15). The discussions commence with definitions: what *hametz* is, and so forth. Even in modern times, no precise biological definition has been found for the process of leavening, and it was certainly a great mystery in ancient times. The regulations on the ways of conducting the search within the home for *hametz* are so ancient that even in the first century C.E. the Houses of Hillel and Shammai had several disputes about the precise meaning of the ancient *mishnah* that contains them. Here too the Talmud does not confine itself to the matter at hand and branches out into other spheres: what constitutes property; how far does the ban on *hametz* extend, and so on. According to one age-old tradition, a Jew is not obliged to destroy *hametz* belonging to a non-Jew even if it is located in the Jew's own home, but the ownership must be established with great care. All these injunctions call for strict observance, but at the same time the Talmud leaves room for maneuvering—not generally exploited until the late Middle Ages—through the formal sale of *hametz* to a non-Jew, who is then regarded as the owner for the duration of the festival. The legal procedure involved and the theoretical substantiation of this activity call for a combination of fiscal law and Passover *halakhah*.

The Talmud also devotes much thought to the Passover *seder*, the festive meal on the eve of the holiday that is the most important religious family occasion of the year and has preserved its ancient form to the present day. The dramatic description of the Exodus from Egypt and the injunctions to preserve the memory of that day and to celebrate it are part of a tradition dating back to the First Temple. The *seder* customs had been stylized to some extent by the Second Temple period. The four questions asked by children during the ceremony are extremely ancient, although without certain details that were eliminated after the destruction of the Temple as no longer relevant. Many problems arose over the centuries, from the common question of the integration of different customs and traditions to the problem of composing a uniform version satisfying the stringent demands of the *halakhah*. Talmudic theoreticians needed to adapt customs developed at a time when the people worshipped and sacrificed in the Temple to new times in which this ritual was but a memory, and they had to learn how to perpetuate Temple traditions without resorting to empty imitative rituals.

The Passover festival, based to a large degree on the public ceremonial offering of the paschal sacrifice, is linked to the whole range of sacrificial laws. Half of the tractate devoted to Passover *halakhah* (*Pesahim*) deals with sacrifice, a very different sphere of halakhic discussion. The differences between the two sections of this tractate—one purely ritual and the other devoted to *hametz* problems—eventually led to its division into two separate tractates. Discussions of the ritual of the paschal sacrifice belong in the *Kodashim* order rather than in *Moed*.

Similar problems emerge in the tractate dealing with *halakhah* for Yom Kippur (the Day of Atonement). The Torah dwells at length on the unique and involved ritual of this holiday, carried out in the Temple almost exclusively by the High Priest. The exact details of this complicated procedure take up most of the *Yoma* tractate (the tractate devoted to this festival). These *halakhot* contain thousands of details that could have been determined only through the continuous living tradition of the Temple priests. For several generations some of the High Priests favored the Sadducean viewpoint and, in order to ensure that the ceremony was carried out in strict accordance with tradition, the High Priest was obliged to swear before a special court that upon entering the Holy of Holies, which he alone was permitted to enter, he would not deviate from tradition. The Sadducean priests apparently respected tradition since they too recognized the fact that it was a body of laws and regulations evolved over generations, rather than a series of innovations introduced by the sages. Although certain priests favored other interpretations of

The Festivals

biblical verses, they did not introduce actual changes into rooted customs.

Because of the great theoretical importance and complexity of the ritual ceremonies, scant attention was devoted to other aspects of this holiday—the prohibition of work, the fast, and the penitential aspects. Yom Kippur, though classified among the usual run of festivals, differs from them in that, like the Sabbath, it is a "day of rest" on which work is forbidden. It was therefore superfluous to enumerate the *halakhah* for such a festival, since it was discussed at great length in reference to the Sabbath. Although from the purely halakhic point of view there are variations between the prohibitions relating to Sabbath and Yom Kippur—and it is clear from the Torah and even from tradition that the Sabbath interdicts are even more stringent than those pertaining to Yom Kippur—there are no great practical implications.

The Yom Kippur fast was also closely examined by the scholars since the phrase employed in the Torah: "And you shall afflict your souls" (Numbers 29:7) lends itself to numerous extreme interpretations. It was possible to deduce from the text itself that physical mortification was called for. The halakhic tradition, which specified abstinence from food and drink (and, on a lesser level of stringency, from washing, sexual intercourse, and wearing shoes), established the boundaries of mortification. The talmudic debate was concentrated on determining precise definitions, which are as necessary here as elsewhere. To what degree is eating forbidden? Does the obligation to fast apply to the entire congregation without exception? The Samaritans, for example, who accepted the Torah without the oral tradition, apply the injunction of fasting to babes in arms as well, whereas halakhic tradition exempts small children, although it recommends limited participation for educational purposes. What is more, in light of the theory that the precepts were given as *Torat haim* (teaching pertaining to life) and that men "should live and not die according to them," the sick, whose lives would be imperiled by fasting, are exempted from fasting. Various yardsticks were established for determining the age of maturity and defining sickness. It was decided, for example, that if, in the opinion of a physician, fasting could prove dangerous for a patient, then the latter was forbidden to fast even if he thought himself able to do so. On the other hand, a man who felt himself too weak to fast was exempted from the precept even without medical confirmation, the assumption being that *lev yodea marat nafsho* (the heart knows its own sorrows), and a man is qualified to judge his own subjective feelings. These rulings again raised questions: for example, what if two physicians gave conflicting opinions? Each case was examined separately.

In addition to the festivals specified in the Torah, there is another category based on *divrei sofrim* (the words of the scribes), established in various periods. The *halakhah* includes in this category all the festivals referred to in the various books of the Bible, such as the fast day commemorating the destruction of the Temple (Book of Zechariah), or the Purim festival (Book of Esther), and those introduced after the completion of the Bible. Everything done or decided by the sages over the centuries derives from the fact that the Torah authorized the judges of each generation to create laws and render justice to the people of Israel, from the days of the prophets to the last days of the Second Temple. A list of all the festivals established over the ages—days of rejoicing on which mortification and public mourning were forbidden, as well as commemorative fast days—was contained in *Megillat Taanit*, the first section of the oral law to be recorded in writing. This *megillah* (scroll), most of which was redacted toward the end of the Second Temple period (apparently at the beginning of the first century C.E.), is not included in the Talmud, although it is often quoted there and may be regarded as a kind of *baraita*. It contains a list of the days of commemoration, most of them recalling joyful events, such as military victories (often during the Maccabean wars), redemption, or the death of tyrannical rulers. In the second century C.E., the life of the Jews in Palestine became

The Festivals

so intolerable that the sages noted sadly that it was no longer possible to celebrate these days, since suffering was so great that the people no longer took note of events. They therefore cancelled most of the commemorative days recorded in the *megillah*, leaving only the festivals of Purim and Hanukkah.

The Book of Esther specifies a number of variegated precepts for observance of Purim, from the injunction to recall the events (fulfilled by the public reading of the Scroll) to the festive meal, the dispatch of sweetmeats to friends, and gifts to the poor. The sages provided the basis for the later carnival-like character of this festival when they expressed the view that "a man must become intoxicated on Purim until he can no longer distinguish between 'cursed is Haman' and 'blessed is Mordecai'." The gay and festive aspect of Purim has been preserved throughout the centuries, even in times of trial and tribulation.

Unlike Purim, the feast of Hanukkah was not accorded a special tractate in the Talmud, since the sages were not anxious to add to the calendar festivals on which labor was prohibited, particularly in times when Jews barely managed to find sources of livelihood. The first Maccabeans apparently wanted to lend this festival greater weight than it later enjoyed, but when the people were again deprived of their liberty, it became impossible to commemorate ancient redemption and victories on a wide scale. Instead, another aspect of the festival was emphasized, namely the fact that it was the first expression of an ideological struggle, since the people then fought not so much for political liberation from alien subjugation as for spiritual freedom. The tale of the vessel of oil which burned for eight days found in the profaned Temple inspired the injunction to light candles on Hanukkah and was the foundation of a whole outlook. The talmudic view of the importance of these two festivals is epitomized in the saying: "If all the festivals were abolished, Hanukkah and Purim would never disappear."

This assessment of the vital significance of the two festivals was not extended to the days of mourning for the destruction of the

Temple. Like the prophet Zechariah, the sages believed that these fast days would remain valid only as long as Israel was troubled. When the Temple was rebuilt, and peace reigned at last, the fasts would be abolished, replaced by days of rejoicing. Of the four fast days mentioned in the Bible, the Ninth of Av is the most important. The others were light fasts, when eating and drinking were forbidden from dawn to dusk, while the Ninth of Av was observed as strictly as Yom Kippur (from nightfall to nightfall), with the same stringent restrictions. But whereas Yom Kippur is basically a day of rejoicing, spiritual purification, and catharsis, the Ninth of Av is a time of gloom and mourning. This is not only because the day marks the destruction of the First Temple, but because it later became a day "singled out for catastrophe." On the same date the Second Temple was destroyed, as was Betar, the last stronghold of Bar-Kokhba. It is interesting to note that the Jews were expelled from England in 1290 and Spain in 1492 on the Ninth of Av, and that other national tragedies also occurred on this date.

The *Taanit* tractate, which deals with these fast days, was not devoted exclusively to days of national mourning; it also discussed those fast days on which the people mourned recurrent troubles. They were linked in particular to the frequent droughts, which threatened the livelihood of the entire Jewish population. The drought fast days continued to be observed in other times and places, though not in such ceremonial fashion as depicted in the Talmud, and they reflected the firm conviction that when the entire people assembled to pray in unison, their prayers would be answered. In ancient times the entire congregation attended prayers, and there are numerous anecdotes in the Talmud about common people, sometimes even those who appeared to others to be sinners, whose prayers were answered by God in times of trouble.

17

Marriage and Divorce

THE RANGE of problems pertaining to Jewish matrimonial law can be divided, as far as sources are concerned, into two categories: the various incest laws and the prohibition of intercourse, and the regular laws of marriage and divorce. Whereas the Torah goes into great detail on the first subject, from the commandment "Thou shalt not commit adultery" to the list of strict interdicts in the book of Leviticus and the additions in Deuteronomy, it almost never refers to permissible marital conduct. From the many injunctions relating to violation of matrimonial laws, we infer that such legislation did in fact exist, but its essence is implied rather than elaborated in the Torah itself. The great structure of *halakhah* on marriage and divorce was based on the tradition of many generations and on the conclusions drawn from the combination of these suggestions with the hints in the Torah and their comparison with other areas of *halakhah*.

From the Mishnah and the Talmud there emerges a very detailed and complicated but consistent network of matrimonial law. There are two facets to marriage in Judaism: the relationship between a man and a woman, and the attitude of others toward them. Where the couple is concerned, the act of marriage almost totally lacks sanctity and is essentially a mutual agreement between two people to live together as a family and undertake to respect the obligations of a marriage contract. Since the act is not a sacrament, there is no need for priestly or rabbinical sanction. Talmudic law establishes that when a man and woman decide to wed, the man need only say to the woman, in the presence of two witnesses (who establish the legality of the occasion not through testimony but as part of the essence of the ceremony), that she has now become his wife through one of the accepted forms of marriage—symbolic handing over of money, written guarantee, or sexual intercourse. When the act takes place with the concurrence of both parties, a marriage has occurred. There are two stages to the legal procedure. In the first stage there is betrothal, which has all the validity of marriage but does not bestow rights. Subsequently, in the presence of ten adult males, the man brings the woman into his home; for this purpose, the *huppah* (canopy) is erected as a symbolic home to enable the ceremony to be held in any chosen location. She then becomes his wife. When the proceedings are conducted in accepted fashion, certain benedictions are recited during the betrothal and marriage ceremonies, but, basically, marriage is an act of legal-civil nature. The Jewish custom of inviting a rabbi to conduct the marriage ceremony dates from the late Middle Ages and is partly an imitation of the Christian ceremony, with no religious significance. Therefore, although there is moral (and, to some extent, halakhic) condemnation of sexual relations outside marriage, it has no bearing on the children born of such a relationship, whose legal status is not dependent on whether their parents were married. As long as the relationship between father and mother does not violate incest prohibitions, the child born outside wedlock has the same legal status as any other child.

The other aspects of marriage concern the relationship of the couple to other people. From the moment that the marriage relationship is established, sexual relations with close relatives of the marriage partner are regarded as incest, as in the case of a married woman. The children born of any type of incest, whether the parents were married to one another or not, are branded as bastards. Although in some ways the bastard is considered the son of his natural father (as regards blood ties, or from the financial point of view, since he also inherits), he is forbidden to marry into the Jewish community in the limited sense of the word.

Since marriage is largely a mutual agreement between two people, great significance was attributed to the marriage contract, known in the Talmud as the *ketubah*. The very idea of a written contract between husband and wife is very ancient, and is mentioned in Hammurabi's code, long before the Torah was written. But the form and content of this contract vary from period to period and according to the nature of the civilization in which it was composed. The sages insisted on the drawing up of such a contract and said that to maintain a wife without a *ketubah* or without specification of fair conditions should be regarded as prostitution. The essence of the *ketubah* is enumeration of the conditions that the husband guarantees to fulfill vis-à-vis his wife and of financial and other guarantees. It contains certain minimum binding conditions (thus, even when the copy of the *ketubah* is not available or at times when Jews were forbidden to write *ketubot*, standard conditions were observed), but it is permissible to add or change certain details by special agreement between the husband and wife.

One basic condition in the *ketubah* is the husband's guarantee to pay a certain sum on divorcing his wife or if he should die before her. The minimum was fixed in accordance with injunctions set in the Torah. In ancient times a sum of money or a precious object of equal value was set aside for this purpose, and the husband was forbidden to make use of it. Simeon Ben Shetah thought that this encouraged husbands to divorce their wives without giving the matter due consideration, since the *ketubah* was ready for this eventuality at any time. He therefore amended the ruling so that the sum of the *ketubah* was calculated as part of the husband's assets; therefore, any man wishing to divorce his wife was first obliged to produce this sum, thus having respite to reconsider his actions. This amendment also enabled young men who lacked ready cash to take wives without being obliged to wait many years until they could amass the necessary sum.

The *ketubah* also contains various agreements on inheritance of property in the event of the husband's death, as well as the obligation to support any daughters born of the marriage and supply all their needs until they reach maturity. Present-day *ketubot* contain other rules and agreements, some of which need not appear in writing, since they constitute an inseparable part of matrimony and of the conditions laid down by the sages for normal marriages. These basic conditions are known, in the language of the Bible, as *she'er, kesut ve-ona* (food, raiment, and conjugal rights), and they encompass the husband's duties toward his wife, to feed and clothe her and engage in sexual intercourse with her at agreed times. The details of the conditions depend on the circumstances and on the parties involved, but there are always certain minimum requirements. According to one general rule, when a man takes a wife "she ascends with him and does not descend with him," that is, if he takes a wife from a lower social or economic stratum he is obliged to treat her according to the customs of his own class. Alternately, if she is of a higher social class, he has no right to reduce her standard of living without her explicit agreement.

As regards the other conditions of marriage, an attempt is made to create a certain balance between the obligations of both parties. On the one hand, the husband must support his wife, provide her with medical care in sickness, redeem her from captivity, and pay the costs of her burial. On the other, he is entitled to enjoy the profits of the assets she brings with her from her parental home (*nikhsei melog*)—usufruct—although he has no ownership rights thereof. She is obliged to work in order to help support the family, although this depends on whether she has brought a large dowry with her. These aspects of marriage are largely a question of

Marriage and Divorce

agreement between husband and wife. Every man has the right to announce that he waives the rights extended to him by the law, and in many marriage contracts the husband forgoes the right to manage his wife's property and assets. In other cases, the wife may give her husband leave and authorization to manage and even sell her property. This balance of duties and rights is incomplete, and we should recall that matrimonial law in the Talmud is based on the assumption that a man is entitled to take several wives, while a woman may wed only one man. The moral sanctioning of polygamy also encompasses the husband's right to divorce his wife (but not vice versa), since he can always take another wife in addition to his first spouse. The biological consideration that provides the sanction for polygamy also grants the initiative to men where matrimony is concerned. In the Middle Ages, Rabbenu Gershom of Mainz, known as Light of the Diaspora, pronounced a *herem* (ban) on polygamy and, incidentally, also on divorce without the wife's consent. This ban, which was accepted by the majority of the Jewish people, gave legal substantiation to the existing situation, since even in talmudic times it was most uncommon to take two wives. Among the mishnaic and talmudic sages, of whom so much is known, we know of only one who had two wives. But this does not alter the fundamental fact that laws of marriage and divorce recognize the validity of polygamy.

Where divorce is concerned, it is anomalous that formal *halakhah* permits divorce with relative ease, though such a step is considered morally reprehensible. (It was said that "even the altar sheds tears for he who divorces his first wife.") There are cases where the separation is voluntary, that is, when the man (or, according to later *halakhah*, both parties) agrees to separate, and then there is no need to provide reasons. But there are also cases in which divorce is compulsory. A man is obliged to divorce his wife if it is clear to him that she has committed adultery or if she demands the divorce on the grounds that he is impotent, or if he is suffering from an infirmity which makes married life intolera-

[133]

ble, or if he forces her to do things she is not obliged to do (such as to move to a new location differing drastically from her first married home).

Practically speaking, divorce occurs when the husband gives a *get* to his wife. *Get* is the mishnaic term for what is referred to in the Torah as *sefer kritut* (bill of divorcement), which is basically a simple written note. After recording the date and place, it contains a declaration that a certain man hereby divorces his wife, who is now permitted to remarry. The *get*, like the *ketubah*, is written in Aramaic, since this was the language commonly spoken in the Second Temple period and later. Such documents are traditionally written in Aramaic, though there is no valid halakhic reason for this. A *get* may be given by an individual who writes it out himself or entrusts the task to a scribe. From ancient times strict attention has been paid to the wording of the *get* and, since it releases a woman from her marital bonds and permits her to remarry, its halakhic authority is annulled in cases of significant error. There were often cases in which men maliciously gave their wives irregularly written divorce papers in order to create legal complications. This led to the rabbinical ruling that "he who is not acquainted with the nature of the laws of divorce and marriage should have nothing to do with them," hence the ordinance prevailing in most Jewish communities that a *get* may be given only by a court, ensuring that it will be written clearly and unambiguously.

A number of problems may arise from even the simplest bill of divorcement, such as the question of the exact spelling of the names of the parties or the exact definition of the location. One of the important principles pertaining to divorce is that it entails complete breach between man and wife, and it is therefore forbidden for the *get* to specify any condition which binds the woman to her ex-husband in any way. (For example, he may not state in the *get* that she is forbidden to marry a certain man.) The time problem may also be complicated, particularly when a man decides to give his wife a *get al tenai* (decree nisi). An example

Marriage and Divorce

of this (the ruling dates back to the beginning of the First Temple period) is the soldier who grants his wife a *get al tenai* before going off to war, in order to preclude personal and legal problems should he be declared missing without proof of death. Such cases call for meticulous wording in order to give legal sanction to the *get* and to prevent exploitation of the document by one of the parties for base purposes.

Matrimonial laws are a combination of fiscal and social arrangements and of laws relating to the sanctity of the marriage bond, and because of the nature of the issue a tremendous number of details call for constant clarification. Since marriage and divorce were essentially private matters, determined and settled between the interested parties, new questions tended to emerge from time to time as unforeseen circumstances arose. For many generations scholars tried to establish formal frameworks for marriage, and to a large extent they succeeded in this. But since the *halakhah* permits private marriage and divorce, there is always room for doubts and problems. It should be recalled that the Jewish law court can only discuss the legal aspects of acts but has no authority to intervene in marital relations, nor can it annul a marriage unless its existence explicitly violates *halakhah*. Only the incest laws restrict the legality of marriage to some degree, and it is only rarely that courts can annul marriages that have already taken place.

The various laws prohibiting marriage are mostly to be found in the Torah itself, and the sages who studied them tried to classify them into various categories. The discussions went on for generations, and on various points agreement was only reached at the height of the talmudic era. As long as there were differences of opinion, the sages could only endeavor to ensure that married couples or their descendants would not encounter legal complications. The details of the debates are extremely involved, but generally speaking, three types of prohibition were recognized. There are cases in which a man is forbidden to marry a certain woman, but if he breaks the law and marries her nonetheless, the marriage is legally valid and can only be dissolved by divorce. An example of this is a man who marries his divorced wife after she has been married to another man and subsequently divorced or widowed. The Torah defines such a marriage as an "abomination" since it could encourage "legal" prostitution. If such a marriage takes place, the court will do everything in its power to persuade the man to divorce his wife, but the marriage is regarded as legal and binding, and in most cases the children born of the union are not affected. Another type of marriage is that in which incest is involved. Even if the marriage ceremony was performed in accordance with normal procedure it is not legal, and the couple are not regarded as married to one another, so that no *get* is needed in order to dissolve the ties. The children born of the union are branded as bastards, but are recognized as the issue of their parents as regards both rights and duties. A third type of marriage is not only invalidated but the man's paternity of any issue resulting is not recognized. This rule applies, for example, to a marriage between a Jew and non-Jew. Whether a marriage ceremony was conducted or not, it is not considered a legal marriage, and any child born of the union is regarded as having been born parthenogenetically, that is, he is always classified according to his mother's origins. If the mother is Jewish he is regarded as a Jew; if she is not, then he too is not Jewish.

This is but the general outline of matrimonial law, and there are various marginal cases and subcategories. A special set of laws relates to members of priestly families, and to the High Priest in particular, and specifies various restrictions on marriage. A separate series of laws deals with non-Jews or freed slaves. Most of the *halakhah* relating to these questions and their fiscal and legal aspects appears in the *Nashim* order of the Talmud.

18

The Status of Women

TALMUDIC LAW excludes women, in many ways, from several important spheres of life. It exempts them, for example, from those positive precepts that depend on a given time of the day or year for performance. These include many of the familiar rituals of Jewish life: wearing the *tzitzit* (fringed four-cornered garment), laying *tefilin* (phylacteries), reciting the *Shema Yisrael* prayer, blowing the *shofar*, constructing the *sukkah*, and pilgrimage. Women are not permitted to join a *minyan* (quorum of ten) for prayer, nor are they assigned active functions within the community. As for their social status, they are not eligible for administrative and judicial positions. And, most significant of all, they are exempt from the important *mitzvah* of studying Torah, a fact that inevitably precludes them from playing a part in Jewish cultural and spiritual life.

One might have expected all these restrictions and exemptions to create an inferior caste, and to relegate women to a totally marginal role in Jewish society. Yet they were active in many different spheres and made their presence felt not only through the activities they undertook as wives and mothers but also in what

[137]

appeared to be exclusively male provinces. The reason is apparently inherent in the nature of the talmudic approach to life and to Torah. The *halakhah* is regarded as more than merely a philosophical and intellectual structure in need of justification and substantiation through incessant theorizing. It is seen, rather, as a network of practical laws—in a sense, laws of nature—the attitude toward which is completely pragmatic and, hence, totally flexible. For example, it was not because the sages thought women intellectually incapable of learning that they exempted them from study. On the contrary, they believed that "women are endowed with greater *binah* [understanding, intelligence] than men" and did not bar the way to those few women who chose to study. It is true that R. Eliezer, who was known for the severity of his views, once told a learned female proselyte that "there is no wisdom for a woman except at the distaff." On the other hand, Ben Azai believed that every man should teach his daughter Torah. Furthermore, one of the more eminent *amoraim* effectively deflated an arrogant student by saying: "Even Berurya, who once learned 300 laws from 300 *tannaim* in one day, spent a long time on this particular text. What makes you think you can study it faster than she?" The renowned Berurya, wife of R. Meir, one of the most brilliant scholars of his day, and daughter of another eminent sage, often took part in halakhic discussions. What is more, her opinion is known to have prevailed over those of her male contemporaries on several occasions.

We learn of the existence of another learned woman through a marriage contract—undoubtedly unusual—between the son of R. Akiva and his bride, in which she guaranteed "to feed and keep him and to teach him Torah." But interest in learning was not confined to a few singular women; many women came to hear the sages expound *aggadah* and *halakhah* in the synagogues, sometimes despite husbandly disapproval. R. Judah Ha-Nasi's servant girls were cited by the sages as a source of information on the use of the Hebrew language.

The Status of Women

Although, as we have noted, women enjoyed no official social standing, this did not prevent them from wielding considerable influence as the wives and daughters of prominent men. There is a particularly illuminating anecdote about Rabba and his second wife, whose love for one another began in early childhood. Rabba's wife, "the daughter of Rav Hisda," was present at a court session when a certain woman was about to take the oath and mentioned to her husband that she knew the woman to be a liar; he accepted her evaluation and passed judgment accordingly. This action aroused no particular surprise among those present, who included several of Rabba's pupils. Some time later, under similar circumstances, one of Rabba's most distinguished pupils, the *amora* R. Pappa, cast doubt on the honesty of a certain litigant. Rabba rejected his opinion politely, saying: "You, sir, are the sole witness, and I cannot act on the evidence of only one witness." "Am I to be trusted less than your wife?" asked Pappa, to which Rabba replied: "I know my wife extremely well, and I rely on her judgment. I do not know you, sir, to the same extent." It is interesting to note that R. Pappa was not offended by this remark; in fact he utilized the incident in order to draw general conclusions on the validity of such evidence when submitted by a reliable witness.

The fact that women were not obliged to perform many of the positive precepts was regarded as an exemption rather than a ban. Men persisted in regarding themselves as the more fortunate sex, privileged to fulfill a greater number of precepts; this is attested to by the benediction recited each morning in which a man praises God for not having made him a woman. However, those women who sincerely wished it were permitted to undertake additional *mitzvot*. Thus it is related that "Michal, the daughter of Saul, laid phylacteries" or "the wife of Jonah went on a pilgrimage." Women were also allowed to offer sacrifices in the Temple "in order to give them pleasure." There is no clear theoretical distinction between those precepts from which women are exempt and those which are binding on them. Although they were exempt from reciting the *Shema* prayer, prayer in general was obligatory, as in the case of men, since it was "supplication to God."

Some sages were slightly daunted by the prospect that women might dedicate themselves too thoroughly to prayer or asceticism, particularly in cases where their motives were suspect. The list of *mevalei olam* (idlers, wastrels) includes the *betulah tzalyanit* (devoutly praying maiden) and the *almanah tzaymanit* (ascetic widow). It was not that the sages regarded women as unworthy, since they themselves said: "We have learned from the maiden to be sin-fearing, and from the widow that virtue is its own reward," but rather that they feared that pious behavior might sometimes be aimed at outward show. It was the idea of the woman who "fornicated for apples, in order to distribute them to the sick" that troubled them. As a general rule, however, the God-fearing woman who busied herself with good works was a familiar figure, and it was accepted that certain women were extremely righteous and even paragons of virtue. The activities and status of the ancient prophetesses were taken for granted and were not deemed to require explanation. In fact, there was a well-known saying that "the patriarchs were inferior to the matriarchs in prophesy."

The equal status of women in penal and civil law also had considerable social implications. Even the most restrictive of marriage contracts allowed the wife a high degree of economic independence, and since women, even after marriage, enjoyed a certain measure of control over their property, many wives engaged in commerce and were parties to various business deals. In some families, particularly those of prosperous merchants, the women conducted completely independent households. A wife who brought her husband a sizable dowry was not obliged to occupy herself with housework, and some of these ladies of leisure—like their counterparts centuries later—passed their time playing chess or in the company of pet dogs. Although the sages disapproved of the study of Greek poetry and sophism, some permitted them to women as "an ornament to the sex."

We know little about the education of girls in the talmudic era, but, in the more prosperous communities and families at least, daughters were apparently given a basic grounding in Jewish studies. A smattering of knowledge of the Bible and *halakhah* seems to have been common among girls, and the more learned the family, the greater the likelihood that the girls would be educated, either through regular studies or by attending their brothers' lessons. This was one of the reasons the sages thought it worthwhile for a man to sell all his possessions in order to marry the daughter of a great scholar. The assumption was—and it is borne out by many anecdotes in the Talmud—that such a girl had been well educated by her father, so that if her husband died or was exiled, she would be capable of educating her children alone, in the spirit of the Torah. The halakhic ruling that "the wife of a *haver* [scholar] is as he" reflects the degree of loyalty and of knowledge of *halakhah* attributed to the women of scholarly families. The ruling was of considerable significance since, as a result, the wives of the sages were treated with the same respect as their husbands and therefore enjoyed higher status than the common people.

In order to comprehend the basic aspects of the status of women in law and in everyday life, it is necessary to ascertain the attitude of the talmudic sages toward marriage. In contrast to Christianity and several of the Eastern religions, Judaism never regarded marriage as a "necessary evil," necessary for the perpetuation of the species but otherwise an institution to be despised. The sages treated the sexual urge as a natural instinct like any other, rather than as something to be condemned. Although they themselves advocated extreme modesty and chastity and the greatest possible purity in relations between husband and wife, they did not ignore the implications of the sexual instinct for men and women. R. Hisda, who greatly admired and liked his daughters (and even said of them: "As far as I am concerned, daughters are better than sons"), instructed them in sexual matters; his teachings are cited in the Talmud and complement the extensive guidance offered to men. In general, the sages were aware of the power of the sexual drive, and their view is epitomized in the saying: *Ein epitropus le'arayot* (there is no guardian over sexual affairs). Accordingly, even the most chaste and pious of men, who was above suspicion, could never be wholly trusted and should not be entrusted with the task of guarding a woman alone. It is a measure of their profound awareness that the sages claimed that "he who is greater than his fellow man is also greater in desire," and several stories are told of men renowned for their piety who were almost tempted into sexual misdemeanors. The purpose of these anecdotes was not to denigrate these saintly men but to emphasize the need for chastity and self-control.

Judaism regards the taking of a wife as an important precept, binding on every man. Even a man who is no longer capable of fathering children is urged to avoid the celibate life. Thus the sexual instinct is seen not merely as a means of perpetuating the species but as part of the human personality, and it was said that "he who has no wife cannot be called a man." An unmarried man, in the eyes of the sages, is only half a body and becomes a complete human being only when he marries (the story of the creation as related in the Torah was interpreted by most scholars as meaning that Adam was created with a dual image and was later separated into two bodies—man and woman).

From the social aspect, the family—the male-female unit—is the nucleus of life, and any discussion must take both sides of this unit into consideration. The emotional and spiritual relationship between husband and wife is also taken into account not only in regard to child-raising but also from the point of view of the couple. The Talmud quotes the case of a certain woman who was married to a scholar and used to tie the *tefilin* around his arm; after his death, she married a tax collector (an occupation that the sages associated with avarice and blackmail) and now tied a collector's armband around her new husband's arm each morning. On the other hand, the Talmud brings the example of a pious man married to a pious woman; after their divorce she remarried and guided her new husband into the paths of righteousness, while her first husband remarried an evil woman who corrupted him. These two examples of the reciprocity of relations point to a realistic evaluation of the role and status of woman in the family. Although there were few ways in which women could express themselves in public life, their practical influence was considerable, and this was neither frowned upon nor camouflaged. There are tales galore about the firm-willed wife of the sage R. Nahman, who was a scion of the family of the exilarch and made no attempt to conceal her influence and power, insisting that she be treated with proper respect. Under the impression that the important Palestinian scholar R. Ulla had insulted her, she sent him an offensive message: "Wanderers are filled with words as rags are infested with fleas." Few women could permit themselves such frankness, not to say rudeness, but the story attests to the universally acknowledged influence of women in the talmudic period.

The standard *ketubah* did not deprive the woman of ownership of her own property, although management thereof, unless otherwise specified, was entrusted to the husband. Since a married woman did not forfeit the right to appear as a litigant in civil-law claims, the Talmud enumerates many cases where women were active in fiscal disputes—and not necessarily only in matrimonial-law cases. A woman's degree of subservience to her husband is clearly defined by a network of laws that do not basically alter the balance of rights and duties after marriage. The Torah permits a husband to annul vows taken by his wife, but the scholars restricted this right considerably—the husband is permitted to revoke only those vows pertaining in some way to marital relations but is forbidden to intervene in any other obligation his wife has undertaken. Similarly, although a father may marry off his daughter and cancel her vows, his authority is limited to minor daughters who have not yet reached the age of sexual maturity (twelve). They become completely independent after puberty.

Neither a father nor any other individual may impose his will on an adult daughter or attempt to force her into a marriage against her will. Jewish parents always concerned themselves with finding mates for their children, but this was not because the father enjoyed special rights over his daughter; it was rather the accepted custom for parents to serve as the emissaries of their daughters' or sons' wishes, serving as go-betweens in matches.

Thus we see that the talmudic sages did not regard women as inferior creatures but, as one sage succinctly put it, "as a nation apart." They assumed that there was a separate feminine network of ideas, rules, and guidelines for conduct differing from that of men. And although women were exempted from many of the important precepts that men were obliged to observe, they were not regarded as less important from the purely religious point of view. It was even said that "the Holy One, Blessed be He, made a greater promise for the future to women than to men." The distinction between the sexes is based on a functional division of tasks, which are seen as separate but equal.

19

Civil Law

CIVIL LAW—or, as it is usually called, *dinei memonot* (monetary law)—is one of the most fertile areas of talmudic thought and creativity and was defined thus by one of the mishnaic sages: "He who wishes to acquire wisdom should study *dinei memonot*, since there is no greater subject in Torah; it is a bubbling spring." Unlike other law codes, which are largely dependent on a relatively inflexible framework of statutes and rules, civil law, which defines an important area of human relations, is flexible and incessantly changing. *Halakhah* pertaining to biological or ritual matters may be preserved unchanged for long periods because of the stability of the objects under discussion, but this is not so in the case of civil law. The sages noted the difference between those areas in which only a limited number of people are involved and the sphere of monetary law, in which all may at some time or other be involved.

One of the principles underlying all *dinei memonot*, which influences halakhic procedure in various ways as well, is the assumption that money may be given as a gift. This seemingly unimportant point serves as the foundation for the entire code, which is

founded on public consent to the establishment of various monetary frameworks. All other types of legislation are perceived as
natural substances that do not proceed from the community and
are therefore not subject to its control and supervision. But since
money can be possessed by the individual, he is entitled to arrive
at an agreement with another party and to waive or amend certain
basic legal requirements. The "custom of the land"—the tacit
agreement of the population to conduct their lives in accordance
with a certain legal code—has greater impact here than in any
other legal sphere. It is assumed that a man residing in a certain
place will undertake to observe local law and custom and will
therefore waive some of the rights that the Torah grants him.

Another basic point that renders monetary law more flexible
than other categories is the knowledge that money "can be replaced." Errors in other spheres are often irreversible, while in
cases where money is involved it is always possible to reverse an
erroneous judgment, to recover stolen funds, and so forth. Thus
despite numerous exhortations to behave justly and fairly, and
the strict prohibition of theft and robbery, the lawmakers were
able to establish legal frameworks for certain acts, despite the fear
that errors might occur. Furthermore, the court was granted
wider powers in civil cases than with regard to other types of
halakhah. In theory, the court can introduce ordinances and pass
sentences that do not derive from the law of the Torah, but it is
permitted to do so, on the explicit instructions of the Torah itself,
in the general interest. The most far-reaching rule is that *hefker bet
din hefker* (the decree of a court can render property ownerless),
and it was on the basis of this ruling that Jewish courts were authorized to initiate new laws and enactments and to appropriate
money from one man and hand it over to another, even though
this right was not specifically granted them by law.

For these reasons, the monetary laws recorded in the Torah
were greatly elaborated and were adapted to diverse needs and
changing conditions. The ancient *Nezikin* tractate was divided
into three "gates" more or less in accordance with the types of

Civil Law

problems dealt with by monetary law. The laws pertaining to damages in the limited sense, encompassing direct or indirect injury inflicted by one man on another, are mostly contained in the first "gate" of the tractate, *Baba Kama*. Monetary disputes, work disputes, and loans are discussed in the second section, *Baba Metzia*, while laws pertaining to partnerships, sales, and legal documents appear in the third section, *Baba Batra*.

The types of injury were enumerated in an ancient *mishnah* as "the four *avot* [principle categories] of injury," and these were eventually expanded to twenty-four. The basic *mishnayot* were very ancient and their enigmatic brevity soon aroused controversy over the precise significance of certain terms, although there was general agreement on the main issues. It was later agreed that the "four *avot*" do not include directly inflicted injury, but only damage caused by property for which an individual is responsible. The mishnaic definitions of "ox and cistern, grazing and conflagration" should be seen as mere technical symbols; as one sage put it: "He who believes that the ox in the Talmud is a real ox has not even begun to understand the *halakhah*."

A slightly later classification, which also served as a prototype, divided injuries into those caused by horn, tooth, foot, pit, and fire. The first three are caused by animals and the other two by inanimate objects. The *keren* (horn) is based on the biblical description of the "butting ox" that inflicts injury on human beings or other oxen, that is, harm caused by an animal through injurious intent. Thus a dog that bites a man comes under the category of *keren*, as does a cockerel that pecks another bird to death. The laws relating to this type of injury are not simple because a distinction is drawn between the responsibility of the owner for an animal that has never before caused damage (known as *tam*, that is, innocent) and for a beast that has already gored in the past (*muad*). There is also a difference between an animal that gores or inflicts some other fatal *keren* injury and is always put to death, and cases of plain injury or killing of other animals. *Shen* (tooth), on the other hand, is a relatively simple category of responsibility for damage. A man is responsible for damage caused by his animal through eating or any act which causes it satisfaction. A classic example of the expansion of the concept of *shen* is the animal which rubs against a wall and causes it to collapse. *Regel* (foot) covers damage caused by a trampling animal, but is extended to encompass any damage that an animal causes by its normal movements or actions without deriving direct pleasure from them. The responsibility of the owner for such damage covers almost every eventuality, excluding the unfeasible or those cases in which the injured party acted with excessive negligence. The general concept of *bor* (pit) damages is borrowed from the biblical example of the responsibility of a man for a pit that he digs, thereby causing damage. More abstractly, the "pit" was seen as the prototype for any nuisance created in a public place, whether a pit or some other object. This was why it was possible to speak of a "rolling pit," a public nuisance that is not confined to one spot, and can be moved. Various reservations about the responsibility of the person causing the injury take into consideration the degree of negligence of the injured party and the extent to which the person creating the nuisance was entitled to place the object where he did.

Esh (fire) damages include not only direct lighting of a fire on the property of others but also the lighting of a fire without sufficient supervision, even if it is located within the property of the responsible party. More profound study of *halakhot* on *esh* entailed examination of the nature of the responsibility. Should fire be considered the indirect continuation of the man himself, it would substantiate the concept of responsibility for one's property. This particular view was summed up in the saying: "His fire is like his arrows," in other words, just as a man is responsible for the arrows he shoots, so he bears responsibility for the fire he lights. Another view was that responsibility for fire should be more remote, specifically regarding actions that a man caused directly, although without direct contact.

The range of problems linked to this question and the various

Civil Law

limitations on responsibility were related to the overall question of the infliction of damage. A distinction was drawn between two concepts that were similar in name and essence: *grama be-nezikin*, a state in which a man becomes the cause of direct damage (for example, if he sends his herd to his neighbor's field); and *dina de-garmei*, laws for the perpetrators, relating to indirect damage. A simple example of the latter is the man who burns a promissory note belonging to another. The direct damage is loss of a slip of paper, for which he must undoubtedly pay. But the owner of the note may, as a consequence, lose a large sum of money. This raises the question of the degree of responsibility for damages of this type. Should the burner be regarded as having inflicted direct damage, for which he bears direct responsibility, or is he merely the cause of the damage (the borrower refusing to repay the loan in the absence of the note), though not fully responsible for the outcome? After generations of dispute in this sphere, the talmudic conclusion was that responsibility exists in the second category as well, although there is no actual participation in the damage.

The minority opinion was that such a case should be regarded as *nezek she-eno nikar*, damage that is not evident and therefore does not entail full criminal responsibility. An example is a man who defiles a burnt offering belonging to another. The damage may be caused by merely touching the offering without actual diminution, but the offering is nonetheless considered inedible and almost valueless. In this case, the behavior of the damager can scarcely be regarded as a deliberate action, according to normal criteria, although the damage may be extremely severe. Those scholars who believe that there is no obligation to pay for such damage agree that this is one of the cases (which are numerous) in which the person causing damage is "exempt from the laws of man and bound by the laws of Heaven," that is, he bears no legal responsibility but is morally bound to pay. The court cannot force him to pay damages but he is morally obliged to recompense the victim. There is a whole network of laws pertaining to the individual who wishes to fulfill his moral obligation even though no legal pressures are brought to bear on him. Here too there are *halakhot* that establish what a man must do in order to pay his moral debt and even when this responsibility no longer exists.

Another legal problem with implications for the entire civil-law code is the question of how to act in the event of *mamon ha-mutal be-safek* (money in doubt), when there are two claimants to a sum of money (or an object) and neither can supply adequate proof of ownership. According to one legal method, the disputed sum is divided between the litigants. Various arguments were voiced against this view (which was rejected), both because it does not punish the false claimant and because in most cases it is clearly unjust, since any disputed object must belong to one of the parties by right and to deprive him of it is unfair. This was also the argument cited against the tendency to seek compromise between the claims of the litigants, for compromise brought "peace" but not "truth." On the other hand, the accepted view in the *halakhah* is that "the onus of proof is on the claimant." As long as the claimant is unable to prove the justice of his claim, the disputed objects remain in the possession of the present holder. Many monetary claims were decided in the light of this basic rule; ownership, in practice, was retained by the holder, and the onus of bringing evidence rested on the other party. There are certain disputes that cannot be dealt with in this fashion, for example when two claimants both hold the object, or when neither has it in his possession. In some of these cases, the rule of "money in doubt will be divided" is sometimes applied, while in other cases the judges are instructed to decide in accordance with their free judgment, without any legal restrictions. These questions, and all the attendant details, are discussed at length and in depth in the Talmud and in the great range of talmudic literature.

This same subject is related to the concept of *hazakah* (literally taking hold) in one of its several meanings. There are three meanings to this term in the Talmud, and to a certain extent they are logically connected, though they differ in detail. *Hazakah*, or possession, is a legal term that exists, with variations, in many legal codes where the question of proof of ownership is concerned. In Jewish law *hazakah* is related to property regarding which "onus of proof is on the claimant," that is, the right of the person in possession to retain ownership is presumed until disproved; but it is both more detailed and more concise. Although the claimant and not the holder is ostensibly obliged to provide proof, Jewish law does not extend to *hazakah* the same validity it does to actual evidence. It is a rule in torts that "*hazakah* that is not accompanied by reason is not *hazakah*"; in other words, possession of an object is not in itself proof that the object belongs to the holder. The argument: "I have had possession of this object for many years and no one has claimed it from me" is not sufficiently valid. *Hazakah* bears weight only if it follows on a claim of ownership (purchase, inheritance, receipt of a gift), and therefore *hazakah* laws do not substitute for laws of evidence, but are aimed at freeing the possessor from the obligation of retaining proof of his ownership *ad infinitum*. After a certain period of time, determined in each case by degree of use, the possessor need not produce evidence, documentary or by witness, of his ownership; it is sufficient to prove that he holds possession of the object by force of a certain claim to ownership. *Hazakah* is, therefore, a technical regulation based on the assumption that within a certain period of time the owner of an object or of land will discover that his property is being used unlawfully and will take the appropriate legal steps to regain his rights, and that in the absence of such a claim the possessor need not guard the note in perpetuity.

A completely different issue from that of damage caused by a man's property is that relating to a man's responsibility for damage he himself inflicts. In such cases the rule of *adam muad le-olam* (a man is always forewarned, that is, lack of intent is no defense) applies. No man can evade responsibility for his actions, whether committed with malicious intent, through negligence, or through lack of concern for the rights of others. The sole argument that may exempt him from responsibility is that of *oness* (coercion), whereby the defendant must prove that he was compelled to commit a certain act, whether because of an external factor over which he had no control or because he lacked the power of judgment (as in the case of a child or lunatic). In damage caused to another individual, a distinction is drawn between five halakhic categories known as *shevet, ripui, boshet, tza'ar,* and *pegam* (loss of time, healing, humiliation, pain, and damage). Only in isolated cases must the inflictor of injury pay all these claims, and in most cases only one or two categories are significant. A man who injures another must pay damages in recompense for the lessening of his value in the labor market or corresponding sphere. If he causes the amputation of an arm, he must pay a certain sum, altered from time to time, for the loss of the limb. Similarly, anyone who disfigures a woman must pay damages for the decrease in her worth, although her ability to work has not been affected. Another category of payment is for the pain caused by the injury. There are, of course, cases in which this is the sole payment demanded, since pain may be the only consequence of assault. *Shevet* is payment for the period of enforced unemployment during convalescence, and *ripui* covers payment of medical costs. If, as a result of the damage, the injured party suffers humiliation, separate payment may be extracted, and there are varying criteria for this, according to place, time, and so forth.

All these payments, like most of the damages enumerated in the sphere of torts, imply that the injured party is being recompensed for his injury. The Torah also contains *dinei kenasot*, according to which the individual inflicting injury not only pays for it but also pays a fine. The talmudic *halakhah* states that in every case in which the Torah demands payment that does not correspond to the actual damage, such payment should be regarded as a fine, even if it is less than the real cost of the damage. These punishments by fine include the Torah law obliging the thief to pay twice the sum of the theft to his victim, or the obligation to pay fourfold or fivefold the value of a stolen ox or sheep. There

[152]

Civil Law

are several differences between the laws pertaining to claims and to fines. Since all monetary claims are demands for justice and are vital to the regulation of normal life, any authorized court may deal with them, whereas only specially authorized judges may try cases where fines may be imposed. Since this special ordination was abolished at the beginning of the Middle Ages, this type of law was thereafter only applied in unusual cases.

Another area of civil law pertaining to responsibility is that known in talmudic terminology as laws of *shomrim* (guardians), which defines the responsibility of a man for the property of another that has been entrusted to him for safekeeping. The *shomrim* are divided into four types, all implicit in the Torah: *shomer hinam* (the unpaid keeper), who bears less responsibility; *shomer sakhar* (the paid keeper); *sokher* (the lessee); and *shoel* (the borrower), whose responsibility is greater. The Talmud defined the precise responsibility of each, since the biblical text is not always clear. For example, only one enigmatic reference is made to the lessee: "If it be a hireling, he loses his hire" (Exodus 22:15). It also engages in detailed discussion of where and when the laws of *shomrim* should be applied in everyday life, since the theoretical distinction is not always clear, and it is sometimes hard to determine the status of a person guarding an object and the degree to which he is responsible. There is a well-known dispute, for example, concerning the person who finds a lost object: is his responsibility that of the unpaid keeper or of the paid keeper?

The laws of *shomrim* are linked in the Torah to the laws pertaining to oaths, in cases where the keeper loses an object and denies ever having had it in his keeping; or offers another interpretation of his responsibility; or claims that the object was taken from him in a way that clears him of all responsibility (armed robbery, for example, which annuls most kinds of responsibility); or the parties differ as to the value of the lost object. There are some cases in which the facts can be clarified through the testimony of witnesses or written evidence. But in many cases, one is faced with two conflicting claims that cannot be examined fully, and this is why the law instructs the defendant to take an oath that "he has not stretched out his hand to his neighbor's labor." After swearing, he is cleared of the charge. There was a restriction on such oaths, namely, that a man was not obliged to take them unless there was a certain amount of incriminating evidence against him, given by one sole witness (the Torah specifies that two witnesses should give evidence), or when the defendant "admits in part," that is, admits the claim in principle but argues certain details. The taking of such an oath, which later came to be known as "the Torah oath," to distinguish it from other kinds instituted by the sages, was regarded as a solemn occasion during which the person taking the oath held some sacred object in his hand.

In the talmudic period another kind of oath, the *shevuat heset* (oath of exemption), attributed to the *amora* Rav Nahman, was added for a defendant in monetary claims, even when he did not admit any of the details of the charge. This oath was apparently introduced in order to regulate prevailing social relations after people began to deny charges in order to avoid taking oaths. It should be noted that the emphasis on the heavy responsibility involved and the fear of taking a false oath, even by mistake, increased the tendency to avoid all kinds of oaths in any situation and to prefer statements without oath.

Halakhot relating to losses are connected with the laws of *shomrim*. The Torah obligates the finder to restore an object to its owner and prohibits not only appropriation but also the discarding of the found object. This rule is easily applied in cases where the finder is acquainted with the object and with its owner, but in general it arouses problems and is inoperable. The *halakhah* tries to clarify which lost objects are identifiable, and must therefore be restored to their owners, and which cannot be identified. For example, money, though it may be clearly marked, is not restorable, since it is customary for money to be transferred from person to person; although an individual can prove that a certain note or coin was once in his possession, he cannot usually provide proof that he was the most recent owner. The key to many of these *halakhot* is the concept of *ye'ush*, that is, de facto renunciation of ownership of a certain object on the assumption that it has been irretrievably lost. From then on it is *hefker* (unclaimed, ownerless) and may be taken by the finder.

The problem of *ye'ush be'alim* (owners' despair) has implications where laws of theft and robbery are concerned. Although theft is prohibited from the religious viewpoint, it is considered by Jewish law to be a civil offense rather than a criminal act calling for physical punishment. The thief is obliged to restore the stolen object and in certain cases to pay a monetary fine to the owner (twice or more the value of the object), but he suffers no other punishment. Study of the nature of the stolen object itself is, however, called for: until when is it regarded as the property of its owner, and when does it become the property of the thief, who is then obliged to repay the value but not to restore the object itself? On this issue there are two illuminating points made in the *halakhah*, one of them related to *ye'ush*. When a certain period has elapsed or when there is a declaration (not necessarily formal) by the owner that he no longer believes that the object will ever be restored to him, it then becomes the property of the thief. If the thief alters the essence of the stolen object in irreversible or significant fashion (for example, steals wood and turns it into furniture), the original owner forfeits his right to the wood itself, although he is entitled to receive restitution from the thief. This problem is of practical significance in several ways. For example, when the price of a stolen object increases, the question is whether the thief is obliged to repay the value at the time of the theft or at the time of restitution. What happens if the thief sells the object to others? Can the original owner then demand that the new owner restore the stolen object itself, or can he only demand recompense of the thief?

It is interesting to note that the *halakhah* differentiates in a most unusual way between theft and robbery. The thief sometimes pays a fine, but the robber who takes openly and by force is merely obliged to restore the object or its equivalent in cash. The talmudic explanation is intriguing: the robber is preferable to the thief since he acts openly, and his attitude toward God, in transgressing against his commandments and committing a robbery, is equal to his attitude toward his fellow men, from whom he steals openly, without fear and shame. The thief, on the other hand, demonstrates that he fears men more than he fears God, since he hides himself from his fellow men but not from the Almighty; he therefore deserves to be fined.

The question of property and methods of purchasing it is of great significance where *halakhah* on theft is concerned and is, in fact, a key issue in many spheres of civil law. It exists in every case of transferral of legal ownership: at what point exactly is an object considered to have changed hands and come into the possession of the purchaser? There are various aspects to this question. Until what stage is it permissible to withdraw from a deal and when is it regarded as final? If the object that changes hands is damaged or lost, or gains in value, who bears the consequences? According to the *halakhah*, an object changes hands through one of several defined methods of purchase, which vary according to the type of object. Generally speaking, the handing over of money by the purchaser is not regarded as concluding the deal, and only actual holding of the object in some way denotes legal transfer. The sages were divided as to whether the concept of *meshikhah* (literally grasping) as the basic method of purchasing movable goods was really implied in the laws of property or was a later addition aimed at safeguarding the purchaser against exploitation of the law by the seller (who could claim that the object was burned or damaged after the sale, when this had really occurred prior to it).

Be that as it may, the transfer of goods is carried out in practice by the act of grasping and pulling or moving, and this criterion was also applied to intangible things. For this reason the laws of sale and barter determine that if one of the parties has "grasped" one of the objects the deal is concluded. *Halakhah* created the general concept of *kinyan agav sudar* in order to ensure the fulfillment of obligations. The party undertaking an obligation commits some symbolic act of grasping an object, such as a *sudar* (head-covering), and pulling it away from the other person's grasp, which denotes the legal conclusion of the agreement and cannot then be rescinded. This act of taking possession is carried out in many spheres of *halakhah* to establish the validity of various legal actions—the guarantees contained in the marriage contract, transfer of property through gift, agreement of both parties to arbitration, etc.

In clarifying these problems the Talmud also touches on the question of bi-metallism. Should silver or gold be taken as the basis for the monetary system? Is silver the basic currency and gold an "object," or is the reverse true? The talmudic sages never arrived at complete agreement on this question.

The laws of sale and barter also deal with questions of fair trading and the permissible margin of error. Although there was never complete accord on this issue, it was usually assumed that the percentage should be one-sixth of the value of the goods. If one of the parties erred by less in his evaluation, it was assumed that he was renouncing the claim, while a higher percentage of error cancelled the deal. The same percentage was also estimated to constitute a fair profit for traders selling staple foodstuffs; a higher profit margin was regarded as profiteering and thus immoral and even punishable by law. Commercial law in general takes an ambivalent stand, since some acts may be legal from the formal point of view but are nevertheless regarded as morally reprehensible. A man who has given or received money for goods is legally entitled to change his mind at any time without concluding the deal, but such a man is regarded as dishonest, and it can even be said of him: "He who punished the people of Sodom will punish the man who does not keep his word."

The laws of sale also dealt with interpretation of sales agreements and contracts. It was accepted that these inevitably vary in accordance with conditions of time and place, but attempts were made to establish comprehensive definitions of various problems.

For example, what is entailed in renting or selling a house? What does the seller transfer as part of this deal? What does sale of a field encompass?

Changing conditions are also an important factor in labor legislation, which deals with day and hourly laborers, artisans and contractors, lessees and renters. Cognizance is taken of the law of the land in these cases, but at the same time, detailed laws were drawn up as general guidelines, to be followed wherever clearly formulated legislation was lacking or when local law was not sufficiently clear. There are several generalized statements in labor legislation, and one of the most important relates to the right of a laborer to cease his work. This is based on a formula which is theological in origin, but is applied in this sphere as well. The Torah states: "Unto me the children of Israel are servants" (Leviticus 25:55), and from this it was inferred that Israel cannot be "the servants of servants." Therefore a worker is entitled to stop working at any time, and his employer cannot force him to complete his task. At the same time we find an interesting balance between this concept and the general concept of justice. A worker may abandon his task, but at the same time, his employer is entitled to sue him for damages. This is a mutual right. The employer who invites a laborer to work and does not employ him must also pay damages. This combination of laws that gives the worker the right to strike but effectively prevents him from utilizing it creates a situation in which worker and employer are obliged to negotiate whenever working conditions or wages change, so that unjustified "wildcat" strikes are unlikely to occur.

There is another labor law, also based on Torah precepts, that prohibits delayed payment of wages. The employer is obliged to pay the worker within a few hours of completion of the job. Furthermore, it was determined that this was one of the few exceptional cases in which the claimant (that is, the worker) takes an oath and is then awarded the sum of his claim if there is any doubt as to whether he has been paid.

Short-term labor contracts or the placing of orders with ar-

tisans were usually carried out orally, without excessive specification of conditions, on the assumption that "everything is done in
accordance with the law of the land." We find one exception—the
case of a sage who advised his son to settle in advance with his
workers which meal he would provide as part of their wages,
since, by feeding them at times that he himself determined, he
would not be fulfilling his obligation to them as "sons of Abraham, Isaac, and Jacob." But this was an exceptional view; according to the *halakkah*, the "law of the land" always prevails.

In long-term labor contracts, including those relating to the
leasing of land, the agreement was recorded in writing. The laws
of deeds contained numerous halakhic problems, one relating to
the validity of the guarantee to pay a fine for nonfulfillment of the
contract. In certain contracts extremely high fines were specified
in order to exert pressure on the recalcitrant party, and the query
arose as to whether such a document was legally valid. This
problem is related to the basic talmudic controversy over the *asmakhta*, that is, a guarantee or agreement to pay a fine for nonim-
plementation when it is clear that the guarantor never expects to
arrive at such a pass. The majority view of the early sages was
that such a guarantee was not legal, and anyone who insisted on
extracting payment of the fine was regarded as a thief. The *asmakhta* is usually cited in the case of exaggerated monetary demands in documents, since the man signing such a bond has no
real intention of paying the sum and is fully confident that the
need will never arise. In short, the sages thought that any guarantee that was not backed by true intent was not valid. A fine that
compensates a man for real loss is not regarded as an *asmakhta*, although here too there were differences of opinion. We can also
understand, in the light of *asmakhta*, why the sages regarded all
forms of gambling as a kind of robbery, since the loser in a dice
game starts out with the conviction that he will win and therefore
does not seriously intend to pay.

The question of the conditions specified in a contract is not
merely a part of the fabric of civil law, but also relates to matri-

monial legislation (marriage or divorce performed in accordance with certain conditions) and other laws. In addition to the question of which conditions are illegal (the fines, according to some schools of thought, or the condition in a divorce contract forbidding a woman to remarry, for example), there is the problem of the relationship of the conditions to the body of the contract. When does nullification of conditions render the entire contract invalid, and which conditions are binding but are not an inseparable part of the contract? Certain contracts do not make it clear when conditions becomes applicable. Is it after the contract is enforced or from the moment of signing?

Other discussions were devoted to the dates of certain documents and bonds and the way in which they should be verified by witnesses. The sages distinguished, for example, between loans agreed on orally and those drawn up by a document signed by witnesses. The latter type constitutes a public obligation, and since, in most such documents, there was also *ahrayut nekhasim* (responsibility for property, *i.e.* the borrower mortgaged his entire property), the lender was permitted, in the event of nonpayment, to take a sum equivalent to the sum of the loan from the borrower's property and assets. In such cases, the mortgage became valid from the time of composition of the document and if the borrower sold his property subsequently, the lender was permitted to extract payment (or, in talmudic terminology, *litrof*, to take prey) from the purchaser, who, in his turn, could demand compensation of the seller. All these conditions apply to written contracts signed by witnesses. Oral agreements or unwitnessed notes (in the handwriting of the borrower, for example) are binding on the borrower but are not regarded as public documents, and the purchaser cannot be forced to restore the property.

Since every individual undertakes certain obligations in the course of his life—the marriage contract is such an obligation—there were always questions of how to divide up remaining property. There were also cases where two conflicting notes written on the same date were found. In Jerusalem it was the custom to record the hour at which a deed was written, but this was not done elsewhere, and complications ensued. The sages also discussed the problem of "early notes," where it was clear that the document had actually been written after the date recorded on it; these were always invalidated to prevent the parties from conspiring against future purchasers. "Late notes" were accepted despite the inaccuracies.

There were two main types of documents: simple notes, to which the witnesses affixed their signature to the written text, two witnessing sufficing, and a special type of document that was considered safer, since it was folded in a special way, each witness signing each fold. The *halakhah* on legal documents is extensive and complex, with discussions on the reliability of witnesses, the likelihood of forgeries, and so forth. The *geonim* composed several works devoted exclusively to such talmudic legislation.

Inheritance laws belong within the civil code. Here too the basic legislation is to be found in the Torah and is elaborated in the Talmud. Basically, the talmudic sages believed that a man cannot be permitted to decide arbitrarily how his property is to be distributed after his death, and the law always prevails over the wishes of the deceased. The inheritance laws could be evaded by handing over property during the owner's lifetime, and there were special legal formulas facilitating this. Even then the sages held that it was wrong to transfer property from one son to another, even from a bad to a dutiful one. The basic laws of inheritance award the prior claim to the descendants of the deceased, sons and their offspring taking precedence over daughters (the daughter of a son coming before a daughter). If the deceased has no issue, the inheritance goes to his father or grandfather. The rule is that "the father precedes all his offspring"; accordingly, if there are no brothers or uncles, family history is investigated until a man who was survived by his sons is located. In practice, however, this designation was not so simple, as the *ketubah* specified certain obligations regarding the wife and her issue.

Civil law is infinitely more detailed and comprehensive than this brief survey can indicate, and its discussions, in the general spirit of the Talmud, are a combination of solutions to practical problems, elucidations, and conjectures.

20

Criminal Law

THE TALMUD sees no basic distinction between criminal and civil law, just as there is no clear division between offenses committed by one man against another and religious transgressions "between man and God." All the spheres of legal activity are seen only as different aspects of one comprehensive body of teaching. At the same time, certain distinctions are made between the laws pertaining to monetary matters and those dealing with criminal offenses and corporal punishment. In practice, the view of the comprehensive nature of the legal system as a whole is valid almost solely in connection with those *halakhot* where corporal punishment is involved.

The legal system was no longer a comprehensive unit throughout most of the mishnaic era and in the talmudic period, and even during the Second Temple era it was not in force in all generations. To a large extent this situation was the consequence of the internal independence of the Jewish people, which was to reach the point where severe action was taken against those who transgressed against the Mosaic code. A relatively high level of autonomy existed in many Jewish communities throughout the world, but this usually developed after *semikhah* (ordination) ceased, and Jewish law could no longer prevail. *Semikhah* is an ancient ceremony of transmitting judicial authority from rabbi to disciple. The chain of authority extended from the ordination of Joshua by Moses through the generations to the beginning of the Middle Ages. We know of at least one case in the mishnaic era where only one ordained scholar survived, a venerable sage who defied the Roman ban on *semikhah* and sacrificed his life in order to ordain five disciples to continue the Jewish legal tradition. But since, according to the Torah, ordination could only be carried out in Palestine, and the Byzantine rulers of the country became increasingly brutal in their methods of suppression, *semikhah* gradually died out. A later attempt to revive it proved unsuccessful. The fact that this comprehensive judicial system disappeared relatively early should not suggest compliant renunciation on the part of the people; they endeavored to adapt themselves to a situation in which it was temporarily impossible to conduct life in accordance with a comprehensive legal code.

There were three judicial categories in civil law, which, to a certain degree, operated side by side. The highest level was a court of three ordained judges authorized to pass judgment on laws of indemnity, as well as other monetary cases. Below it was the court of three laymen (*hedyotot*), sometimes chosen by the two litigants by mutual agreement, sometimes by each party selecting one judge and the two judges subsequently choosing a third member of the court. The courts of laymen were sometimes arbitratory bodies that demanded the prior agreement of the litigants to accept the proposed compromise. But sometimes this court passed independent rulings, and although the judges had been chosen by the litigants themselves, the latter were not permitted to reject the decision. What is more, since the Jewish legal system was not hierarchic, there was no high court of appeals. In the event that the court of *hedyotot* erred in its judgment, because its members were not sufficiently acquainted with the *halakhah*, the case was retried by the same court or another court. If the judgment had caused irreversible damage, the judges were obliged to compensate the injured party; this was not the case with the court of legal experts, who were exempt from payment even in the event of error. Of equal standing with the three lay judges was the court consisting of a single ordained judge who, in certain cases, was empowered to pass judgment alone. Despite this authorization there was a binding rule, morally rather than legally valid, that no judge should sit alone. Thus even when the experienced *dayyan* was, in practice, the sole arbiter, it was the custom to appoint another two judges, if possible also experienced, to sit with him and share the burden of judicial responsibility. The court of three experts was the most authoritative, since, according to the *halakhah*, it could even decide on corporal punishment, though not on execution.

Capital offenses were tried by a specially composed court of twenty-three judges, known as the *Sanhedrei Ketana* (Small Sanhedrin). Not only were the judges all ordained, but other strict criteria had to be observed. Since there were standing instructions to courts to refrain, insofar as possible, from passing the death sentence, it was customary to remove from the bench any man who was believed incapable of maintaining an impartial attitude toward the defendant. For example, if the members of the court had witnessed the crime with their own eyes, they were forbidden to try the case, on the assumption that their personal resentment would distort their ability to pass fair judgment. Childless men or aged persons were also disqualified from serving on such courts, since, as the Talmud said, "they have forgotten the sorrow of raising children," and therefore might be more eager to apply the strict letter of the law than to consider the motives and emotions of the defendant.

The twenty-three-man court was authorized to pass the death sentence in most cases, but some matters were outside the scope of its authority because of their wider national implications. These were tried by the Great Sanhedrin, the supreme court, composed of seventy-one members and permanently located in the Chamber of Hewn Stone in the Temple. This court alone was empowered to try a man accused of being a false prophet, or a sage who had transgressed and instructed people to act in violation of *halakhah*. The Great Sanhedrin tried those accused of grave offenses (for which the death sentence could be imposed) against the High Priest and the monarch. Unlike the Small Sanhedrin, it was not merely a judicial institution, but was regarded as the continuation of the *bet din* of seventy sages, which Moses himself had founded. This great law court was the expression of supreme religious authority; its power included the right to declare war, to decide the legality of the enactments of other courts and judicial institutions, and to promulgate new enactments binding on the entire nation. It should be recalled that the area of jurisdiction of the Great Sanhedrin was not limited to one place and extended beyond the borders of the Jewish state. It appointed the judges of the twenty-three-man courts in Jewish centers throughout the world, and its influence encompassed the entire Jewish people.

The procedures of Jewish courts, as detailed in the Talmud, differed considerably from modern custom. The courts that tried civil cases were much more flexible both in their methods of deliberation and their attitude to evidence, but they too were ruled by a stable legal system. Most of the talmudic sages believed that all subjects discussed in the Torah should be treated with the same degree of precision and punctiliousness, but practical observance of this rule would have proved extremely cumbersome, and precious time would have been wasted without producing clear results. It was therefore agreed that courts were empowered to expropriate property as they saw fit for the common good and to discuss monetary law in a more flexible fashion. Most of these considerations applied to the sphere of corporal punishment as determined by the law, whether offenses punishable by flogging (imposed on those who transgressed against the negative injunctions) or capital offenses.

Criminal Law

The first qualification was applied to laws of evidence. According to the Torah, evidence is valid only if substantiated by two witnesses. These must be men who have attained their majority, have never been accused of criminal offenses of any kind, and are not related to the litigants, the judges, or one another. Written testimony was not accepted by the courts, the principle being that every witness must stand up to cross-examination. In civil monetary claims, various documents were cited, and it was said that "witnesses who have signed a document are regarded as having had their evidence accepted by a court," but this was not true of criminal law. The restrictions applied to the types of evidence acceptable in court rather than to the witnesses themselves. The latter faced examination and cross-examination, and if significant contradictions emerged in their evidence or between various testimonies, the testimony as a whole was rejected. In certain cases, the examination was so searching that witnesses could only withstand it if they adhered strictly to the facts and admitted to having forgotten certain details.

Another important qualification related to acceptability of the confession of the accused. If the defendant in a civil case admits the charge, there is no need of further clarification, and sentence is passed accordingly. The basis for this procedure is not the assumption that the defendant is telling the truth, but the belief that every man is entitled to give away his money as a gift. Therefore, if he decides to state that the charge against him is a just one, it is not the concern of the court to seek further facts. This is not so where criminal law is concerned. The basic assumption in *halakhah* is that a man does not belong only to himself; just as he has no right to cause physical harm to others, so he has no right to inflict injury on himself. This is why it was determined that the confession of the defendant had no legal validity and should not be taken into consideration. This rule, which has its own formal substantiation, served courts for centuries as a powerful weapon against attempts to extract confessions by force or persuasion.

Not only can no man be forced to incriminate himself through his own testimony, but self-incrimination has no significance and is unacceptable as evidence in court.

Study of the sphere of criminal law furthers our understanding of the fierce urge to arrive at the absolute truth that inspires all talmudic examination. First, the courts do not accept circumstantial evidence even if no other interpretation of the facts is feasible. An extreme example of this cautious attitude is cited by the Talmud itself when it states that if witnesses see a man, sword in hand, pursuing someone, both enter a building, the pursuer emerges alone with a blood-stained weapon and the other is found dead inside, the pursuer cannot be convicted on the basis of this eye-witness evidence. Witnesses can only attest to what they have actually seen with their own eyes, and neither conjectures, theories, nor hearsay evidence will be accepted by the court. Evidence concerning a crime is valid only when the witnesses actually saw the crime occur.

Another important factor is clarification of the intentions of the defendant. According to the Torah, a man cannot be sentenced to punishment (flogging or execution) unless he committed the deed with malice aforethought. How can such intent be proved? In most countries the law assumes premeditation on the basis of the actions and preparations of the criminal, but Jewish law does not acknowledge such a method of drawing conclusions and demands real proof of intent. This is the purpose of the warning (*hatra'ah*). A man cannot be condemned to death unless witnesses attest not only to the deed but also to the fact that he was cautioned, that is, told just before committing the crime that the act he was about to commit was forbidden by law and that the punishment for violation of the law was death. Furthermore, it was not sufficient to utter the warning; it was necessary to verify that the defendant had taken note of it and accepted it by saying: "I know and I take it upon myself." Without these elements there is no possibility of proving malicious intent, and consequently of punishing the criminal.

[168]

Criminal Law

Another factor that helped weigh the balance in favor of the defendant was the policy of the courts to take his side as far as possible. This is why the defendant could only be found guilty by a majority of three (thirteen against ten), while a majority of one sufficed to clear him; he was also cleared if the court could not arrive at a decision. In addition, any individual had the right to plead for the defendant in court, but only the members of the court itself could prosecute him. A judge who expressed an opinion in favor of the defendant was forbidden to change his view, while the opposite was always permitted. It was, of course, extremely difficult to find a case that answered all the requirements according to all these conditions and restrictions. And it was said, not without cause, that a court that passed a death sentence once in seven years was known as "the killing court."

These stringent restrictions led sages to ask how lawlessness was to be prevented in a country where the courts found it so hard to impose severe punishment. How was the state to prevent the exploitation of this excessive caution by various criminals? The problem was discussed as long ago as the Second Temple period, and two practical solutions were found. One was based on the powers of the monarchy. According to the *halakhah*, the king could establish his own special courts whose main task was to maintain public order, and they were not bound by the various restrictions on testimony that guided the actions of regular courts. Since they were granted greater powers, they could ensure that no criminal acts were committed against citizens and that, if committed, they would be suitably punished. But there was an additional method, based on the fact that Jewish courts are not law courts in the limited sense of the word. To a certain extent, the *bet din* is the institution that ensures that the affairs of the state, or of the town or region under its jurisdiction, are conducted normally. Thus the courts themselves initiated certain steps when convinced that public order, religious law, or morals were imperiled. When the *bet din* sat as an administrative institution rather than a court of law, it wielded extremely wide-ranging authority. It was empowered not only to extract various monetary fines but also to impose heavy prison sentences, even life imprisonment (punishment by incarceration is nonexistent in the basic Mosaic code) or flogging, as it saw fit. This latter punishment, known as *makot mardut* (punishment for rebelliousness), was applied to those who rebelled or offended against the Torah. The court was also authorized to impose the heaviest penalty of all—the death sentence. The *bet din* therefore considered certain problems not only in the light of the guilt of the defendant according to the law, but sometimes on the basis of whether the precept "And thou shalt pluck the evil from thy midst" should be applied to him. In accordance with these powers, the courts sometimes dealt out severe sentences ("not from the words of the Torah and not in order to transgress against the Torah") determined not by the general code of law, but in accordance with exigency. These powers were exercised not only while the Sanhedrin existed, but later as well (apparently until the fourteenth century in Spain). The court could also wield the weapon of *herem* (excommunication) in varying degrees (starting with *nidui*, which is relatively light, and extending to full excommunication), which was utilized until modern times.

The law court as depicted in the Talmud also had its own trial procedures. The members of the twenty-three-man *bet din* were seated in a semi-circle to enable them to see each other. On each end stood one of the two court scribes who recorded the arguments of the judges. Three rows of scholars sat opposite the bench, the rows being arranged by standard of scholarship, and when the need arose to ordain a judge to complete the requisite number, he was chosen from the front row. In certain cases these scholars were permitted to take part in the discussion and voice their own opinions, although, as a rule, their votes were not counted when the final tally was made. In all courts the examination of witnesses was conducted in the presence of the audience and the litigants, but during the judges' deliberations, the public, the witnesses, and the litigants were apparently excluded from the courtroom. Those disciples who were present during the deliberations were cautioned, as in the case of closed sessions in the academies, not to disclose anything of what they heard. Even in civil cases, the different opinions of the judges were not published, although unanimous rulings were phrased differently from majority rulings. Severe disciplinary action was taken against those who revealed the secrets of closed sessions. It is related in the Talmud that on one occasion a man who revealed something that had occurred in the academy twenty-two years earlier was banished from it forever.

Litigants in Jewish religious courts did not employ counsel to plead their cause, and the concept of legal advice, which existed in Greek and Roman law at that time, was viewed negatively, as lawyers were thought to distort the truth by offering dishonest advice to clients. On rare occasions the defendant was permitted to appoint someone to represent him in court, and sometimes a guardian would plead on behalf of an orphan. But in criminal cases no representatives were allowed to appear on either side. The case for the prosecution was conducted by the witnesses to the crime, who were not allowed to speak for or against the defendant but merely to describe what they had seen. After the clarification of testimony and cross-examination of the witnesses by members of the court, the judges pondered the weight and reliability of the evidence and the legal aspects of the case. They would then divide up and argue for conviction or acquittal, according to their personal views of the case. In criminal trials in particular, it was incumbent on the judges to seek evidence in favor of the defendant and to accept any weighty evidence in his favor.

The penal laws and the possibilities for punitive action were extensive even if we discount the special punishments that were not an integral part of the Mosaic code. Suspects who were obliged to await sentence because the court had not yet arrived at a decision were detained for a specific period. The courts were cautioned not only against miscarriages of justice but also against *inui din* (delay of justice), that is, leaving a defendant in suspense as to his fate. Judges were urged to expedite the passing of sentence, particularly where the death penalty could be invoked. In addition, a man who caused grave bodily harm to another was detained until it was determined whether the injury had proved fatal, in which case the offender was charged with murder.

The most common punishment was flogging. The Torah specified a fixed number of lashes (thirty-nine) as punishment for any person deliberately transgressing against the negative ("thou shalt not . . .") injunctions. Excluded from this ruling were monetary offenses (theft, robbery, etc.) or "offenses that contain no action," that is, where no physical act was involved. These included not only acts committed in thought alone (like hatred, which is a grave misdemeanor, but cannot be judged), but also curses. Graver offenses were punished more severely. Floggings were administered by the court beadles under the supervision of physicians who determined whether the offender could endure the punishment. Sentences for acts of rebelliousness were left to the discretion of the court; sometimes the punishment was flogging, for various offenses not covered by the Torah, or to force a man to carry out the decision of the court. A case in point is the man who refused to divorce his wife despite the explicit order of the *bet din*.

Kipa (life imprisonment) was imposed on recidivists and on defendants who tried to exploit lacunae in the regular laws of evidence. For example, when the court was convinced that a man had committed murder deliberately but had not been sufficiently cautioned of the possible consequences, he was sentenced to life imprisonment.

The Torah imposed a special sentence on the *rotzeah bi-shegagah* (accidental murderer). The legal definition of *shegagah* in this case is negligence and lack of caution without malicious intent. In this event, the defendant was condemned to exile in one of the cities of refuge specified for this purpose. He could return home only after the death of the High Priest.

Where the death sentence was concerned, there was a differentiation among four types of implementation, according to the severity of the crime. The harshest, stoning, was imposed on those found guilty of idolatry, profanation of the Sabbath, and the graver kinds of incest, including the rape of a betrothed girl. The witnesses who had testified against a convicted man carried out the sentence. He was thrown off a high place and a heavy stone was hurled after him. Under the circumstances, totally incriminating evidence was rarely submitted to the courts. Violations of the less severe incest laws were punished by burning at the stake, adulterers were put to death by strangulation, and murderers were beheaded.

To these penal laws we should add the special laws pertaining to the right to self-defense. It is a basic assumption in the Torah that "if anyone comes to kill you, you should kill him first"; what is more, every individual has the right to kill those about to commit a grave crime (murder or rape). There is no room for cautioning the legal deliberations where self-defense is concerned, nor is there a prescribed method of implementation. At the same time, it is stated emphatically that violence should not be employed in self-defense beyond the necessary and feasible minimum dictated by circumstances. A man who kills his pursuer when he could have saved himself in some other way may himself be charged with murder. The special law relating to informers was an expansion of the concept of self-defense. Anyone bearing tales against others to the alien authorities—even if his evidence pertains to civil law, and even more so if a capital offense is involved—places himself outside the law by his action, and members of the community are permitted and even encouraged to kill him. Even when the death penalty was abolished in certain communities, informers were still sentenced to death. It is interesting to note that in medieval Spain the Jewish courts sentenced Jewish informers, but the sentence was carried out by the Spanish authorities, despite the fact that the informer had been acting on the latter's behalf. The courts continued to judge informers in this severe manner throughout the centuries, and informers have received death sentences within living memory in Soviet Russia and Nazi-occupied territories.

21

Sacrifices

BOTH written and oral law devote extensive space to sacrificial laws. The prophetic tradition roundly condemns those who substituted the offering of sacrifices for true penitence, but at the same time the prophets never objected to sacrifices as such and denounced those who spoiled sacrifices by choosing flawed animals. In the Second Temple period, the sages stated that the world rested on three things: the Torah, Temple worship, and charitable deeds. The profound emotional attitude to Temple ritual did not wane in intensity after the destruction of the Temple. Not only did the Jews continue to pray for the rebuilding of the Temple and restoration of worship and sacrifice (in the *Shemoneh Esreh* prayer and in part of the *Musaf* prayer on ceremonial occasions), but they continued to discuss and amend the laws of sacrifice. Despite the historical and geographical distance, the Babylonian sages devoted considerable attention to the laws of sacrifice, their justification being that "he who engages in study of the laws of sacrifice should be regarded as if he had offered up a sacrifice himself." Accordingly, an entire order of the Babylonian Talmud, *Kodashim*, is devoted to this subject.

In line with the general policy of the Talmud we find no systematic attempt therein to explain the ideological basis of the injunction on sacrifice, and the issue can be understood only through the hints dispersed throughout the text and from the various commentaries written over the ages. There seem to be three basic elements to sacrifice: the giving, the substitution, and the coming close. The idea of giving implies the renunciation by the worshipper of something he owns, given as a gift to his Creator. On the basis of this idea, "one may give much and another little as long as his heart is directed at Heaven." Since it is not the quality of the sacrifice that counts but the effort made by the sacrificer, the meager offering of the poor man may be worth more than the rich man's large sacrifice. Another basic concept is substitution—the sacrifice substitutes for self-sacrifice or death. The sinner deserves to die for his sins, but the Torah grants him the opportunity of offering up a sacrifice, on condition that he realizes that this symbolizes sacrifice of his own self. Everything that is done to the sacrifice should have been done to him. This approach is implicit in the *midrashim* and is expressed in the story of the sacrifice of Isaac, where a ram is placed on the altar and sacrificed in his stead. The talmudic sages often speak of "Isaac's dust," which is the foundation of the altar, the reference being to the ram slaughtered in place of Abraham's son. It is always emphasized in this sphere that the sacrifice alone cannot atone for sins and can only be offered up after the sinner has repented, whether through expressing regret and swearing never to sin again, in cases of sins against Heaven, or through restitution of the theft, in cases of sin committed against his fellow men. An atonement sacrifice offered *after* the act of penitence was considered the most profound and basic ritual sacrament. Offering the sacrifice, pouring its blood on the altar, and burning the flesh are ceremonies of communion with God, and this aspect is strongly emphasized when the sacrificer eats part of the flesh. At this moment, the sacrificer communes with and is as one with God.

Sacrifices

The priests or other persons offering sacrifices participate in symbolic fashion in the meal.

The laws of sacrifice as they appear in the Torah itself, particularly in Leviticus, are comprehensive and complicated, though not exhaustive. There was undoubtedly an extremely detailed priestly tradition on how to deal with each type of sacrifice, both as regards the actual ceremony and the various flaws that might be found in the sacrifice itself. Sacrifices were rejected when the animal itself was flawed or when the thought or intention was unworthy, thus invalidating the offering. Even in the talmudic era, the laws of sacrifice were regarded as the most involved in the Talmud; as a certain sage said to one of his disciples: "Such a difficult problem belongs, from the point of view of gravity, with the laws of sacrifice." The complexity results not only from the abundance and intricacy of the details but also from the basic intellectual theories underlying this type of law. Unlike civil law, for example, which is essentially rational, laws of sacrifice are based on very ancient traditions and customs for which no apparent explanation exists. In the talmudic period it was emphasized that, unlike other *halakhot*, laws of sacrifice should be studied and analyzed with great caution, and methods of study appropriate in other spheres were not always effective in this area. The scholars cited extensive proof that halakhic methods relevant and applicable elsewhere cannot be employed in deliberations on laws of sacrifice, which constitute a world apart. At the same time, the scholar who becomes reasonably erudite in this field begins to discern a special kind of logic that can serve as the basis for more profound examination.

The many different types of sacrifices are classified in the *halakhah* according to various criteria. There is clear differentiation between public sacrifices, those offered up at fixed times (like the *tamid* sacrifice offered every day or the *musaf* sacrifice offered only on Sabbaths and holidays), and private sacrifices, whether obligatory, offered by individual worshippers to atone for sins or as an act of purification, or free-will offerings. There were also sub-divisions into offerings of *zevah* (cattle, sheep, or poultry) and *minhah* (meal: flour, wheat, or barley). In addition, there was classification by degree of sanctity of the sacrifices, determined by other criteria. Thus a distinction was made between sin-offerings (as on the Day of Atonement) whose blood was brought to the Holy of Holies; other sacrifices, known as "the holiest of holies," which were particularly sacred and were only consumed to the extent that they were edible by the Temple priests; and sacrifices of "lesser sanctity," the majority, which could be consumed by the individual offering them.

The *Kodashim* order does not deal solely with sacrifices or with various disqualifications; it also deals with principles clarifying the nature of various sins that call for atonement offerings. It is a basic rule, to which there are very few exceptions, that a man cannot offer a sacrifice for an offense committed with malicious intent. Such a deed must be punished by man, that is, by a court, and only in cases where the court is powerless for lack of sufficient evidence is the sinner punished by Heaven. Sacrifices are offered only for unintentional offenses; deliberate offenses cannot be atoned for by sacrifice alone. On the other hand, if a man sins through *oness* (that is, having been coerced or because of lack of knowledge), he is not regarded as bearing responsibility for the deed. When he offends because he forgot a prohibition and transgressed against it, he is obliged to offer a sacrifice. It is assumed in this case that although no man bears full responsibility for inadvertent errors, and cannot be tried for them, his forgetfulness results from an inner deficiency and calls for atonement.

In addition to sacrifices, numerous voluntary gifts were brought to the Temple and the priests. Some of the priestly gifts were taken from the field crops and have almost no connection with the Temple itself, pertaining by subject and by talmudic classification to the *Zeraim* order. There were other gifts brought to the Temple for specific purposes. In the days of Moses we find a contribution of half a shekel for Temple maintenance. It was

[178]

Sacrifices

given at that time for the express purpose of building the Tabernacle, but when the Babylonian exiles returned to Palestine and built the Second Temple, the need arose for regular popular participation in Temple maintenance, and it was decided that every person would make a fixed contribution to the Temple. This sum, which continued to be known as the half-shekel, although its value fluctuated from era to era, became the main source of financing Temple expenditures, covering public sacrifices, restoration of buildings, or the purchase of utensils and instruments for use therein. In due course giving a half-shekel became the expression of national participation in Temple worship. Contributions were collected not only in Palestine but from the Diaspora as well. After the destruction of the Temple, the Roman authorities forced all the Jews within their area of jurisdiction to continue payment of this sum as a tax to the Roman treasury.

Participation in Temple worship was not restricted to monetary contribution: arrangements were made for establishment of a suitable popular representation for purposes of Temple worship. Generally speaking, there was no need for all the priests in Palestine to attend Temple ceremonies, and, as a result, from David's reign onward, the priests and Levites were divided into twenty-four *mishmarot* (watches). The priests of each watch spent one week every six months serving in the Temple and, in addition, all the priests came up to the Temple on the three main holidays, the times of popular pilgrimage and mass sacrifices. In addition to the priestly watches, the sages also established *ma'amadot* (stations), a corresponding division of worshippers. Whenever it was the turn of a certain watch to go up to Jerusalem, some of the members of its station would go up with it and participate as spectators in the ritual ceremonies as representatives of the people. The members of the station who remained at home devoted the week to a series of special prayers, fasts, and assemblies. Thus ritual worship became the concern of the entire nation, and people felt that they had their own special emissaries to the Temple.

Expenditure of the sums allocated to the Temple through the

shekel contributions, as well as the sums given in accordance with vows and in other ways, had to be supervised, and this called not only for reliable financial arrangements but for a special attitude toward Temple funds. The basic *halakhot* on this subject appear in the Torah itself, where a monetary fine, an extra one-fifth above the basic value, and extra atonement offerings are demanded of those who unintentionally benefit from objects or money earmarked for sacred purposes. An entire tractate of the Talmud, *Me'ilah*, is devoted to clarification of *halakhot* on this theme: determining the exact moment at which monetary contributions become sacred, when utilization should be regarded as embezzlement, and so forth. Since Temple funds were regarded as sacred (until utilized for their specific purpose), there was, as a rule, no fear of theft or robbery. In fact, people sometimes marked their money chests as Temple property in order to prevent theft.

The Temple funds were not earmarked exclusively for sacrificial purposes, and in the First Temple period (and, to a certain extent, in the Second Temple period as well), the Temple treasury served as the national exchequer. The money was usually expended on daily worship in the Temple and payment of clerks' wages. Clerks and appointed officials were not usually paid from public funds, but in cases where they devoted all their time to their task they received a special allowance from the Temple treasury. Restoration work in the Temple was also financed from contributions, and a certain sum was allocated for building Jerusalem, which, as a holy city, was also regarded as sacred to a certain degree. In times of crisis, when no other source was available, the Temple treasury also served as an emergency fund, particularly when there was no monarch and the High Priest was also a political ruler.

A large amount of evidence is extant on the architectural structure of the Temple, its procedure, and ritual. Some of the information was supplied by Josephus Flavius, himself a priest, who described those aspects of the Temple with which he was per-

Sacrifices

sonally acquainted. But the mishnaic sages also felt the need to perpetuate details of Temple worship; they devoted a short tractate to the description of ritual and another tractate to external description. The Second Temple was based on two models: on the one hand, it was reminiscent of the structure of the First Temple, but several details were copied from the model Third Temple as envisaged by the prophet Ezekiel for the epoch of true redemption. The Second Temple was built at a time of considerable financial and political instability, and even when it was improved and enlarged by King Herod, who transformed it into one of the most glorious structures in the entire region, it was felt that the time was not yet ripe for building the Temple in accordance with Ezekiel's aim.

The basic layout of the three models is identical and is based, to a certain extent, on the Tabernacle built by Moses in the desert. Mount Moriah, on which the Temple was built, was commonly called *Har ha-Bayit* (the Temple Mount). Surrounded by a wall, it was a separate sacred area, like the original "Levite camp" in the Sinai desert. Inside the wall of the Temple Mount was another wall encompassing a smaller area, that of the Temple itself, consisting mainly of a great open courtyard with many rooms utilized for various purposes. Several of these rooms were storehouses, others were reserved for the priests or for various preparatory tasks (for example, preparing the incense and the shewbread), or for the courts that sat regularly in the Temple, headed by the Great Sanhedrin. Most of the area of the great courtyard, known as the *azarah*, was reserved for the worshippers who came to pray or to watch the ceremony of sacrifice. It was known as the *ezrat nashim* (women's court), because both men and women stood there. A narrow area in the front was known as *ezrat Israel* and was reserved for those bringing sacrifices. Inside stood the great sacrificial altar to which the priests ascended by ramp. By the side of the altar were all the instruments and utensils needed for the ceremony. At the forward western end of the Temple stood a tall building 50 meters high in which were located the *kodesh* (Holy Place) and the Holy of Holies. In the *kodesh* were the inner utensils of the Temple, the gold table for the shewbread, the *menorah* (seven-branched candelabrum), and incense altar. At the front end was the closed chamber of the Holy of Holies. In the First Temple period the Ark of the Covenant was in the Holy of Holies, while in the Second Temple the chamber was empty. Only the High Priest was allowed to enter the Holy of Holies on the Day of Atonement, at the culmination of the ceremony on this solemn day. The Temple faced west, the holiest direction, so that the Holy of Holies was at the western end of the building. The wall now known as the Western (Wailing) Wall was then the western wall of the Temple Mount, closest to the Holy of Holies. The direction in which modern synagogues face is not related to this ancient layout but is determined in accordance with the direction of Israel and Jerusalem and varies according to the geographical location of the synagogue vis-à-vis Israel.

The most important and sacred tasks in the Temple were carried out by the High Priest. In ancient times this position was handed down from father to son within a few select priestly families, although there was no law regulating this procedure, and efforts were later made to insure that the outstanding priest of each generation was elected to the position. This tradition was undermined, to a certain extent, by the Hasmoneans, who, themselves priests, appropriated this lofty position. After the rise of the Herodian dynasty and in the days of the Roman governors, corruption was involved in the appointment of priests, and the high priesthood was sometimes awarded to people who paid enormous sums in order to purchase the honor. The High Priest played a twofold part: he carried out the most hallowed tasks in the Temple, and he was obliged to observe the ritual laws of purification and asceticism more strictly than the other priests. In addition to the special sacrifice he offered up every day as part of the daily ritual, he was entitled to offer any sacrifices he chose in place of any of the other priests. But his main task was carried out on the

Sacrifices

Day of Atonement, when he alone was responsible for the Temple rituals described most precisely in the *Yoma* tractate and other sources. Since there was no possibility of conducting the Day of Atonement ceremonies without the High Priest, there was a special post, that of the Deputy High Priest, who was ready to substitute if the High Priest were unable to perform his duties for any reason whatsoever. In addition to his ritual obligations, the High Priest was also the supreme supervisor of the Temple, and all of the Temple clerks were under his jurisdiction, and were apparently appointed by him. During the Persian occupation and in the Hasmonean era, the High Priest was, for all practical purposes, ruler of the country.

Routine work in the Temple was supervised by the Deputy High Priest, who was also responsible for order and discipline. Special clerks selected from among the priests managed the details of Temple affairs, each bearing responsibility for one particular department, from sacrifices to medical care. The fiscal affairs were managed by an intricate network of officials whose task was to prevent embezzlement. They included two *katoliki* (overseers), seven *amarkalim* (administrators), and thirteen *gizbarim* (treasurers), all of whom held keys to the treasury (which could only be opened, however, when all thirteen were present). Strict attention was paid to the conduct of the Temple staff, who were expected to be scrupulously honest and of irreproachable character.

There was a certain hierarchy among the priests themselves: the heads of the watch, who supervised the entire watch; the *rashei bet av*, each responsible for one-sixth of the watch carrying out its duties on a certain day of the week; the elders, who also served on the special courts of priests; and the younger priests, who were apprenticed and who, together with the Levites, made up the permanent guard of honor of the Temple.

22

Dietary Laws

THE DIETARY LAWS specifying which foods are prohibited and which permitted are associated with several extremely diverse areas. A food may be forbidden because the tithe has not been set aside, because it serves directly or indirectly for idolatrous worship, or because it was the object of theft or robbery. It may be banned because it is *hametz* during Passover, because it belongs to a species regarded as unclean, because it has not been prepared in accordance with halakhic instructions, or for many other reasons.

All these dietary bans have several common halakhic characteristics, and the codification of dietary laws (*kashrut*) called for the integration of many subjects into one significant whole. Very generally speaking, the various bans may be divided into two types that are usually (though not always) related to one extent or another to the primary prohibition. There are general bans on consumption according to which it is forbidden to enjoy or consume a certain food, utilize it in any way, or even sell it to a non-Jew. Such foods are irreparable and must be destroyed. An example of such an interdict is that against all objects that serve for idolatrous worship or that against *hametz* during Passover; these are never permitted under any circumstances. As to other objects, there is no prohibition against enjoyment, meaning that it is permissible to handle them though not to eat them, as in the case of blood, abdominal fat, or poultry dishes cooked in milk. These may be handled and even sold.

The essence and applications of the prohibitions may be divided into three categories. Some are forbidden because the Torah prohibited their consumption or enjoyment, for example, the pig or the fruit of a tree in the first three years after planting. Other objects are forbidden because they have not been properly prepared for consumption, that is, fruits from which the tithe has not been set aside or cattle that has not been slaughtered according to the *halakhah*. The third category includes those objects forbidden because they entail some transgression or abomination and are prohibited on the basis of the verse: "Thou shalt not eat any abominable thing" (Deuteronomy 14:3).

Most of the bans on consumption, apart from those deriving from the nature of the object, have no rational explanation, nor did the sages try to supply one. Over the centuries many implausible explanations have been offered, mainly on pseudo-medical grounds, but none is in either the Mishnah or the Talmud. The prohibitions apply to objects from the animal and vegetable world and never to mineral objects, except for the ban on enjoyment of idols. Most of the vegetable interdicts are related to the laws of the Torah concerning Palestine, and their discussion is mainly concentrated in the tractates of the *Zeraim* order, which deals, in the main, with agriculture; they were hardly ever applied outside Palestine. There were strict interdicts against the consumption of the fruit of trees that had not yet reached their fourth year (*orlah*) and against certain types of *kilayim* (diverse kinds of seeds sown together). Other prohibitions are associated with the laws of *shemitah* (sabbatical year), when the land must be left untilled and its fruit abandoned to man and to the beasts of the field, or with the laws of tithes. In most cases, produce from which the tithe had not been allocated to the priest, the Levites, or the poor was strictly banned until the tithing had been carried out.

A wide network of prohibitions relates to animal foods. The invertebrae are usually forbidden, the only exceptions being several types of locusts enumerated in the Torah. Only one Jewish community still maintains this tradition and sometimes consumes locusts. All reptiles are strictly forbidden, according to the dietary laws.

The Torah enumerates various ways of distinguishing between permitted and unclean fish; only fish with both fins and scales are permissible, and all others are forbidden. This division corresponds to a large extent to the biological classification into bony and cartilaginous fish; the latter were prohibited. Many fish may be classified, biologically speaking, halfway between the two categories, and these aroused many problems. The Talmud tried to arrive at more precise definitions and to explain which scales were significant for the classification, where they were located, and so forth. At the same time, certain types of fish were the subject of controversy between different schools of thought for generations, and when the Turkish Jewish community debated the question at great length, the dispute extended to other and more personal spheres as well.

Whereas the Torah provided explicit definitions of fish, the situation regarding birds was more complicated. A list of more than twenty species of unclean birds was given, and the problem of identifying them arose in the talmudic era. It transpired that there were no longer living traditions relating to several of these species. The sages tried to uncover biological traits that could guide them in this matter by seeking the common denominator of the permitted species and the ways in which they differed from the forbidden ones. They found various external traits, anatomical differences, and variations in behavior that enabled them to establish certain natural biological classifications. There were, however, many marginal cases, and the sages were well aware that there was no way of arriving at a perfect solution. They therefore prohibited the consumption of birds except those traditionally known to be clean, thus restricting the number of permitted birds to domestic and related species.

The classification of mammals is clear and unequivocal. According to the Torah only cud-chewing and cloven-hoofed animals may be consumed; these constitute a very clearly defined group from the zoological point of view, including all types of cattle and sheep, gazelles and rams, as well as giraffes and okapis. The particularly emotional attitude toward the eating of pig is noted in talmudic sources. The ban is no stricter than that against the consumption of horse or camel flesh, yet the Talmud says: "Cursed is he who grows pigs." There was apparently some historical source for this particular interdict, which is not clear to us. It is possible that the peculiarly intense reaction was the result of the Seleucid attempt to force the Jews to eat and sacrifice pigs, and it may be the consequence of the fact that one of the accepted symbols of the Roman legions (especially those that fought in Palestine) was the pig.

In addition to forbidden birds and animals, there are special laws relating to parts that may not be consumed. An important prohibition is that against the consumption of blood. The Torah emphasizes that "blood is the life and thou mayest not eat the life with the flesh" (Deuteronomy 12:23). In the case of warm-blooded animals, the blood is removed before consumption and the meat rendered fit for cooking ("kashered"—a word that, incidentally, does not appear in the sources) by *melihah* (salting), the salt serving as a hygroscopic factor. There is another way of carrying out this process, namely, roasting. Another forbidden portion is the *helev* (lard or tallow of sheep and cattle). Many talmudic sages discussed this question and sought the correct distinction between permitted and forbidden fat, which is based on anatomical and physiological differences. These two prohibitions are indirectly associated with the laws of sacrifices. Both blood and *helev* were offered up on the altar in all sacrifices and were therefore set aside and forbidden for consumption. Some sages understood these bans in other ways, unrelated to sacrifice.

Another kind of ban, also connected with warm-blooded animals, was that on the consumption of animal flesh torn by wild beasts (*terefot*). This prohibition is mentioned in brief in the Torah, but practical need led the sages to expand it and to discuss its various aspects. The ban on eating carcasses pertains to animals or birds that were not slaughtered according to the ritual that renders flesh fit for consumption. The laws of *shehitah* (ritual slaughter) are not elaborated in the Torah, but their existence is implied in the verse: "And thou shalt sacrifice . . . as I have commanded thee" (Deuteronomy 12:21). These laws appear to be very ancient, to the point where the talmudic sages could not agree on the meaning of several of the basic concepts. The original and most prevalent meaning of *terefah* was an animal mauled by wild beasts, though not killed outright. The sages understood the word in the widest possible sense as encompassing all animals so seriously diseased or injured by other beasts or men that they were unable to recover. The Mishnah and the talmudic commentary on the subject discussed specific cases at great length and laid down several important rules for defining the categories of *terefah*. The basic rule was *kol she-ein kamoha hayah—terefah* (any animal whose like cannot survive is *terefah*). This obliged the scholars to clarify numerous aspects of the anatomy and physiology of animals and birds in order to determine which flaws rendered the animal *terefah*. In this context we find that several sages engaged in various scientific experiments on dubious animals and some even established private collections of *terefot* in order to instruct their disciples.

It was the proliferation of problems relating to the law of *terefot* that led to the introduction of the post of *shohet* (ritual slaughterer) in the Middle Ages. The *shohet* undergoes strict training in the practice of his profession: preparation of the instruments, study of the various types of *terefah* and ways of distinguishing between

Dietary Laws

deviations from the norm that remain within the sphere of permitted foods and those which render the animal unfit for consumption. Thus although in the talmudic era any individual could slaughter animals, later ages imposed the task on specially trained experts, and in many communities the *shohet* was second in status only to the rabbi. Hence also the custom of awarding to ritual slaughterers special certificates attesting to their expertise and knowledge (*kabbalah*). In some communities women also fulfilled this task.

Another prohibition connected with the flesh of birds and animals is that against the mixing of meat and milk. The biblical passage "Thou shalt not cook the kid in its mother's milk" (Exodus 23:19) was understood from very ancient times, and, at least in the middle of the Second Temple era, as a ban on cooking any animal flesh in milk. Over the centuries it was extended until (from about the time of the Houses of Hillel and Shammai) it encompassed birds as well. The fear of violating this prohibition engendered various laws and customs aimed at distinguishing between meat and milk dishes to the point where they are now not even eaten at the same meal, and a certain length of time must elapse between the eating of milk and meat and vice versa. There are many customs relating to dietary laws, and one of the sages remarked: "In this sphere I am the wicked son of a righteous father [literally vinegar, son of wine]: after eating meat he would not partake of milk for twenty-four hours, whereas I abstain only from meal to meal." The fear that milk and meat might be cooked together also led to the introduction of separate sets of dishes and household utensils.

The various prohibitions pertaining to food are sufficiently detailed in themselves to necessitate extensive perusal and study of minutiae, many of which cannot be studied in abstract fashion but call for practical experience and demonstration. Any scholar who specialized in dietary laws was obliged to work for a time at a slaughterhouse in order to learn how to act in each specific case. In addition to the technical aspects, there are problems of theoretical importance. These problems are related to questions of doubt and of mixtures of materials and are not restricted to dietary problems; they are found in any area of the *halakhah* where there are interdicts. The basic issue is simple: we know that a certain object is forbidden for some reason, but it is not clear what should be done in the event of doubt. What should a man do if he is faced with a piece of meat and does not know its origin and exact condition? This problem may appear in another and more complex form, namely, what is to be done when a banned object is blended with permitted objects? The Talmud cites the analogous situation of an object that is dangerous. From the halakhic point of view it is forbidden to eat an object or commit an act that imperils life, and the Talmud cautions against such objects and acts. When a suspicion of risk is present, the sages usually take a strict view and advise the reader to avoid any doubt. But here again practical queries emerge, and the scholars must consider the chances that a certain object will be banned or dangerous on the grounds of probability or circumstance. If an object is blended with others, should the prohibition (or the risk) be regarded as annulled on the calculation of percentage, on the assumption that a small concentration cannot be harmful?

These problems led the sages to develop their own independent approach to the theory of probability and to develop a series of rules for the clarification of all types of problems. When discussing *halakhah* on matters in doubt, they utilized various methods of consideration. The basic assumption was that the majority predominated, and this theory was cited in most cases. But at times the rules had to be qualified; in certain spheres a simple majority, however small, sufficed, while in others, especially in matters of particularly grave importance, a large majority was demanded. Another question that arose is found in different form in modern statistical studies. If we are speaking of majority and minority, how do we select our model? On the basis of which sample do we determine our attitude? A classic problem served as the model for the solution to various problems as early as the mishnaic period.

Dietary Laws

Let us assume that in a certain locale there are several stores selling meat—the minority selling *terefah*, the majority selling ritually clean meat. If a hunk of meat is found in the vicinity, should it be regarded as *terefah* or kosher? Several facts need to be taken into consideration here, for example the question of *rov o-karov* (majority or vicinity). Should the object be examined in relation to the nearest location, or should the condition of the majority of stores (or purchasers) be the decisive factor? Another problem, related to the question of the randomization of the sample, is that of *kavua:* to what extent should the majority prevail when the elements are not entirely independent and a certain factor hinders complete homogeneity? On this problem the sages ruled that whenever it is clear that the sampling is not entirely random, the statistical majority can no longer be relied upon, and the doubt should be restored to the primary logical sphere of uncertainty or fifty-fifty probability.

The question of the hybrid belongs in the same category. If a prohibited object is blended with permitted objects, which considerations prevail? Here too the general assumption is that the majority should be followed and the minority is regarded as annulled. But even then care should be taken to ensure that the blend is such that there can be no fear that any part of it will not represent the necessary majority. Distinctions are therefore drawn between liquid mixtures and blends of solid objects. In other cases, taste was the determining factor, and wherever possible an examination was made of whether the taste of the forbidden object was evident in the blend. In practice the sages suggested that an expert non-Jewish cook be consulted. In certain areas a simple majority sufficed; in others it was demanded that the prohibited object be nullified within a much larger majority, the usual proportion being one to sixty. In certain cases they insisted on a high percentage, one to one hundred or even more. In cases where the ban was particularly stringent, they did not accept the possibility of annulment and said that "even within one thousand it is not annulled." They took a particularly strict view of prohibitions on which there were time limits, where the rules of nullification are not relied upon, as a high degree of factual uncertainty is involved.

It was because of these problems, among others, that basically uncomplicated *halakhah* pertaining to the various dietary laws became the inexhaustible subject of study. In practice, even relatively simple questions, such as the repurification of utensils in which forbidden foods have been cooked, can involve the scholar in a wide range of questions, from the practical halakhic problems of the penetration of infinitesimal portions of the forbidden object into the utensil—where physical and chemical evidence was cited and distinctions were drawn between the various materials from which utensils were made—to the question of how long a certain object remains unclean. If it has undergone transformation through various processes, has it not changed its essence to the point where it is no longer prohibited? The scholars cite a wide range of examples of "defective reasoning," when it may be assumed that the forbidden object not only adds no advantage to the *heter* (permit), but has been damaged to such an extent that the ban is nullified. Then there are the questions of the ratio of forbidden and permitted objects in a mixture, the nature of the forbidden object, and the probability of obtaining a complete or incomplete blend.

The *halakhah* on problems concerning dietary laws is discussed at great length in the *Hulin* tractate of the Talmud, but the wider theoretical aspects, which touch on many areas of *halakhah*, are to be found in almost every tractate of the Talmud and constitute an involved but fascinating subject of study.

23

Ritual Purity and Impurity

THE LAWS of ritual purity and impurity take up a whole order of the Mishnah and, even more than sacrificial law, constitute a self-sufficient unit that is perhaps the most recondite section of the Talmud. Although these *halakhot* were discussed in various parts of the Jerusalem and Babylonian Talmuds, it is almost certain that no entire commentary was written on them, apart from the *Nidah* tractate—for which there was great practical need. One of the reasons for this apparent neglect is that these laws are almost completely confined to Palestine and to the periods in which the Temple existed. In the absence of a Temple and of sacrifices, there was little justification for observing the rules of ritual purity, and when sacrifices were no longer offered it was impossible to observe the full scope of these *halakhot*.

The laws of purity are essentially a complex, unified network of laws, interrelated within a special logical structure. Although the Torah devoted considerable space to them, it offered no explanations. In mishnaic times it was related that Rabban Yohanan Ben Zakkai once succeeded, through his wise responses, in persuading a non-Jew of the value of these laws, but his disciples then said to him: "You have fobbed him off with a vague answer, but what have you to say to us?" To this Rabban Yohanan replied that these matters did not derive from rational consideration and that they pertained to one of the spheres of which the Holy One, Blessed be He, said: "I have passed laws, decreed decrees, and you are not permitted to reflect on them." In fact, this legislation is extremely involved and contains a plethora of detail that seems to have been determined at random with no clear rationale.

At the same time, the general structure of these *halakhot* may be comprehended with the aid of several basic principles. First, it should be recalled that purity and impurity are not concepts related to the sphere of cleanliness or hygiene. Observance of the laws of purity may in some ways serve as an aid to hygiene, but this is neither the reason nor the explanation for their issue. As regards the basic outlook, there appear to be two main spheres: life, the most complete expression of which is anything pertaining to sanctity (regarded as the primary source of life); and death and the void, seen as the opposite of life and of sanctity. Generally speaking, it may be said that that which is living and healthy contains no impurity and that impurity increases as an object comes closer to death. Thus the most impure thing, "the supreme cause of impurity" (*avi avot ha-tuma*), according to talmudic terminology, is a corpse, and the lower degree of pollution is that of the leper, the *zav* (victim of gonorrhea), and carcasses of animals and reptiles. The impure object is usually not only impure in itself but also transmits its pollution to objects that come into contact with it. The higher the degree of pollution, the greater the ability to pollute other objects in different ways. The corpse, for example, pollutes whatever comes into contact with it, which is then sometimes polluted to so great an extent that it, in its turn, becomes an independent source of pollution. Pollution is usually conveyed by touching the impure object, but sometimes even by remaining under the same roof or by carrying the polluted object without touching it.

Not every object can be polluted: the more sensitive the person or object touching the source of pollution, the more easily it is infected. Certain foods and drinks take on pollution with great ease; wooden objects and fabrics are affected to a lesser degree; metal objects are regarded as more sensitive to certain types of pollution; and human beings are defiled only by a specific degree of pollution. Living animals, growing plants, and unfinished objects cannot be infected with pollution. According to the *halakhah*, changed slightly by later enactments, the laws of impurity are only significant for Jews. Non-Jews are not sensitive to pollution and cannot transmit it to others.

Purification from pollution does not always take the same form and depends both on the nature of the polluting agent and of the object it pollutes. Pottery, for example, cannot be cleansed and must be broken, while most other utensils can be purified in the same way as human beings. All types of purification have one factor in common—immersion in water.

Immersion is carried out, as specified in the Torah, in a spring or other source of water (*mikveh mayim*). Later this term was shortened to *mikveh*, which came to mean a place where enough water has gathered to serve for purification purposes. The polluted individual enters and immerses himself in the *mikveh*, thus cleansing himself to a certain degree of his impurity. Immersion in the *mikveh* is not necessarily a matter of cleanliness; since the source of purification is merely a natural gathering place of water, it was necessary in ancient times to utilize the standing water in caves, which was not always salubrious. From the mishnaic era onward, special structures were built for this purpose and more convenient facilities were introduced for the bathers.

Even when most of the purification laws were no longer observed in practice, the *mikveh* retained its importance. It served women as a place for purification from the ritual uncleanliness of menstruation or childbirth, and men utilized it for purification before study or prayer. The obligation for men to immerse themselves was no longer binding in the talmudic era. Although the decree of immersion was attributed to Ezra, the practice was actually abolished. In later times, and mainly as a result of the intensification of the Kabbalistic strain in Judaism, immersion took on renewed significance as a means of spiritual purification, and it is still practiced to a large extent among Hassidim.

In addition to immersion in water, which is a component of all purification rituals, there are special ceremonies for specific kinds of pollution. The *zav*, the leper, and the woman after childbirth cannot be completely cleansed except by offering a special sacrifice, not for atonement but for purification. Defilement by the dead (the gravest, and also one of the commonest forms of defilement) could only be overcome by sprinkling water mixed with the ashes of a red heifer. This purification ceremony is specified in considerable detail in the Torah, but since it was a very important one, and it was not easy to find a red heifer, according to the Mishnah the ceremony of burning the carcass of the heifer was carried out only eight times in the course of Jewish history. This ceremony was hedged by a number of restrictions and qualifications over the centuries in order to emphasize its vital significance. In the days of the Temple, the carcass of the heifer was burned on the Mount of Olives opposite the Temple, and this is one of the reasons why this spot is considered sacred; a special bridge was constructed between the Temple Mount and the Mount of Olives lest there be any suspicion of pollution en route. The ashes of the red heifer (or the ashes of all the heifers, since, according to tradition, some of the most ancient ashes still remained at the end of the Second Temple era) were carefully preserved and used for the purification of those defiled by contact with the dead. For several generations after the destruction of the Temple—some scholars believe that it was as long as 300 years—such ashes existed and were used for the ceremony. When the ashes were used up, it was no longer possible to purify the polluted, and thus there was no logical reason for observing the purifi-

Ritual Purity and Impurity

cation laws. The assumption from the Middle Ages onward was that "we are all polluted by the dead," either directly or indirectly, so that it was no longer feasible to observe the laws.

In general, the laws of ritual purification apply only in direct relation to sacrifices and to sacred objects. Religious law does not oblige a man to be pure, with the exception of the *kohanim* (priestly tribe), who were forbidden to come into contact with corpses. The prohibition still exists, and descendants of the priestly clans are still forbidden to handle a corpse unless—as the Torah specifies—it is that of a close member of the family or of a *met mitzvah* (a man found dead by the wayside who has no one to bury him). No defiled person was allowed to enter the area of the Temple or to participate in worship, and this rule was violated on pain of grave punishment. The priest was forbidden to consume any of the priestly gifts while in a state of pollution. It is therefore clear why in Temple times any man bringing a sacrifice or entering the Temple on a pilgrimage was obliged to purify himself. Priests and members of their families were also obliged to cleanse themselves in order to be permitted to eat the offerings. The hour at which the priests ate their contributions, after immersing themselves and being purified, was so regular that it served as a recognized designation of time.

Despite the fact that most members of the congregation were not obliged to maintain themselves in a state of purity, there were those who nevertheless observed the rules of ritual purification out of a desire to live fuller lives, because purification was perceived as the perfect state. They included a few individuals who observed the laws so strictly that they ate only foods that were in the state of purity required for the priests, but there were many more "who ate *hullin* [common foods] according to the rules of purity." They were apparently quite numerous and created their own religio-social movement, known as *haverim* (comrades). It was composed of those people who ate only pure foods and strictly observed the tithe rules. The groups of *haverim*, who evolved special initiation ceremonies, were diverse in composi-

[197]

tion, and most of the disciples of the sages were apparently members at some time, although only the academy heads were eligible for membership without benefit of special ceremonies. Women were also accepted for membership, and it was decreed that "the wife of a *haver* is herself a *haver*." The various Essene sects were apparently closely linked with the *haverim* but tended to asceticism, while most of the *haverim* did not.

After the disappearance of the ashes of the red heifer, the purification injunctions could no longer be observed in full, and they were abolished for all practical purposes. At the same time, two types remained applicable: those relating to the pollution of woman by *nidah* (menstruation and childbirth), and the laws of priestly pollution and purification. The impurity of the *nidah* has implications for the marital relationship, for sexual relations are prohibited as long as the woman remains impure. Most of the *mikvaot* from the mishnaic period onward, and possibly also at the end of the mishnaic era itself, were dedicated to this type of purification. It is not surprising, therefore, that *Nidah* is the sole tractate in the order of *Toharot* to which both the Babylonian and the Jerusalem Talmuds devote commentaries.

The prohibition of priestly pollution through contact with the dead also survived. Here too there was a special reason why this particular interdict remained. In modern times the *kohanim*, like all of Israel, are defiled by contact with the dead, direct or transmitted through others. The Torah ban, however, is directed not at the condition of the priest but at his actions, and thus the law continued to be observed even after the laws of purification had, in practice, been invalidated.

24

Ethics and *Halakhah*

HALAKHAH is essentially law, but, by virtue of its structure, it contains elements of ethics and of a certain general outlook on life. From the point of view of its general composition and its inflexibility, it resembles other legal codes that cannot be adapted to every eventuality or circumstance that arises.

In discussing the question of why the Second Temple was destroyed when the people at that time led blameless lives and studied Torah, the Talmud comments harshly that "Jerusalem was only destroyed because the law of Torah was delivered there." This perplexing statement is elaborated: the people of Jerusalem were punished because they judged only in accordance with the laws of the Torah and did not advocate leniency. This implies that although existing laws bind all men, there are various considerations for tempering the law, in certain cases, with mercy. If those authorized to pass judgment do not act with temperance, their behavior denotes the onset of destruction. Thus the law—particularly the statutes regulating relations between man and his fellow men—is but an external framework containing other frameworks that must also be taken into consideration. The concept of justice, which is so important in Judaism, does not lose its force, but other factors are taken into consideration in order to alleviate the harshness of the law.

Jewish law is also based on the Torah injunction: "Thou shalt not favor the cause of a poor man," which prohibits the perversion of justice, even for the sake of the poor. The very fact that such an injunction, unique in world legislation, was created demonstrates that the tendency to defer to the poor was so great that it was necessary to caution the people. The Torah instructs the just judge in how to conduct a case involving a poor man and a rich man. He must act in accordance with the law, and sometimes even compel the poor man to pay his debt, but he must then recompense the poor man from his own pocket. This rule of leniency—*li-fnim mi-shurat ha-din* (literally inside the line of the law)—is not universally applicable, but it serves as a kind of inner code, binding on all those who aspire to higher spiritual standards. It should be recalled that this code does not suggest that the borderline between good and evil should be ignored or blurred, but merely that mercy and self-renunciation should be exercised. Generally speaking, it seems that this range of ethical *halakhah* was denoted *mishnat hassidim*, and one of the tractates of the *Nezikin* order, *Avot* (Ethics of the Fathers), is sometimes known by this name as well. *Avot* is the living illustration of ethical teaching that extends beyond mere moralizing and is contained within the supreme legislative work, the Mishnah itself. The injunctions in this work are not binding on the entire people, as is the case with the general legal code, but are valid for those who wish to reach beyond the *halakhah* to the inner circle, the domain "inside the law."

The talmudic definition of a *hassid* is a man who acts and conducts himself "inside the law." This may be illustrated by a story related in the Talmud after the discussion of *halakhah* involving the responsibility of workers and artisans for property on which they worked. The debate is summed up by the statement that in every case of harmful negligence on the part of workers, they are obliged to pay damages to the owner. It is then related that one of the sages hired workers to transfer clay barrels filled with wine from place to place. The workers behaved negligently and broke the barrels, and the owner acted in accordance with the law in appropriating their outer garments in order to ensure that they would pay the damages. The workers complained to the great *amora* Rav, and he ordered the sage, who was his disciple and relative, to return the clothes. The sage accepted the judgment but asked Rav: "Is this the law?" to which Rav replied: "Yes, for it is said 'that you may walk the path of righteousness.' " The workers then complained to Rav that they were poor men, had worked hard all day, and now had nothing to show for their pains. Rav then ordered his disciple to pay them their wages, and again the disciple asked whether this was the law. "Yes," replied Rav, "for it is said: 'And the ways of the righteous he shall preserve.' " This dialogue should undoubtedly be interpreted as the rabbi telling his disciple that for a man of his caliber, who can afford the loss and who aspires to do more than is dictated by the inflexible legal code, *mishnat hassidim* is not only a question of free choice but a duty.

A number of laws within the civil code pertain to the question of moral responsibility in cases where a man "is exempt from human law and culpable according to divine law," that is, when the damager bears no legal responsibility enforceable by a court but is morally obliged to compensate his victim. The laws of damages contain so many moral injunctions that one of the sages said that he who wanted to behave piously could do so merely by observing the rules laid down there.

The tensions within the sphere of the law and beyond it find more profound expression in the basic viewpoint of the laws of priority and precedence. In many spheres it is ruled that when there is conflict between two similar obligations certain people should be given preference over others. But the legal norm is:

"Your own has priority over that of any man," that is, no man is obliged to suffer loss through aiding a friend. If the restitution of a lost object involves loss of time and money on the part of the finder, he is not obliged to carry out this precept. The wider implication of the ruling, when there is conflict of interest, is "your own life takes precedence." Here too the reader is cautioned against excessive adherence to the law, and different views are taken of the obligations of various types of people. Conduct considered legal and fair in the case of an ordinary man is unacceptable in a man of higher standards. A talmudic saying that reflects this approach evaluates people in accordance with their attitude to property: "He who says 'Yours is mine and mine is mine' is a wicked man; 'yours is yours and mine is yours' is a pious man; 'mine is mine and yours is yours,' this is the average, but there are those who say that it is a Sodomite rule [*i.e.*, cruel]." Tension therefore exists between the view according to the law, "mine is mine and yours is yours," and blind adherence to the letter of the law in every event, which is "a Sodomite rule."

There is an aggadic tradition that regards Sodom not necessarily as the center of wild and indiscriminate corruption but as a place in which the legislation was evil because of a combination of malice and excessive respect for the letter of the law. If a man repents of an oral guarantee and goes back on his word, no court can force him to carry out his promise, but he is cursed: "He who punished the men of Sodom will punish those who do not keep their word." And, generally speaking, a man who insists on his legal right to deprive another of enjoyment when he himself has nothing to lose is accused of *midat Sodom*.

The courts were even known to intervene and help those who were being deprived of some benefit, even though the giver was not liable to lose thereby but was merely insisting on his rights. Sometimes the court would enforce payment, in other cases it would publicly humiliate the man who had acted so inflexibly. There were also cases in which the court acted more severely

[202]

toward people against whom there were moral claims; a person who had behaved badly toward others on the basis of the formal requirements of the law was often repaid in his own coin by the court, which exercised its full rights and sentenced him on the basis of certain strict laws that were not normally cited.

A painful moral predicament arose in situations where a man could escape some threat or danger only by abandoning some other individual to his fate. One of the examples cited was that of a group of people threatened with mass execution if they did not hand over one of their number. In such an event, the *halakhah* rules that the whole group should give itself up rather than abandon one member. They are permitted to hand over one of their number only when a specific person has been demanded and this individual is indeed a wanted criminal. But even here the issue is not clearcut, and the moral decision is not always the same. The sages cited a case in which a man accused of killing a Roman princess fled and concealed himself in a community. When the authorities learned of his presence there, they threatened to kill the entire population unless they handed over the wanted man. When it became evident that the community was really in danger, the local sage went to the fugitive and explained the situation, and the latter agreed to give himself up. But, it is related, Elijah the Prophet, who had previously appeared to the sage every day, ceased to come to him. When the sage prayed and fasted in the hope that Elijah would return, the prophet spoke to him, saying that he would never again visit him because the sage had caused the death of the fugitive. The sage protested: "But this is our teaching" (*i.e.*, the mishnaic ruling permits it), to which Elijah retorted: "But is it *mishnat hassidim?*" In other words, a great man has higher obligations than other people.

The same problem is raised in another famous example cited by the sages. Two men are travelling in the desert and one has enough water to enable him to survive until he reaches civilization. If the water is divided between the two, both will die en route. What should they do? The mishnaic sages argued the point extensively, but the conclusion that was accepted as *halakhah* was that the man in possession of the water should drink it alone and save himself, on the assumption that "one's own life has priority." It was noted, however, that this halakhic conclusion applied only to common people. Scholars should divide the water between them, even though aware that this act spelled death.

These basic problems, which were sometimes defined as dealing with the relationship between "truth" and "peace," were never easily resolved. Should justice (which is truth) be preferred to compromise (which brings peace), or is absolute truth always unattainable? Some sages believed that the concept of compromise conflicted with the idea of justice and that no judge should ever propose to litigants that they seek a compromise, while other scholars believed that any compromise was better than a decision—however just—that was disadvantageous to one of the litigants. The halakhic conclusion on this issue is approximately as follows: the judge should propose a compromise before he hears the claims of the litigants or when he cannot arrive at a conclusive decision on the justice of their claims; but he must not compromise when it is clear to him that one of the parties is in the wrong. The question of "truth" and "peace" also arises in relation to the strict injunction against falsehood, on the one hand, and the injunction to avoid causing pain, on the other. This problem is of metaphysical significance. The sages say that "truth is the seal of the Holy One, Blessed be He," but they also state that "the name of God is peace." And, indeed, they explicitly permitted "changing for the sake of peace," that is, telling a falsehood if it appears that thereby two litigants can be reconciled or suffering can be avoided.

The overall solution to the question of the law versus private moral considerations is as follows: a man may go as far as *shurat ha-din* (the limit of the law) in making demands of others; in his conduct toward others he must act "inside the law." In addition to these halakhic restrictions, there was a well-known concept in civil law and interpersonal relations of the man who acts with forbearance. It was said of such a man that God would forgive all his sins as a reward for his behavior. The ideal man was described as follows: "Those who are insulted but do not insult, hear their shame but do not reply, act out of love and rejoice in suffering, of them it was written: 'And those who love Him will be as the sun in its splendor.' "

25

Derekh Eretz
(Deportment)

THE TERM *derekh eretz* has various meanings in talmudic literature. Above all, it is "the way of the world," the way in which people behave, accepted deportment. It is not contained in a fixed code within the *halakhah*, and, although rendered in detail in the Talmud, these *halakhot* are not binding. *Derekh eretz* is regarded as the foundation for any kind of progress, rather than as law. Rules change from time to time and place to place, but a man is generally expected to behave in accordance with prevailing custom. *Derekh eretz* is demanded of every individual. Although the sages deplore the unlearned man, they concede that he may be a decent human being even without a formal education; but "he who knows nothing of Mishnah or the Bible or *derekh eretz* is not a civilized person." In other words, those who do not observe the accepted rules of behavior place themselves beyond the pale. It was even said that such people were ineligible as witnesses.

The demand for *derekh eretz* directed at every individual was stressed even more strongly in the case of scholars, for two reasons. The first was external: the scholar must be "beloved by Heaven and pleasant on earth," that is, respected by his fellowmen. If he does not observe the rules of deportment and conduct, he demeans the Torah by displaying himself in an unfavorable light and must therefore act so that people will be able to say "that a man who has studied Torah behaves well and his conduct is correct." But there is another aspect to the injunction to follow *derekh eretz*, since correct behavior is part of the whole undefinable range of actions and thought known as *da'at* (knowledge, wisdom). This is not merely the sum of knowledge, but practical understanding, common sense, and general behavior, as well. *Da'at* guides a man in how to behave with his family and others; it determines his way of speaking; it is the ability to decide when to persist and when to forbear. And although it is not in itself written law, every man connected with Torah is expected to be endowed with *da'at* to a reasonable extent. For generations scholastic tradition referred to the "fifth *Shulhan Arukh*," an additional section of that famous work dealing with non-halakhic human relations. The sages believed that *da'at* was a most important asset, and they said: "If you have acquired knowledge, what do you lack? If you lack knowledge, what have you acquired?" Scholars were strongly urged to acquire *da'at*, and the Talmud was emphatic in its view that "a scholar in whom there is no *da'at* worse than a carcass."

Da'at is to a large degree a natural quality, since some people will always know instinctively how to react appropriately to different situations without training or instruction. But even those not blessed with this quality were expected to acquire knowledge, to learn it from others in order to be worthy of bearing the honorable title of scholar. The saying that "the service of Torah is greater than its study" implies that he who was privileged to serve a great sage, even in prosaic and simple matters, learned more from him than those disciples who merely attended his formal lessons. And sometimes the most important acquisition was *da'at*, the knowledge of how to behave in various situations and toward different types of people. There are hundreds of anecdotes in the Talmud about disciples who took note of details of the conduct of their rabbi, not necessarily in spheres related to formal study.

The etiquette and customs of the talmudic era were collected in a small tractate entitled *Derekh Eretz*, which is a treasury of information on the morals and conduct of that era. The *halakhah* on *derekh eretz* encompasses diverse spheres of life. Many laws, for example, are devoted to rules of etiquette at formal meals. This was important in an age when it was the custom to hold protracted feasts (where the guests reclined on sofas) involving considerable ceremony and formality. These rules included such pearls of common sense as, "It is forbidden to talk during the meal lest the food be swallowed the wrong way," as well as instructions on how to eat various dishes. The tractate also relates, with humorous intent, how R. Akiva invited two disciples to his home in order to test their knowledge of manners and etiquette. He set before them meat that had not been cooked sufficiently; one of the two, who was well mannered, tasted the meat, found it inedible, and left it on his plate, while the other tried to tear his portion apart by force. Said R. Akiva mockingly to the latter: "Not thus, my son. Put your foot on the dish and pull."

Many of the rules of behavior were based on purely aesthetic considerations, such as instructions on how to lay a table or how to eat certain dishes. But there were other rules of more fundamental significance, for example, the prohibition against defiling various foods. This derives, to a certain extent, from the general interdict against wanton destruction or defacement, which is fully valid from the viewpoint of the *halakhah*, being based on the law of Torah, though considerably expanded by the sages. It was also based on an attitude of respect for food as man's sustenance. It is related that a certain man came to visit one of the sages and rested his plate on a slice of bread. The sage removed the bread from under the plate and ate it. Since the visitor did not take the hint, the sage said to him: "I thought you would be scalded by lukewarm water, and now I see that even boiling water does not

Derekh Eretz (Deportment)

affect you," admonishing him for having failed to grasp that food is not eaten after having been spoiled or treated with disrespect.

Another aspect of the rules of etiquette is reflected in the saying of the sages that when the Temple still existed, the altar atoned for sins, whereas after the destruction each man's table atoned for him. This concept was aimed at encouraging people to invite poor guests to their homes, since their participation in meals could compensate for the material and selfish aspects of eating and lend it a dimension of sanctity. The view of a man's table as an altar also influenced the rules of table etiquette, for eating was viewed not only as satisfaction of an urge, but as part of a whole way of life and of worship of the Creator. This was the basis for the custom later practiced in many Jewish communities of placing salt on the table at every meal, recalling the salt placed on the altar, or the custom of removing knives from the table during the grace after meals. Iron was not placed on the altar, since it could shorten a man's lifespan when used as a weapon and thus could not be placed in proximity to the Temple, which extends his life.

There was yet another dimension to the rules of *derekh eretz*—the obligation cited in the Torah to respect certain people and treat them in specific ways. There was a general exhortation to respect parents ("Honor thy father and thy mother"), scholars, and the king. Distinctions were drawn between the ways in which each category should be treated, but an attitude of respect toward one's elders and toward the wise was part of biblical law itself and was developed and elaborated in the rules of conduct. In whose presence should one rise? Who should enter or leave a room first? Who should be accorded the honor of doing something first? All these subjects, which are largely optional but became part of formal halakhic tradition, are dealt with in the code of *derekh eretz*. The guiding rule is that when an honor is to be bestowed the person most worthy is given precedence over others; where indignity is involved, the least important member of the group acts first. For example, the most important member of a group takes precedence upon entry, but the least important exits first.

The *halakhot* pertaining to respect for one's father or rabbi are numerous and emphasize that betters should be revered. In daily family life it is, of course, not possible (particularly in the case of children) to observe all the niceties of good conduct and ceremony, and there were those who said that the father or rabbi who agreed to forgo honor was honored nonetheless. On the other hand, a monarch is forbidden to forgo honor since, unlike the case of the father or rabbi, the king's honor is not his alone, and respect is paid to the monarchy as such. The rabbi, whose wisdom is self-accomplished (or, similarly, the father), is entitled to renounce honor and ceremony. Therefore, although it was said that the son was forbidden to sit on his father's chair, to contradict him, or do anything in his presence without his permission, particularly if it entailed disrespect, these injunctions were not observed strictly and were generally applied only when the sons reached adulthood and were themselves eager to honor their parents. An amusing illustration of this attitude is found in the talmudic sources. A father's will stipulated that he was leaving his property to his son on condition that the son become a fool. The sages could find no logical explanation for the strange document and appealed to R. Joshua Ben Hananiah, who was renowed as a great scholar and a very shrewd man. When they arrived at his home, they found him crawling on all fours, his small son riding on his back. The sages waited respectfully, lest they disturb their rabbi at play. When they eventually asked his opinion of the will, he replied: "You yourselves have seen the meaning. The father meant to say that his son should come into the inheritance when he himself had children."

Correct deportment and conduct were part of that *da'at* which it was incumbent on every man to acquire, and, as the sages themselves emphasized time and time again, this also encompassed the ability to discern when it was permissible to deviate from *halakhah* and the laws governing conduct.

26

The World of Mysticism

THE TALMUD usually mirrors the issues studied in the academies over the centuries, but it undoubtedly contained many *halakhot* and legends that did not originate in public discussions there. Some are anecdotes from the lives of great men, others the tales or sermons of sages, but despite these exceptions, the Talmud is basically the public record of deliberations in the academies, the lessons taught by scholars to their disciples, who were regarded as trustworthy because of their high scholastic standards. The fact that the Talmud contains extremely intimate details of the lives of various sages does not alter this basic picture, since the private life of a teacher was also the source of inspiration and study, even if he had not originally intended it to become public knowledge.

Together with the public statements uttered before all the academy students, there were various subjects that were discussed in closed sessions. We know, for example, that the discussion of the lineage of certain families was usually conducted in secret. We also find that lists of ineligible families that had married into the community unlawfully or families unjustly disqualified were not common knowledge, but were handed by rabbi to disciple at certain intervals (approximately every seven years) lest they be forgotten. The *midrash* on the Book of Chronicles, which apparently contained an extremely detailed discussion of the genealogy of families, was handed down in semiclandestine fashion, and it was claimed that certain people were not worthy of studying it. In fact, this work disappeared from view in the talmudic era.

In addition to details of this type, however, there was a whole world of mysticism and mystery that was concealed from the general public and transmitted only to a chosen few. Thus we find it written that "one should not teach the Act of Creation to two, or the Divine Chariot to one, unless he is wise and understands by himself." These esoteric subjects were therefore taught by the rabbi to only one chosen disciple and, in some cases, the teacher confined himself to the outlines of the subject without going into detail. We know very little of this mysticism, and the few details available to us are indicated obliquely in various tractates of the Talmud, which refer to sages and the subjects with which they dealt without providing a satisfactory explanation of the nature of these issues. In these areas assumptions and conjectures outweigh facts and certainties, and in some cases it is impossible to arrive at a conclusive answer. We find books dealing with mysticism that date from ancient times, several of them attributed to mishnaic and talmudic sages. It is, however, impossible to ascertain which were indeed written by these authors. The stringent restrictions on esoteric interpretation were relaxed gradually during the Middle Ages, and from the period of the *geonim* onward we find much clearer statements. By the beginning of the modern era, the Kabbalah (literally tradition, transmittal) was an important and even central element in Jewish thought. Much of what we can surmise of the esoteric world of the talmudic sages is based on this literature and the light it casts on the hints contained in the Talmud.

Esotericism was apparently first taught in ancient times. The

The World of Mysticism

schools established by the prophets ("sons of the prophets") certainly discussed ways of preparing individuals to receive the gift of prophesy and dealt with the inculcation of specific intellectual methods of comprehending these matters. Such secret groups continued their activities in the Second Temple period, and the various Essene sects were apparently influenced by their secret teachings, as may be ascertained from sources outside the Talmud (Philo of Alexandria, Josephus, etc.). The mishnaic and talmudic sages who engaged in esoteric studies were the heirs of this ancient tradition, which is rooted in the days of the prophets and has survived to the present day.

The sources state that *torat ha-sod* (mysticism) was divided into two parts: *Ma'aseh Bereshit* (Act of Creation) and *Ma'aseh Merkavah* (Divine Chariot). The former was more theoretical and dealt with the creation of the world and the first divine revelations. *Ma'aseh Merkavah*, based on the prophet Ezekiel's description of the Divine Chariot, is a study of the prevailing relations between God and the world and apparently contained the seeds of what later came to be known as *Kabbalah ma'asit* (practical kabbalah). As we have noted, all these matters are shrouded in mystery. We know only that most of the great Jewish scholars engaged in esoteric studies, some extremely intensively, others as an essential part of religious study in general. There were also scholars who did not regard themselves as worthy of such knowledge, and they therefore only dabbled in the subject.

Among the themes known to have been contained in esoteric teaching were the names of God. From the mishnaic period onward, the explicit name of God was never uttered except in the Temple, and we learn from the Septuagint that this was an ancient tradition. But even the name uttered in the Temple during prayer was not what is known as the "explicit Name," which was known only to a select few. A certain sage who had served as a Temple priest in his youth reported that the name was uttered during the priestly blessing, but was intentionally drowned out by the singing of the Levites so that even the young priests never heard it. There is therefore no known tradition (except in the Kabbalah) on ways of uttering the Divine Name. (There were apparently a number of ways, expounded upon in later kabbalistic works, and modern attempts at transcription are not even viable guesses.) Furthermore, we know that the four-letter name, despite its sanctity, was not the explicit name and that there was a twelve-letter name, a forty-two-letter name, and even one with seventy-two letters. These are referred to several times in the Talmud, but without explanation, and even the classic talmudic commentators did not always understand the reference. The High Priest apparently uttered the explicit name on Yom Kippur, but because of its length and complexity, it was almost impossible to grasp it. The name aroused great awe, as the Mishnah related: "When the priests and the people heard the great and terrible name uttered by the High Priest, they would kneel and bow down and say: 'Blessed be the name of His honored kingdom for ever and ever.'" The Talmud explains that only those few disciples who were outstanding for their spiritual qualities and profound moral standards were taught the name by their rabbis.

The mystic and esoteric world was kept hidden for several reasons. One basic reason was that it was considered that matters pertaining to the greatness of God should be left to those worthy of studying them. But it was also feared that unworthy use might be made of the powers a man acquired from knowing the names and the secrets according to which the world was constituted. The sages regarded knowledge of "the letters according to which Heaven and earth were created" as an instrument lending mortals the power to engage in acts of creation. They even said: "If the righteous so chose, they could create a world," and we sometimes read of sages who studied a "book of creation" and created various objects. It is related that one of the scholars created a man through reciting names, and this is the first reference to the legend of the *golem*, which appears in medieval esoteric literature.

[214]

The World of Mysticism

This power to create—and even destroy—wielded by the *Baal Shem* (possessor of the name) was undoubtedly a powerful argument for concealing such matters from the knowledge of people who might exploit such powers for evil purposes.

There was another consideration: study of esoteric teachings was not merely theoretical; it seems to have been accompanied by profound mystical experiences which were apparently dangerous for those imperfectly prepared. These experiences were known, we believe, as *pardess* (entering the orchard), and there is a well-known story in the Talmud about four sages who entered this "orchard": R. Akiva, Simeon Ben Zoma, Simeon Ben Azai, and Elisha Ben Abuya. They were guided by the wisest and most experienced among them, R. Akiva, and it is related that he warned them of certain dangers awaiting them in words that could have no meaning for those who had not travelled in those spheres. Despite his guidance, however, the group was unable to withstand the dangers: Ben Azai died, Ben Zoma lost his reason, and Ben Abuya "uprooted plants," that is, arrived at heretical views, apparently under Gnostic influence. Only R. Akiva "went in in peace and came out in peace." This story is the most detailed but not the sole description extant, and its intention was to emphasize the dangers awaiting those who entered into this domain.

The teaching of *Ma'aseh Bereshit* was therefore never carried out in public, and was always confined to one disciple. Thus a student whose qualifications were closely examined did not receive detailed instruction but was merely taught outlines of the subject. In this way, if he did not display aptitude and did not himself arrive at a mystical experience, he would not be harmed by the knowledge imparted to him. We find, for example, that R. Elazar Ben Arakh lectured on this subject to his teacher, Rabban Yohanan Ben Zakkai, who was amazed at the understanding he displayed. Other disciples told Yohanan of their discoveries in this sphere, and he replied: "These words were said to Moses on Sinai." But, as noted, only the bare facts of the stories are known and no explanation beyond vague hints is conveyed on their content.

It should not be assumed, however, that there were two separate areas of "revealed" and "hidden" material. To a certain extent, these were thought of as components of the all-embracing Torah. A well-rounded disciple who absorbed his rabbi's teachings also learned esoteric wisdom. It was related of Rabban Yohanan Ben Zakkai that he left out nothing and learned from his teachers both "great and small things." The explanation was "great things—*Ma'aseh Merkavah*, small things—the problems which Abaye and Rav discussed," but both great and small were contained within Torah. What is more, the talmudic outlook sees all worlds—that of material nature and the higher metaphysical spheres—as a single unit, with no barriers between its parts. Talmudic discussion of everyday affairs often takes flight into metaphysical realms. An example of this is the story told by R. Yossi, disciple of R. Akiva. One day he went into one of the ruins of Jerusalem to pray, and when he came out he saw Elijah the Prophet awaiting him at the entrance. Elijah asked him whether he had heard a voice in the ruins, and Yossi answered: "I heard a divine voice murmuring like a dove and saying: 'Woe is me, for I have destroyed my house and burned my palace.'" Elijah replied: "Not only now does it speak thus; God Himself mourns the destruction of the Temple three times daily." Without pause, R. Yossi went on to tell his disciples what halakhic conclusions he had drawn from this conversation with Elijah. The divine voice and Elijah's revelation are an integral part of a prosaic story of a sage who chose to pray in a secluded spot. Nor are the two worlds remote from one another; the deserving man lives in both without strain. Tales of how Elijah appeared to sages, discussing *halakhah* or esoteric matters with them, are very common in the Talmud and often arise out of various halakhic associations, whether profound or trivial.

This close connection between prosaic and esoteric matters is

The World of Mysticism

one of the outstanding characteristics of Jewish esoteric literature in general. The Jewish mystic is not detached from the *halakhah* and practical questions; on the contrary, the halakhic expert is often also a mystic, and the kabbalist studies legal and mystic matters with the same degree of enthusiasm. In fact, esoteric literature is, in a way, interpretation and theological substantiation of the everyday details of *halakhah*.

This outlook does not differentiate between the "rational" world and the world of mysticism, both being seen as part of a whole. Those same letters from which Heaven and earth were created, which contain infinite creative and destructive powers, are also the letters which make up Torah itself and record and relate all the great and small issues with which talmudic *halakhah* concerns itself.

Man's status within this world is often highlighted, and he is regarded as the perpetuator of the creative process. Esoteric literature implies that the concept that man was created in God's image is a basic structure and that man is able to create independently. One of the most imaginative stories in talmudic literature reflects many of the elemental problems in this area. It is the description of the controversy between the great R. Eliezer and most of his disciples, headed by R. Joshua, on questions of ritual purity and pollution. The dispute was aroused by a seemingly marginal question, namely, whether a pottery utensil could be defined as a broken vessel, one that is unpollutable. When the sages refused to accept R. Eliezer's view, he called on the forces of nature to prove his theory correct, crying: "Let the carob tree be uprooted from its place, let the water change the direction of its flow." To this R. Joshua replied: "You cannot cite evidence from the carob." Then R. Eliezer appealed to Heaven to prove that his ruling should be accepted, and a divine voice was heard saying: "What do you want of my son, Eliezer, whose rulings are universally accepted." Still R. Joshua was firm in his opinion, saying: "Torah is no longer in Heaven. God has given it to men, and it is they who will decide this matter." Most of the scholars then ruled against R. Eliezer. This story, which illustrates the talmudic view that man is a creator, was only concluded several generations later, when it was reported that one of the sages asked Elijah the Prophet what God said on that occasion, and Elijah replied: "God smiled and said: 'My sons have prevailed over me. Yes, my sons have prevailed.' "

PART THREE

Method

27

Midrash
(Halakhic Exegesis)

MIDRASH HALAKHAH (from the root *darash*, meaning to enquire or investigate) is the body of literature that interprets Mosaic law, seeking evidence and suggestions within the text to further comprehension. It constitutes only a small proportion of the
Mishnah itself, but in its efforts to elucidate the mishnaic sources,
the Talmud often cites the *midrash*. It quotes extensively from
midrashic compilations, some of which have survived to the
present day, and other collections of *baraitot* (extraneous commentaries) preserved in the Talmud alone.

The basic problem of *midrash* is the question of whether examination of the biblical text and the various logical methods of interpretation are the true source of the legislation derived from it.
Some important sages, led by Maimonides, believed that the *midrash*, or at least its large part, was not an authentic source of
halakhah. It was their view that the main outlines of *halakhah* had
been contained, by age-old tradition, in the oral law, which con-

veyed all the details of mishnaic *halakhah*. *Midrash*, they claimed, was nothing but a method, handed down from age to age, of linking the biblical text with the *halakhah* by finding associations and implications indicating the connection. According to this theory, the halakhic *midrash* is an important mnemotechnical instrument but cannot be regarded as constituting substantial evidence. Like so many of the statements formulated by Maimonides, this theory is distinguished by its clarity of thought, intellectual brilliance, and provision for the solution to many problems. It also created fresh problems, however, since analysis of the *midrashim* themselves does not always bear out his explanation.

Another theory, advocated by the classic talmudic commentators (Rashi, the *baalei tosafot*, and most of the Spanish commentators) distinguishes between true halakhic *midrashim* and *asmakhtot* (supports). According to this basic distinction, found in the Talmud, some *midrashim* are authentic sources of *halakhah*, while *asmakhtot* are merely aids to memory or devices for linking rabbinical legislation to scriptural texts and do not constitute true proof. The sages themselves sometimes said of biblical verses they cited as evidence, ". . . although there is no proof of this in the Bible". The difference between the two kinds of *midrash* is not always clear, since the mechanics may be almost identical, as was pointed out by the sages and the commentators.

There are certain hermeneutical rules for interpretation of the biblical text, usually enumerated according to the order established by Rabbi Ishmael, who formulated thirteen principles for interpretation. This list is not exhaustive, since not all the possible methods are encompassed, and there is an amplified list of thirty-two rules for aggadic interpretation, most of which also apply to the *halakhah*. But even this number does not cover all the details of interpretive methods in the Talmud, and in recent times these have been estimated at several hundred. At the same time, R. Ishmael's rules cover the fundamental methods, and several are widely utilized.

The most important exegetical principles are: *kal va-homer, ge-*

Midrash (Halakhic Exegesis)

zerah shavah, binyan av, kelal u-ferat, davar ha-lamed me-inyano, and *shnei ketuvim makhishim. Kal va-homer* is a simple method of deduction that exists in all methods of logic, permitting deduction from a minor to a major case or from a light to a severe case. The following example is cited in the Talmud, although for various reasons it is not considered totally satisfactory: according to Torah law, a man is forbidden to marry his daughter's daughter. From this we may deduce through *kal va-homer* that he is undoubtedly prohibited from marrying his daughter. This method is sometimes known, because of its simplicity, as *din*, simple logical consideration, and the assumption is that any man may employ this method and derive new *halakhah* from it. There are many methods of restricting *kal va-homer*, whether by providing accurate proof of flaws in the basic logical structure or mechanism, or by proving the implausibility of the outcome. In the opinion of most sages, there is also a restrictive rule known as *dayo*, according to which the deduced fact is equalized to the case from which we infer, and neither a stricter nor a more lenient view is taken. A clear proof of this rule is in the biblical text itself, where the sages found ten explicit references to *kal va-homer*, and this rule helps preserve a certain degree of logic and order.

Another basic hermeneutical principle is *gezerah shavah*, which may be defined as a philological measure. When the meaning of a word or *halakhah* is unclear, it is inferred by word analogy from another passage where the meaning is clear. *Gezerah shavah* is basically simple, but it is considerably elaborated in the halakhic *midrash* where a certain word may serve as the key to inference on different subjects. The logical structure resembles that of deciphering texts, various key words serving as the basis for interpretation of the entire sentence. This important exegetic rule may prove dangerous if employed indiscriminately, since many words appear in different sentences and any desired conclusion may be obtained. One basic qualification is that a man may not infer *gezerah shavah* unless he learned it from his teacher. Thus the method is a matter of traditional knowledge of key words, and it is necessary only to clarify the significance of the comparison between two related texts. There is an additional restriction: *gezerah shavah* is acceptable only if it can be proved that the key word in both passages was really inserted for this purpose and is superfluous to the text. The method is, therefore, utilized like the figures that denote footnotes, to designate the connection between the text and a note appearing elsewhere.

Binyan av resembles *gezerah shavah* in principle but differs in logical structure. It is an inductive method of proof, where an attempt is made to show that a certain *av* (case) serves as the basis for a whole series of other similar passages constructed in similar fashion. Here too there are several methods and several qualifications.

Kelal u-ferat takes many different forms, but the essence is that it is possible to draw conclusions from the way in which a passage is written, that is, where the generalization appears. When the general principle precedes the particular, we say that "there is nothing in the general principle that is not contained in the particular"; in other words, the general principle adds nothing but merely provides the logical structure. In the opposite case—for example, when it is stated in laws regarding losses: "In like manner shalt thou do with his ass and so shalt thou do with his raiment and with any lost thing of thy brother's"—where the general principle follows the particular, this implies that the details cited are mere examples, and that the precept applies to all types of losses, without exception.

Davar ha-lamed me-inyano is a relatively simple method of deduction from the text. For example, the commandment "Thou shalt not steal" appears twice. The first instance is in the Ten Commandments in a very solemn context (in proximity to the laws pertaining to murder and adultery), and it is therefore explained that the allusion is to kidnapping, for which the penalty is death. On the other occasion it appears among the various laws pertaining to fair trade and so forth and is interpreted there as a ban on the theft of property. Another of the basic hermeneutical

Midrash (Halakhic Exegesis)

rules is that pertaining to two contradictory passages, where the contradiction is either overt or hidden. In this case it is necessary to seek a third passage in order to decide the matter and to explain both in such a way that each is taken to refer to a different subject and the contradiction is prevented.

The halakhic *midrashim* employ a certain extremely precise exegetic method which derives from the assumption that every law or deed recorded in the Torah was formulated accurately and concisely, making each detail significant. Any word that appears superfluous—whether blatantly unnecessary or merely nonessential to the meaning—is a source of study, and superfluity is taken to imply emphasis. When two subjects are discussed in close proximity, it is possible to infer from one to the other to a certain extent, even if they do not deal with the same matter. Even superfluous letters have meaning; for example, if a sentence commences with the conjunctive letter *vav*, this may be regarded as a hint at some essential link with the preceding sentence.

Although *midrashic* methods are relatively simple, the *midrash* in general is not content with random interpretation, and one method is applied on top of another. Except for the laws of sacrifice—which cite, almost exclusively, primary evidence—the *midrash* compares various verses dealing with the same theme and explains each in its own way. The halakhic *midrash* is inflexible to a degree that appears relatively artificial, but in fact when the biblical text is regarded as a primary halakhic source, each word and phrase is important, as is the case with any text of vital legal significance where there is room for study of each minute detail.

There were various methods of interpretation: R. Ishmael's academy developed its own methods, while R. Akiva's developed detailed and comprehensive rules for itself, and the differences between various sages or schools of thought found expression in methods. For example, we find that the Babylonian Talmud cites halakhic proof only from the Torah, considering it to be the sole binding text from this point of view. Wherever evidence is cited from other books of the Bible, numerous qualifications are noted, and it usually appears only in support of other proof, as an *asmakhta*. The Jerusalem Talmud, on the other hand, tends to rely on the other books more, and thus offers simpler explanations of many of the involved theories of the Babylonian Talmud.

Although the basic rules for exegetic interpretation were simple, the mechanics of *midrash* and the interrelations between the various rules, as well as their exact definition and application (in some cases two rules may be applicable), are a subject that the Talmud peruses extensively, and the commentators on the Talmud and the *midrash* also devoted considerable attention and profound thought to it.

28

The Talmudic Way of Thinking

THE TALMUD is unique not only in its subject matter but also, and perhaps to an even greater extent, in the way it discusses its themes. The same issues are handled in other ways by later halakhic and kabbalistic works. Many scholars have pondered the question of whether the Talmud has a logic of its own, and whether it would be possible to arrive at different conclusions on the basis of the same premises and assumptions if another logical method were employed. On various questions, as in the halakhic *midrashim*, it is possible to discern special patterns of analysis, exegetic rules that do not always correspond to the theories of other logical systems. But the question is whether talmudic scholarship created a unique logical structure or merely utilized unique methods of demonstration. Dissimilar subjects sometimes call for varying techniques, and measures that are valid in one sphere may prove ineffective in others. In actual fact, it is possible to find classification of subjects by methods of analysis and discussion even in the Talmud itself. For example, laws of sacrifice constitute a separate area regarding both subject matter and evidence. Of another category of teachings, regarded by tradition as "*halakhah* delivered by Moses on Sinai," it was said that the topic could not be discussed on the basis of any of the regular methods of study of halakhic *midrash*, however logical. Furthermore, in various spheres *ein lemedim min ha-din* (in other words, logical manipulations) could not be relied upon as a source of *halakhah*, but other methods, sanctioned by tradition, were utilized.

Despite all these limitations, the talmudic way of thinking and discourse may be regarded as a unique framework that can be understood from different standpoints but cannot be studied by other means. A basic factor is the attitude toward abstraction. In the Talmud, as in most areas of original Jewish thought, there is deliberate evasion of abstract thinking based on abstract concepts. Even matters that could easily be discussed through abstraction are analyzed, sometimes cumbersomely, by other methods, based mostly on unique logical systems aided by models. The Talmud employs models in place of abstract concepts. We have already noted the models cited in laws of damages, such as "horn" or "foot," which serve neither as examples nor as parables but operate like modern mathematical or scientific models. The model is utilized in accordance with a series of clearly defined steps, approved by tradition. *Kal va-homer*, for example, is a method applied to a certain model in order to adapt it to another model. Thus there is a high degree of mechanical thought, and no attempt is made to clarify practical or logical problems per se; they are seen rather as complete entities, and their conclusions are of practical or logical significance, though it is not always possible to understand the convoluted methods of the operation itself.

On the basis of these assumptions, it is possible to comprehend the method of *danim efshar mi-she-i efshar* (deducing the possible from the impossible). According to this method we choose a certain passage and draw halakhic conclusions on another issue, employing one of the methods permissible in this context. Anyone

The Talmudic Way of Thinking

contemplating the text will immediately discern that the basic inference is "impossible," since the first case, which is our model, appears to be founded on essentially different considerations. An example of such a discussion is the question of whether religious conversion is valid without circumcision. One of the sages wanted to demonstrate the truth of this assumption, citing the fact that women may be converted without undergoing circumcision. Against this, it may be argued that it is biologically impossible to perform circumcision on a woman. But this does not alter the validity of the *halakhah*, according to this sage, since he says: "Although it is impossible, it is an impressive piece of evidence." In other words, the evidence is based on a certain model and operates accordingly, without taking other aspects into consideration.

Such methods of demonstration are utilized in our own century in various areas, but are not usually employed in everyday matters. The talmudic sages, on the other hand, applied exacting methods to every subject under the sun. The fact that their thought processes operated in such ways explains the structure of their world, which contains many models and in which abstract concepts are replaced by many illustrative examples (none of which can be taken at face value) elaborated in a variety of ways. The great advantage of employing such models, as opposed to abstract concepts, lies, *inter alia*, in the ability constantly to supervise the validity of methods of demonstration. The elemental and relatively simple model serves as the basis for examination and enables us to draw inferences or examine whether we have diverged from the fundamental issue through abstract thinking on unclear issues. The weakness of all abstract thought lies in the fact that it is constantly creating new terms and concepts, and since they cannot be defined except by use of similarly abstract terms, we can never know whether they constitute a departure from the subject or are still relevant. Therefore we almost never find abstract terms in the Talmud, even when they would seem to be vital to the discussion and when any other legal system would have introduced them. Words such as *authority, discipline, framework,* and *spirituality* have only recently been translated into Hebrew from other languages and philosophies. The Talmud very rarely employs such terms, although it frequently deals with the problems defined by these words in ways that differ greatly from those of other philosophical or legal systems.

Another unique aspect of talmudic discussion is the attitude toward fundamental issues. The basic talmudic view is always that the subject under discussion is not "law," in the socio-legal meaning of the term, but the clarification of facts and actual situations of intrinsic importance. This attitude produces consequences that are clearly evident in the Talmud itself. One of these is the lack of differentiation between important and minor issues, between the useful and the irrelevant. No value is placed on the practical or basic significance of a certain problem. The objective is to arrive at the truth, which cannot be classified into components by order of importance. When it is necessary to discuss the solution to practical questions, certain restrictive measures are employed that determine the form of pure halakhic discussion. But the Talmud does not deal exclusively with legal solutions that can be put into practice; any problem that calls for clarification and involves the search for the truth is regarded as worthy of analysis. It has already been noted that the Talmud often considers situations that not only border on the implausible but could under no circumstances have practical implications, since they are of strictly historical significance. Study of a remote and irrelevant subject may sometimes produce conclusions of practical value, but these are incidental, and the main objective is truth. Thus the scope of discourse is wider than even that of "pure science," since not only purely theoretical issues but even irrefutably disproved methods are examined thoroughly. As even an incorrect method may prove significant for the attainment of truth, its intrinsic value and veracity are studied closely. It is related that one of the sages once made a remark that implied contempt for a totally rejected halakhic method. After the inner logic of the

The Talmudic Way of Thinking

method had been explained to him, he visited the graves of the originators of the method to beg forgiveness for having slighted them.

Another aspect of this same ardent search for truth is the method of demonstration. Attempts are often made to attain degrees of certainty that are usually attainable only in the sphere of mathematics. The sages are not content with proving that an explanation is reasonable or highly probable in accordance with the simplest method. This may suffice in the natural sciences, or in the sphere of practical legislation, but the talmudic intellectual method is not content with such achievements. It endeavors to prove the validity of its conclusions beyond a shadow of a doubt and to preclude any alternative explanation. This is why the Talmud contains so many methods of rejection. After a certain rabbi has offered reasonable proof, another sage (or even the selfsame man) will seek an alternative interpretation of the issue. This second method, however tenuous and unlikely, can lead to the rejection of the original method and to a renewed attempt to find irrefutable proof. This method of argumentation is referred to in the Talmud as *shinuya*, and although the alternative argument is often highly improbable and based on tortuous logic, the Talmud will not accept the original evidence as long as it is imperfect or incomplete.

The most striking aspect of talmudic *pilpul* (dialectical reasoning) is this inability to accept simple and apparently satisfactory proof, and the continued search for incontrovertible evidence. The quest for the flawless explanation sometimes leads to tenuous conclusions that may restrict *halakhah* to a very limited area. This method is not deliberately encouraged, and attempts are always made to arrive at intellectually satisfactory explanations that adhere to the original texts. We often find a comment implying that if a *tanna* went to the trouble of formulating a comprehensive *halakhah*, he did not intend it to be applied only to one unusual case. But such a comment is in place only when the subject itself obliges the scholar to arrive at bizarre conclusions. In the Talmud, as in various spheres of exact science and knowledge, there is little room for "common sense," which in such cases would mean superficial understanding that fails to fathom the depths of the problem.

Also unique to talmudic thought is the underlying principle of many of the debates—the constant attempt to adapt methods and opinions to one another. In every case the tendency is to avoid controversy, to reduce to the minimum differences between methods and points of view. The sages will do everything possible to locate the common denominator. For example, it is often possible to interpret the method of a certain *mishnah* according to the views of one of the *tannaim* that fit in with the phrasing and inner logic of the text. But the sages usually try to find explanations for each *mishnah* and halakhic maxim to which all methods are applicable, although this sometimes obliges them to adopt the interpretation that seems least plausible from other points of view. The inner logic on which this approach is founded seems to operate in other spheres as well, and should be regarded as implying that *halakhah* does not consist of remote and detached statements but is based on experience, on the facts of life, not conjectures.

It is a basic assumption in modern science, as in the Talmud, that those engaging in research should be regarded as honest seekers of truth. Thus if there is a contradiction between the conclusions of two different experiments, attempts should be made to find a generally applicable theory that takes note of all the experiments. It is always possible that a scholar may have erred in his logical or practical methods, but it is desirable to avoid clashing with any of the methods, even though this attempt at consensus or compromise sometimes entails the construction of an extremely involved intellectual edifice. The same approach is adopted toward the methods of various scholars. It is assumed that each attempted to explore all the possible intellectual processes in his quest for the true answer, and that every one of his statements should be accepted as true and integrated, insofar as possible, with the statements and rulings of other scholars. Therefore, even when it is obvious that there are differences of opinion, the sages try to reconcile the methods and minimize the differences. It was customary to choose two seemingly incompatible methods and ask the authors to defend them against one another, to demonstrate that the two were in accord on most details. If the experiment proved successful, it was possible to show that the discrepancy between the conclusions was not the result of widely divergent approaches but was based on a subtle difference between the basic theories or a mere matter of taste.

These methods of exposition do not aspire to historicity, since they make no attempt to reconstruct the mental processes of the early scholars. But this is not the main issue. Since we regard each ruling as a scientific experiment, each *halakhah* as the determination of an empirical fact, it follows that we must strive to explain matters in the most complete way and to arrive at the truth.

29

Strange and Bizarre Problems

ACQUAINTANCE with the basic talmudic methods furthers our comprehension of an ostensibly odd phenomenon—the bizarre and outlandish issues sometimes debated therein. The problems that are clarified with great thoroughness and seriousness are largely of practical and prosaic interest, and in some cases their solution has practical implications. But the Talmud also relates to questions that are extremely unlikely to arise in everyday life and to some that may not be totally unrealistic but appear absurd because details of infinitesimal importance are discussed with a gravity out of all proportion to their significance.

Those cognizant of the Talmud's patterns of thinking are aware that hypothetical elucidation of an elemental problem can never be regarded as insignificant. Some questions may be insoluble within the talmudic text, but in seeking an answer the scholar presents a certain case, a model, with whose aid he tries to clarify the nature of the problem. There is yet another argument in favor of these discussions. Since the Talmud in general is not primarily concerned with practical application, almost all problems are granted equal weight. It is not the urgent need of a solution that counts, but the intrinsic interest of the issue. Thus the claim that a problem is unrealistic would bear little weight in rabbinical circles. We sometimes find constructions so dense and convoluted that it is almost impossible to envisage their implementation. But what of it? "It is Torah and therefore deserves to be studied."

The sages commented that several *halakhot* "never existed and never will" because of the numerous restrictions on practical implementation. "Why were they written? Study and you will be rewarded." This approach implies that even the Torah laws may be understood in such a way that the possibility of implementing them will be extremely remote. At the same time, there is no restriction on detailed examination of these laws and their implications not merely as an intellectual exercise but as true study, which is its own reward. For example, the Talmud contains an extremely complicated discussion of a mouse that brings bread crumbs into a house cleaned of *hametz* for Passover. The sages launch into an analysis of the mouse, the number of crumbs in the house before and after his entrance, the possibility that a rat might enter after the mouse, and other potential developments. This discourse on rodents takes up almost an entire page of the Talmud and is rich in interesting theories and basic evidence, all aimed at solving the problem of the crumbs deposited by the mouse. There is also an involved debate on childbirth relating to the question of birthrights, in the course of which the sages ponder the problem of the fetus transferred from one womb to another. Elsewhere the text takes up the mythical *golem* and asks whether such a being is entitled to participate in a *minyan*.

Many of these bizarre and imaginative issues are relevant even in the sphere of practical *halakhah* because the principles and rulings derived from the discussion are applicable elsewhere. Since the discourse on mice or on the *golem* is as thorough and precise as the analysis of more practical problems, the conclusions will always be applicable, in some degree, to other cases. The most prosaic problems could sometimes only be resolved in this way. The talmudic stand is reminiscent of pure theoretical research; there too the solutions to marginal or implausible problems are applied to practical issues. Talmudic scholars and students have long known that it is sometimes impossible to anticipate the outcome of a certain study, although it has shown no indications of pertaining to reality.

Other practical consequences of investigating these strange and remote questions are not always immediately evident. A certain question may appear absurd and meaningless in one era and become vitally important in a later age, when technology has made great strides. From this point of view, since the Talmud is open to every type and level of query, it is not surprising that many discussions that once appeared theoretical and unrealistic seem amazingly perceptive forecasts of now-current issues. One of the subjects of talmudic debate, the "tower floating in the air," was cited for centuries as an example of the degree to which the human imagination can run riot. The sages certainly never dreamed that mechanical methods of constructing flying towers and fortresses would someday be developed, nor were they particularly intrigued by the problem. But since one of their number happened to raise the question of what would happen if a tower should float in the air, they settled down enthusiastically to clarify all possible aspects of the problem. These visions no longer appear far-fetched and absurd, and in fact the discussion now helps us solve some very real problems.

Similarly, the talmudic scholars and codifiers devoted considerable attention to the question of the artificial insemination of women and the ensuing complications over the legal and moral status of mother and child. It took almost 2,000 years for this problem to take on practical significance, and many other discourses on subjects that still appear implausible may someday provide answers to important questions. The debate on the *golem*, for example, is only one of many references to the problem of defining the nature of man and his limitations, and some of the discussions touch on extremely bizarre questions. The Jerusalem Talmud, for example, analyzes the case of a man with the head of a beast and a beast with a human head and suggests—partly as an intellectual exercise—the complications that might ensue from this type of "split personality." This particular problem has not yet taken on topical relevance (except to a limited extent in *halakhah* relating to malformed births, which the Talmud discusses at length), but the possibility that it may someday be cited in relation to a modern issue cannot be discounted.

Nonetheless, the sages did not concern themselves with the pragmatic aspects of problems, since their objective was not the resolution of human questions but study for its own sake. They always employed models based on the world around them, even if such constructs seemed unreal in their day. One of the most frequent queries in the Talmud is *hikhi dami?* (how, exactly, can this state of affairs be depicted?). The question is posed when the sages wish to clarify a certain matter with greater precision and depth because the basic ruling is too generalized or too abstract and only the construction of a certain model can help them ascertain the truth. Such models often reveal that a ruling that appears simple and effective in the abstract is actually implausible or anomalous or calls for elaboration.

The advantages of employing models become even more apparent in the course of such elucidation. Even when the models are constructed through the combination of two methods (in accordance with the theory that differences of opinion should be reconciled as far as possible) or through the incessant attempt to solve abstract problems by citing concrete examples, the result, however cumbersome or strange, is more effective than any abstract analysis. Construction of a model makes it possible to examine all the components of the question and the interaction between various issues.

There is nothing surprising, therefore, in the weirdness of some of the more unrealistic explanations. Within the context of talmudic thought, they are vitally important and sometimes produce the most satisfactory solutions. The many practical consequences, some of them astoundingly relevant to posterity, should be regarded as the product of this unique way of thinking.

30

Methods of Study

THE TALMUD, as a many-faceted and diverse work and the main object of Jewish scholarship over the centuries, has been taught according to many different methods and adapted to new locales and different eras. The contrast between the North African-Sephardi exegetic method—with its tendency to contemplate issues as a whole—and the Franco-Ashkenazi method—which studied the Talmud in infinitesimal detail—is an expression of basic differences in ways and objectives of learning. The Sephardi system, to a large extent, focused on the question of *halakhah* and halakhic ruling. Concentration on halakhic conclusions called for a special approach to interpretation and association of the issues. Even when it was not aimed directly at finding practical legislative answers to problems, the Sephardi approach always concerned itself with examining the possible conclusions that might be derived from various opinions and methods. Accordingly, it never ignored the finer points of the debate but tried to find the common denominator, that is, the practical conclusion. After perusing each theory or opinion, those who study the Talmud according to this method will ask: "What conclusion should we draw from this conjecture?" The scholar in search of a solution to his specific problem will often apply discussions of other subjects to his own sphere of interest. The Spanish sages and those who followed in their footsteps often found practical implications or decisive conclusions in even the aggadic portions of the Talmud.

This method of halakhic study declined, to a large extent, after the Jewish expulsion from Spain in 1492. The codifiers were obliged to use it throughout the ages in order to organize their material, but this type of literature (in the important codifications or *responsa* works) is no longer widely studied. Many Ashkenazi sages preferred the Sephardi method and tried to introduce it into wider use among Ashkenazi Jewry. The most prominent of these were the renowned rabbi known as the Maharal of Prague, and his pupils, who wrote a number of works according to this method, which they considered conducive to direct and conclusive thought. Despite these scholarly efforts, the method never took root in Ashkenazi communities.

The Franco-Ashkenazi method was basically different. To a certain extent it should be regarded as the continuation of talmudic ways of thinking, the aim being to create, as it were, a Talmud on the Talmud. In other words, the Talmud itself became a basic text, and its sources and opinions were compared and analyzed by scholars who attempted to arrive at a high degree of compatibility and uniformity. The *baalei tosafot*, who are the classic exponents of this method, brought it close to perfection, and their disciples continued along the same path. In the last two centuries of the Middle Ages, this method was expanded and came to include the works of the classic commentators themselves. In the Middle Ages there already existed studies not only of the talmudic text but also of Rashi's commentary on it, the result of a systematic attempt to understand and interpret his methods.

The methods varied from academy to academy, and we find reference to the Augsburg or Nuremberg methods (named after the towns where they originated), which differed in the key ques-

Methods of Study

tions asked during study. All these methods were elaborated in the same general direction and eventually created what was known as the *hilukim* or *pilpul* (dialectical casuistric) method. The father of the *hilukim* method was R. Ya'akov Polak, who lived in Germany in the sixteenth century. Demanding great keenness of mind, this method attempts to create harmony between incongruent matters and to explain problems by employing relatively inflexible principles that are not always related to true comprehension of the talmudic text itself. An example of one of these methods is the approach to the problems of *makshan* (questioner) and *tartzan* (answerer). We often find two viewpoints in the Talmud, with one sage expressing his opinion, another attacking it and citing evidence in support of his own argument, and the first, the *tartzan*, then defending his original theory.

According to one of the *hilukim* methods, controversies were explained as follows: after the first query, the expounder declares, "You have not understood my method properly, since I was referring to something else. But you are wrong even on the basis of your *own* method and way of understanding." The questioner presses on: "I have understood your theory very well, and my query, despite what you claim, is closely related to the question. But even if I accept your view that I have not understood you properly, my query is still relevant according to your approach." And so on, ad infinitum, according to the number of queries and explanations in the Talmud. Clearly such a method calls for an exceptionally sharp mind. It should be noted, however, that the method was not wholly created in the Middle Ages but is to be found in the Talmud itself, where it is sometimes claimed that a certain sage did not understand the argument of his colleague properly and attacked him on an irrelevant point. Consistent development of this method, although it entails tremendous intellectual effort, is sometimes regarded as a pastime without vital theoretical importance.

The *hilukim* method found fertile ground for development, as it offered wide opportunities for a show of mental dexterity and in-

tellectual brilliance. It was frequently employed to uncover infinitesimal—almost imperceptible—differences between identical
methods or maxims and to establish complicated logical structures that were not always meant to be taken seriously. In later
centuries many anecdotes were told about this method. One
famous parody describes how a rabbi asked his disciple why the
letter *peh* (*p*) was needed in the word *korah*. When the disciple
replied that the letter did not appear in that word, the rabbi
persisted: "Let us assume for a moment that the letter is placed in
this word." "But why should it be needed there?" asked the
disciple, to which the rabbi replied: "That is exactly what I asked
you." The anecdote also shows us another aspect of the method,
namely, lack of attention to the talmudic text, since this theorizing
led to conclusions that did not stand up to examination of the
sources.

The *hilukim* method aroused the opposition of many scholars,
and the Maharal was only one of those who claimed that it encouraged spurious intellectual brilliance and that it would be
more profitable, for that purpose, to study chess than to distort
Torah. Other scholars also expressed their strong objection to *pilpul* methods when these ran riot. The great talmudic commentators, headed by the Maharsha, Rabbi Samuel Edels, rein-
troduced a more systematic method that included study of the
tosafot as a subject of perusal and comparison. But they emulated
the *baalei tosafot* themselves in their attempts to extract all that
could be drawn from the Talmud and to observe intellectual
moderation in drawing conclusions and settling problems. *Pilpul*
and *hiluk* were practiced until several decades ago, mainly in
Poland, where from time to time many of the great sages would
demonstrate their expertise in these methods, although they
usually regarded them as intellectual pastimes rather than as
serious methods of study.

In the sixteenth and seventeenth centuries many of the important scholars again took an interest in *halakhah;* although their
methods of talmudic study were not exclusively halakhic, their

Methods of Study

focus helped tone down pilpulistic tendencies and introduce more serious methods of analysis. The critical methods of the Maharshal and the Gaon of Vilna in the eighteenth century constituted a distinct school of thought, though it did not reach its maximal development. These scholars began to display interest in the nature of the texts they were perusing, and proved that it was often possible to unravel the most complicated problems not by seeking implausible pilpulistic solutions, but by finding better formulations. The Gaon of Vilna, who continued the work of the *baalei tosafot* in one sphere, succeeded in establishing finer distinctions between various strata and approaches in the Talmud itself. It is sometimes possible to understand certain subjects more clearly by abandoning the search for harmony and trying to analyze the issues per se according to the views of their original exponents. Although this method was never perfected, it constitutes the nucleus of most modern scholarship on the Talmud, which is mostly concerned with problems of editing and with the relations between the primary sources and the later commentators. It was not developed to its fullest extent, mainly because it was rejected in favor of more enticing approaches. Distinguished scholars leaned to the critical method, based on analysis of the texts themselves, particularly in basic discussions of elemental issues. Its use was furthered by the discovery and publication of various ancient manuscripts of the Talmud—such as the famous Munich manuscripts—and the publication and dissemination of the works of the first commentators, mainly the great Spanish scholars. The discovery of these commentaries pointed the way to fresh understanding of texts that had been interpreted according to specific methods until then, and also enriched critique of talmudic exegesis.

Both the Spanish and Ashkenazi communities attempted to understand the Talmud in the light of its own methods. Over the centuries a body of work has developed dealing with the "rules of the Talmud," meaning research into its methods of tackling various problems. Some of this literature is highly technical, and it was utilized both by the great commentators and the codifiers, but it can also serve as a means of analyzing the Talmud by its own methods and of classifying and defining these methods. Many of the greatest scholars both utilized talmudic methods and elaborated on them, although this system never became widely popular.

The inculcation of various methods of scholarship was encouraged by research into the halakhic works of Maimonides. Unlike most scholars before and after him, Maimonides did not cite the sources for his writings on the Talmud or the commentaries, although all his rulings were based on the Talmud. Thus his work itself soon became the subject of research, and scholars tried to determine his sources and his methods of selecting them. In every generation this study has been based on contemporary exegetic methods. At first the objective was to find the obvious sources, and some of the commentators did not attempt to defend Maimonides' viewpoint against the criticism of his contemporaries. Later scholars tried not only to decipher his statements but also to substantiate them. They were not content with discovering the origins of Maimonides' rulings, but also set themselves the aim of synchronizing the various talmudic sources, and even reconciling the anomalies. Development of these methods in an attempt to ascertain Maimonides' specific intentions has become an essential part of present-day talmudic scholarship.

In various centers, particularly Hungary, the method of *leshitato* was developed. It was an attempt to expound the teaching of the mishnaic and talmudic sages by compiling material of a single personality from various sources and using a certain degree of *pilpul* to link it together. This method is ancient, and the Talmud itself often engages in the same elemental clarifications to find the common denominator in the theories of a particular scholar on dissimilar issues.

The past century has witnessed the blossoming of the Lithuanian method, largely the fruit of the intellectual efforts of R. Yosef Dov of Brisk, whose many disciples carried on his method, sometimes to extremes. It is, to a large extent, a logical attempt to formulate more general abstract definitions of various talmudic problems by employing various legal distinctions (some cited in the Talmud) to explain different issues or reconcile conflicting statements. The technical means employed by this method include such basic definitions as the distinction between *haftza* and *gavra*, that is, between the obligations imposed on an object and on a man, or "two *dinim*," which is an attempt to distinguish between two theoretical components of a certain act or obligation, such as the negative and positive aspect. These scholastic methods were expanded in various academies, each of which introduced its own innovations and classifications. They resemble somewhat the investigative methods of theoretical law, but their application to the Talmud provided a great stimulus for students and enabled them to elucidate many concepts in totally new ways. They have gained great popularity in modern *yeshivot* but have also come in for their share of criticism for violating the discipline of reference to the Talmud's intrinsic methods and internal patterns of thought. Several of the greatest talmudic scholars of recent decades have chosen to utilize other methods, which are longer established and less speculative.

31

The Talmud and
the *Halakhah*

THE TALMUD, unlike the Mishnah, is not largely a work of
halakhah, although it is undoubtedly the most important and authoritative halakhic source ever composed. In the last analysis, all
halakhah rests on the Talmud, and in every case of doubt this
work is consulted. In other words, the primary source for the
body of Jewish law is not itself a legal work. In using the Talmud
as a guide to legal procedure, it is not sufficient to extract those
sections pertaining to practical matters; it is also essential to utilize several apparatuses developed by the *savoraim* and the *geonim*.
Methods of deriving *halakhah* from the Talmud are to a certain extent inherent in the Talmud itself, and the *geonim* merely expanded them, creating additional rules and methods. The greatest Jewish codifiers not only sought to create new laws or aspects
of *halakhah* but also continued to seek additional principles.

The Talmud contains an immense number of rulings on
various subjects and an even greater number of debates and con-

troversies. The Jerusalem Talmud clearly expresses the practical aspects of a legal ruling: "One should rely neither on the *mishnayot*, nor on the *tosafot*, nor on the *aggadot*, nor on the *midrashot*, but on practical *halakhah*." In other words, the sources within and outside the Talmud cannot serve as the basis for binding *halakhah*, since it is not enough to state that a fact has been conclusively determined on the basis of a certain source. Much more is needed—namely, knowledge of the place of the ruling within the entire legislative process. A statement may appear in a certain *mishnah* and later be revealed to conflict with another *mishnah*, or the general consensus may prefer a third *mishnah*. Therefore only a ruling that can be put into practice, where the scholar decides (or commits a deed) and explains that he is doing this on the basis of *halakhah*, has binding validity.

The Talmud does not often refer explicitly to binding rulings of this type, and it is not always possible to find unequivocal statements. But it was with this end in mind that the first of the *amoraim* began to evolve certain regulations for halakhic ruling regarding the Mishnah. They ruled, for example, on how to evaluate various forms of expression in the Mishnah itself. Several important sages supported the precept *"halakhah ki-stam mishnah,"* meaning that every anonymously recorded mishnaic ruling should be accepted as *halakhah*. This does not solve all problems, but it does make it easier to evolve basic approaches. Many auxiliary rules pertaining to the special relations between *stam* (anonymous *mishnah*) and controversy were added, and the sages also began to consider how to settle disputes between two *tannaim*.

In certain cases fixed rules were established: "When R. Yossi and R. Judah differ, the former's opinion prevails; when R. Meir and R. Judah differ, the latter's view is accepted," and so on. The same method was later adopted to decide controversies between the talmudic sages themselves. On several fundamental issues, more or less fixed norms were established, apparently by the *savoraim*. For example, when Rav and Samuel differ, the former's opinion prevails on questions pertaining to laws of ritual and the latter's in civil law. In controversies between Abbaye and Rava, the latter's ruling is accepted—with some exceptions. These regulations, however few in number, constitute the basis for significant ruling. Several other elemental rulings were established: for example, for a certain number of generations, the view of a pupil cannot overrule that of his teacher, but from a certain generation onward, the ruling is always according to the "later scholars," who are assumed to have had good reason for disputing the statements of their predecessors. The combination of all these rules created a wide-ranging code applicable to a considerable proportion of the disputes in the Talmud and enabling the scholar to deduce *halakhah* when the Talmud itself does not do so.

In addition to these simple principles, there were other rules based on stylistic considerations and on the fact that the Talmud pays meticulous attention to detail. In the event that a certain problem was not solved in the Talmud and the names of the disputing sages are unknown—precluding the application of rules—the principles established by the *geonim* or sages of the first generation may be put into operation. Every *teko* (problem without satisfactory solution) in the Talmud is classified as a doubtful case and is treated accordingly. If the doubt involves a Torah precept, the law takes a severe view; in a rabbinical case it is more lenient. It is generally strict in connection with laws of prohibition, but in civil law cases the onus of proof is on the claimant. On the basis of the Talmud's editorial methods, most codifiers agreed that if the Talmud offers two possible solutions to a certain problem, then the second is the binding *halakhah*. This guide therefore offers enlightenment even when, from the purely theoretical point of view, there is no room for differentiation between different solutions. There was also a question of what to do when talmudic sources conflicted. Here the rule was that halakhic priority should be accorded to the statement made in the *sugiya* actually pertaining to the specific subject.

Above and beyond all the detailed and largely mechanical

rules, there is one principle the Talmud itself regards as the most important test of the validity of a ruling, and that is the clarification of the overall talmudic conclusion on a certain problem. This is not always explicit in the text, and only study of the various *sugiyot* can reveal that the Talmud accepts certain assumptions as fundamental, while others, although never explicitly rejected, are not applied.

Simple mechanical methods cannot suffice to discern such subtle distinctions and must be combined with a high level of scholarship to deduce valid conclusions. Sometimes a source may appear to indicate a certain direction, while another leads to a conflicting conclusion. The great majority of the disputes between sages on halakhic ruling are expansions of such problems. It is sometimes possible to interpret a certain section in two ways or apply *halakhah* to several cases, and there are not always clearly defined ways of determining the truth. Halakhic literature throughout the centuries has concentrated on the attempt to find the binding *halakhah* when there are so many possible theories. Many controversies between codifiers originate in divergent approaches to the question of which *halakhot* are binding or how to interpret them.

One of the acute problems, for example, was that of establishing a clear order of priority not only within the Talmud but for other sources dealing with the same subject. The *geonim* raised the question of the degree to which it is possible to rely on the Jerusalem Talmud when it contradicts or complements the Babylonian Talmud. They usually decided that the latter enjoyed a twofold advantage both because of its later date and its more accurate and responsible editing. But one of the most common questions in *halakhah* is what to do in cases where the Babylonian Talmud failed to rule on a certain issue—because of some doubt—while the Jerusalem Talmud came to a decision. Many sages, including Maimonides, tended to accept the judgment of the Jerusalem Talmud in all such cases, but this view was not unanimous. Nor was there a consensus of opinion on the halakhic status and degree of importance of the *midrashim* on *halakhah* and *aggadah*. Throughout the ages these problems sparked off both halakhic and practical disputes.

In general, study and analysis of the Talmud and the view that it constitutes a comprehensive body of legal work from which deductions may be drawn are still the basic means of halakhic study. Through perusal of a certain *halakhah* and all attempts to solve problems that are not explicitly discussed in the law, compilations direct the scholar back to the source—the Talmud itself. Furthermore, conclusions may be drawn by employing the above-cited rules, comparing various sources, and continuing various ancient debates. For all these reasons, the Talmud—without itself being a book of *halakhah*—has served as the primary source.

32

Aggadah in the Talmud

ABOUT A QUARTER of the material in the Babylonian Talmud may be classified as belonging to the sphere of *aggadah*; in the Jerusalem Talmud the proportion is smaller but still considerable. Since it is extremely difficult to arrive at a satisfactory definition of *aggadah*, it is customary to start with the negative definition: all the material contained in the Talmud that is not *halakhah* or discussion of *halakhah* pertains to *aggadah*. One of the reasons it is difficult to define *aggadah* is that the aggadic material is not all of a piece; it consists of different frameworks divided into a number of categories.

One part of *aggadah* pertains to *misdrash* and is devoted to interpretation of those biblical verses from which practical halakhic conclusions cannot be derived. Another section is devoted to ethical and homiletic teachings on various subjects. The sages not only expressed views on matters of halakhic significance but also offered advice on conduct and ethics. The *Avot* tractate of the Mishnah is an example of a compilation of teachings of this type, but all tractates contain some material of this kind. Also included in talmudic *aggadah* are anecdotes about great men, and here we should differentiate between legends about biblical figures and their activities (sometimes accompanied by suitable verses as evidence) and longer ancedotes and stories about the mishnaic and talmudic sages. In addition there is aggadic material on theological and religious problems that cannot be included within the sphere of *halakhah*, such as the relations between man and God, or the coming of the Messiah. *Aggadah* also encompasses some of the popular legends of the age, proverbs, and folk sayings, and since the scholars devoted attention to almost every subject under the sun, it is a potpourri of travel tales, philological questions, commercial advice, medical hints, and history.

Although these diverse spheres cannot be covered by one precise term, the sages differentiated between *halakhah* and *aggadah;* their definitions, however, were to a large extent individual rather than categorical. Certain sages dedicated themselves almost exclusively to *halakhah* and were not greatly interested in *aggadah*, while others were known as *rabbanan de-aggadata* (*aggadah* sages) because of their preoccupation with the various types of *midrash aggadah*. The division was mostly a question of individual taste and condition. Most of the great scholars were erudite in both fields; Rav in Babylon and R. Yohanan in Palestine, Abbaye and Rava, Ravina and Rav Ashi studied both spheres, and their studies of *aggadah* were as extensive as their conclusions on *halakhah*. But there were sages who did not delve deeply into *aggadah* and regarded themselves as unqualified in this sphere. A certain sage who was asked to explain why the letter *tet* did not appear in the Ten Commandments on the first tablets replied: "Since you are asking me why the letter *tet* does not appear there, you should ask me whether it is a fact that this letter does not appear there. You had better ask some other scholar who is an expert on the subject." In fact, the aggadic scholars offer several explanations. But even those scholars who did not devote attention to *aggadah* or textual interpretation because they themselves did not feel equipped to deal with it—just as other sages felt that they were incapable of solving problems in the area of *halakhah*—regarded it as an important sphere.

There were, of course, scholars who engaged in the study of *aggadah*. One was Abahu of Caesarea, who defended one of his colleagues by stating: "I said that he was a great man as regards his knowledge of *halakhah;* but I did not mean to imply that he is erudite in *aggadah.*" When asked why he was so expert in textual interpretation, Abahu explained that since he was obliged to engage in debate with Christians and nonbelievers, he felt the need to study the subject more closely than his collegaues. It is related that he came to Caesarea with a colleague who delivered a profound sermon on the *halakhah*, while Rabbi Abahu spoke on the *aggadah*. Most of the audience chose to listen to R. Abahu, while only a few came to hear the halakhic address. In order to placate his comrade, R. Abahu offered the following parable: "If two merchants come to a town, one bringing gold bars and the other haberdashery, most of the customers will flock to the latter." In other words, *halakhah* is like heavy and precious gold bars, which not everyone is able to buy and appreciate, while *aggadah* is easily comprehensible and therefore more popular. In later times it was said that as a result of economic pressures and political anxieties, people preferred to listen to comforting *aggadah* rather than to devote close attention to complicated *halakhah*.

This does not mean that *aggadah* was held cheap. Both *halakhah* and *aggadah* were Torah, each reflecting a different aspect of the truth. In one of the sources the sages compare *halakhah* to meat and *aggadah* to wine, emphasizing the difference between the basic nutritious food and drink that raises the spirits. In fact, *aggadah* was often regarded as the path to spiritual elevation, and it was said: "If you wish to know the One who spoke and brought the world into being, engage in study of *aggadah*." *Aggadah* drew constant inspiration from esotericism, but unlike study of the Act of Creation and the Divine Chariot, which was confined to outstanding scholars, *aggadah* could be defined as popularization of esoteric teachings. We often find therein subjects and ideas whose development actually pertains to the esoteric. But since they were expounded allegorically or in simple fashion, they did not reveal mysteries and could also satisfy spiritual needs.

The sermons delivered by the sages in synagogues were usually composed of both halakhic and aggadic elements. Some sages followed the *tanna* R. Meir, whose regular sermon consisted of one-third *halakhah*, one-third *aggadah*, and one-third fables. The sermon sometimes began with aggadic teaching so as to attract the attention of the public, and continued with *halakhah;* sometimes a specific practical halakhic problem was discussed, and *aggadah*, legends, and various homiletic teachings introduced into it. Even on more formal occasions, when the rabbi expounded halakhic matters to the students of the academy, it was customary for him to commence with lighter material—even witticisms—and only when a light, relaxed atmosphere had been created were the more difficult halakhic questions tackled.

The rabbis were as serious in their attitude to *aggadah* as to any sphere pertaining to Torah. This does not mean that they were incapable of humor or lightheartedness, but even when they told humorous stories or related fables or sayings, they did not feel they were stepping outside the bounds of Torah. Even "the everyday conversations of scholars" were regarded as worthy of study, and in many cases the sages themselves demonstrated that conclusions—sometimes of great halakhic significance—could be deduced from the seemingly inconsequential conversations of great scholars. It was emphasized that jesting was forbidden (with the exception of jests at the expense of idolatrous worship, which were permitted and even desirable), but this did not prevent them from making humorous remarks on general subjects, sometimes as criticism of one another. It was stressed, however, that such humor should not smack of malice or profanity and that everyday conversation should not be licentious; even remarks that did not pertain to *halakhah* should be meaningful.

Thus levity is an indication of a positive attitude to life and to

the world as a whole and implies that there is nothing wholly negative in the world and no subject undeserving of attention. Even
unimportant issues are accorded attention, and rabbinical gravity
signifies that a subject is found worthy of discussion—it does not
indicate humorlessness. When a folk saying is quoted, the sages
often peruse it and find that it corresponds to something said in
the Bible or elsewhere, thus demonstrating that the people are
wise in their own way, no less than the learned scholars. When a
scholar is asked, "Why does every creature rule over mice?" he
does not dismiss the question lightly, although his answer may be
humorous. The sages ruled that the biblical injunction "Do not
answer the fool in his folly," which prohibits devoting attention
to foolish remarks, is valid only for questions of custom and manners, when it is best to keep silent. Where Torah is concerned,
however, it is thought desirable to answer the fool. Every question deserves an answer, even though the reply to a foolish question may be on the same level.

This even-handed attitude toward all things and phenomena,
which was adopted by the listeners as well, enabled the sages to
discuss whatever they chose even though their subject matter was
not always part of the general discussion. Rabbi Yohanan delivered a public address on how to prepare a remedy for scurvy, on
the assumption that any matter of public interest should be discussed in public. Seemingly allegorical remarks were sometimes
disguised as riddles or fables that were certain to be understood
by some of the audience on the simplest level. As long as the
teachers believed that their remarks could cause harm to no one,
they did not hesitate to deliver them in this guise. This is why we
find a considerable amount of aggadic material that can only be
understood metaphorically, although the moral is not always expounded, either because the sages were reluctant to enter esoteric
spheres or because they did not want to impart knowledge that
might prove harmful to the unlearned listener. It was almost certainly the picturesqueness of talmudic style that led the sages to
compose many tales in which the Almighty and his angels are

depicted as vivid and human figures. It is very likely that not all the members of an audience understood everything they heard, but they were able to enjoy the lessons or sermons, and the deeper content was reserved for great scholars.

Among the most renowned talmudic stories are the travel tales of Raba Bar Bar Hana, who relates the wonders of his journeys over seas and deserts. Most of them were justifiably understood as allegories on faith, political matters, or other spheres, as, for example, the following tale: "Once I saw a frog that was as large as the city tower. A crocodile came and swallowed the frog, a raven came and swallowed the crocodile. Then the raven perched itself on a tree. Ah, how great was the strength of that tree." Another sage writes of this tale: "If I had not been there, I would not have believed it." This story was rightly interpreted as an allegory on various kingdoms that succeeded one another in history, each devouring its predecessor. The Jewish people are symbolized by the tree, and the fact that the tree has never broken is regarded as a great wonder. The comment of the second sage can then be viewed in a different light—as the sadly ironic remark of a man contemplating the history of his people.

The *aggadah* holds many examples of an anachronistic approach to the heroes of the past. Biblical figures are often depicted in the image of Jewish sages of the mishnaic and talmudic eras. These descriptions were not intended as historical portraits but as attempts to clarify figures and phenomena by means comprehensible to the general public. Instead of trying to convey the audience to another historical era, the talmudic sages thought it preferable, from the educational point of view, to lend historical figures the dimensions of living persons, thus enabling the audience to identify with them, to understand their problems and emulate their examples. As in other cases, wider comprehension was thought to take precedence over historical accuracy.

The commentaries on *aggadah*, although they sometimes appear even more abstract than the *midrashei halakhah* in their interpretation of texts, are also confined to certain fixed frameworks. There are not only codified rules for interpretation, but clear tendencies to reveal the ethical and spiritual content of the texts. In some cases the mechanism of *midrash* does not even try to adhere to *peshat* (interpretation according to simple meaning), but at the same time it serves effectively as *asmakhta*, a mnemotechnic instrument. Those who listened to the *midrashim* were well acquainted with the Bible and could thus associate the texts they studied with ethical teachings, various abstract ideas, and so forth.

It is self-evident that the *midrashei aggadah* do not attempt to create halakhic ruling or unequivocally binding conclusions. When we recall that even in the sphere of *halakhah* the main objective is not the conclusion but study for its own sake, it is abundantly clear that the less-defined sphere of ethics and spiritual matters cannot always produce practical conclusions. This in no way implies that *aggadah* consists only of freewheeling sermons. Just as there are ways of drawing practical halakhic conclusions, the same is true of *aggadah* and *midrashei aggadah* in the Talmud. The various moral exhortations are not included in order to create an effective sermon but to instruct people on how to conduct their lives. The ethical teachings in the *Avot* tractate, for example, may vary in tone, but there is undoubtedly a high degree of consensus regarding principles of behavior. Although there were controversial issues, an attempt was always made, as in the sphere of *halakhah*, to reconcile differences in method, particularly since these were not great. The scholars differ, for example, over the quality of pride. Some held that a sage should posses "an iota" of pride, which would help him maintain his status as a leader of the community. Others stated firmly that he should possess "not one whit," since it was generally agreed that this attribute was to be condemned. These differences of opinion on practical ethics could be interpreted and discussed in depth (and this was indeed done by post-talmudic scholars), but the degree of accord on basic issues is evident. There are, of course, conflicting *midrashim* on various problems, from interpretation of the biblical text itself to weighty theological matters (for example, "Is messianic redemption part of, or extraneous to, nature?"); the attitude toward the subject, however, is always serious, attempts at persuasion are balanced and moderate, and some problems are accepted as insoluble.

After the period of the *amoraim* we find that the sages continued to engage in elucidation of *aggadah*, and most of the commentators also displayed considerable interest in these spheres. In later generations there were always some versatile scholars who dealt to the same extent with ethical and halakhic problems, while others tended to concentrate on the more exact aspects of *halakhah* or *aggadah*. But the greatest scholars always studied both spheres, regarding both as part of one whole—the Torah—which offered theoretical and practical guidance.

33

What Is a Scholar?

EVERY CULTURE has its elite—people who represent the ideal that others strive to emulate or attain. In Jewish culture it is undoubtedly the scholars—*talmidei hakhamim* (literally pupils of the wise)—who constitute this aristocracy. Every Jew dreams of realizing this ideal, and if he himself is incapable of it, he transfers his ambition to his sons. Scholars have always enjoyed preeminent status as favored aristocrats who enjoy advantage in every sphere. In most periods Jewish society was ruled by learned men, the leaders of each community being chosen from among its best scholars. Even when other elements of society wielded considerable influence, they were always to some extent under the sway of the scholars.

This was an aristocracy in the truest sense, "the best of the people." Scholars always encouraged others to study and thus to join their ranks, and they never constituted a hermetically sealed unit, since the only qualification for membership was scholastic ability. The sages never advocated exclusiveness, and throughout the centuries their ranks were swelled by the talented sons of unlearned fathers. Several sages noted sadly in the Talmud that "there are no scholars who have produced scholars," and they provided a metaphysical explanation: the people knew that "knowledge cannot be inherited," since the sons of scholars often had nothing to offer but their family background, while the sons of the unlearned poor could not be despised, "for knowledge emerges from them." Factually speaking, this does not mean that there were no distinguished families in which scholarship was handed down from father to son (such as the sons of patriarchs of the House of Hillel) or in which scholastic distinction was maintained for many generations (Rashi's family is the best example of this). Their status, however, was not the result of social advantage but of hereditary gifts. The same test of pure scholarship was applied to other families, even if they were socially inferior. Examples such as R. Akiva, who began to study at an advanced age and eventually reached the highest echelons of scholarship, were rare, but this was because any child who displayed talent for learning was encouraged by society and was not obliged to postpone his studies until adulthood. Most of the talmudic sages advanced through their own efforts and were not favored by family background. The quality of openness in this stratum was itself a powerful instrument that enabled the deserving to study and develop their talents. Every man was expected to be a scholar to the best of his ability, and all those who arrived at impressive achievements found their place among the upper stratum, which was therefore a true aristocracy.

How can one define a scholar? The first and most important criterion is that he be capable of studying and understanding the Torah, a condition that calls for the highest possible degree of intellectual ability. This, however, is only one facet of the fundamental outlook of the scholar. It is not enough for him to be erudite and perceptive; he must also be a noble human being endowed with spiritual and humanitarian qualities. One whose deeds are not compatible with his theories—either because his morals are not beyond reproach or because he does not strictly observe the precepts—cannot be regarded as a true scholar and is therefore worse than an ignoramus. The sages themselves said: "The deliberate errors of the unlearned are regarded as unintentional, while the unintentional mistakes of the scholars are regarded as deliberate." It is not enough for a scholar to preach; he must also practice what he preaches, and when there is incongruence between theory and practice, a man can no longer be considered a scholar. Furthermore, a learned man is expected to live in the light of his knowledge, so that everything he does or says will itself constitute Torah. It was said of the scholar who transgressed: "His Torah was but lip service," since true Torah must be reflected in personal behavior as in study. These were not merely abstract moral rules but very practical halakhic precepts. The codifiers also regarded them as such and determined that a man, however erudite, whose conduct was contemptible, could not be respected for his learning but should be condemned and despised. It is often related in the Talmud that learned people of dubious character were punished, chastised, or excommunicated.

Thus scholarship is not merely an intellectual standard but encompasses the entire personality, the man becoming the symbol of Torah, his whole essence synonymous with it. We can therefore understand the eagerness to study the deeds and conversations of scholars and to learn from them, given the assumption that anything done or said by the scholar can serve as a guide to others. There is no better description of the qualities of the scholar than the *baraita* that says:

> Torah is greater than priesthood or monarchy, since monarchy calls for thirty qualities and priesthood for twenty-four, while Torah demands forty-eight attributes: audible study, distinct pronunciation, understanding and discernment of the heart, awe, reverence, meekness, cheerfulness, ministering to the sages, attaching oneself to colleagues, discussion with disciples, sedateness, knowledge of the Bible and of Mishnah, moderation in business, moderation in intercourse with the world, moderation in pleasure, in sleep, in conversation, in laughter, by forbearance, by a good heart, by faith in the wise, by acceptance of chastisement, by recognizing one's place, by rejoicing in

one's portion, by putting a fence to one's words, by claiming no merit
for oneself, by being beloved, by loving the Almighty, by loving
mankind, by loving justice, rectitude and reproof, by avoiding honor,
by not boasting of one's learning, by not delighting in giving decisions, by bearing the yoke with others, by judging one's fellow fa-
vorably, by showing him the truth, by leading him to peace, by being
composed in one's study, by asking, answering, hearing and adding
thereto, by learning with the object of teaching, by learning with the
object of practicing, by making one's master wiser, fixing attention
upon his discourse, by quoting things in the name of their author.

This list clearly demonstrates that the scholar must be a well-
rounded personality.

When we understand the stringent demands made of the
scholar we can also comprehend the qualities attributed by
scholars themselves to those of their rank. The scholar is not only
a man who has studied but also the personification of Torah itself.
To honor him is to honor the Torah, and the scholar is instructed
to "fear his rabbi as he does his God," and even from the positive
point of view, the scholar deserves the same degree of respect and
love. It was said: "He who wishes to bring first fruits at this time
must make a gift to a scholar." However, many of the scholars objected to gifts for various reasons, and those who agreed to accept
them specified that they should be small symbolic presents.

This range of moral qualities demanded of the scholar in no
way detracted from the intellectual expectations that were the
basis of his erudition. A scholar should above all be well versed in
Torah, but here too there were clearly defined limits. A man with
expert knowledge of the Bible or even of the Bible and Mishnah is
not yet considered a scholar; in order to win that title he must
know the Talmud as well. Even the student who has a profound
knowledge of the sources does not become a true scholar until he
has "served scholars" and studied the various methods of learning, mainly based on study of Gemarah.

The Talmud itself recognizes the existence of various categories of scholars, classified by character and methods of study.
Some are erudite above all, others are extremely keen minded;

What Is a Scholar?

some are experts in *pilpul* or logical deduction, others excel in discussion but are incapable of arriving at practical conclusions; some are distinguished by their perceptive ruling but are weaker in other fields. But several basic qualifications are demanded of all scholars and their methods of study. A man with expert oral knowledge of the entire Talmud is undoubtedly in possession of an extremely important aid to learning, but this does not automatically classify him as a distinguished scholar. Nor are outstanding acumen and perception in raising questions always the distinguishing traits of scholars. The ideal combination of talents includes close acquaintance with a certain amount of basic material, since without such knowledge he is unable to tackle more profound problems and can only engage in empty speculation. On the other hand, the student of the Talmud must also be capable of analyzing all methods of study in order to arrive at full comprehension. In addition he must be endowed with the special ability to tackle talmudic problems and understand them in context. This unique talent is undoubtedly related to general intellectual powers but is not the same as mental dexterity. A man may be capable of understanding problems expounded to him by others but not of attaining a high standard of independent scholarship. The true scholar is able to identify with the talmudic sages and their methods and to immerse himself in their special world.

There is a point at which we differentiate between the man capable of average scholarship and the person who may develop into a great scholar. Any talented person can understand the text of the Talmud and, after investing a certain amount of effort—entailing quantitative as well as qualitative study—he may be capable of learning independently. But this is where the dividing line is drawn. The talent for studying Talmud resembles artistic ability in some ways: any man who has a predilection for the subject may become a passive savant, and if he is more proficient, may become creative, but greatness depends on a special skill, what in other spheres is called artistic genius. The higher echelons of talmudic scholarship are not reached by plodding effort alone; attainment depends on the quality of the man. There are always a few outstanding students capable not only of passive comprehension of the beauty of the Talmud's intellectual structure but of actual participation in its fashioning. The Talmud is unique in that no student can master it fully without taking an active part in the creative process. He must be responsive to questions and answers, be able to sense instinctively how a subject will develop, and be ready at any time to move the discussion in a certain direction.

A true scholar is therefore always part of the Talmud, himself creating through his study and his own innovations. There was good cause for the demand made of every scholar that he not only study but also introduce new interpretations, since in creating something new he increases his understanding of the source and becomes capable of continuing it. Not every scholar is capable of independent interpretation. The solitary scholar who makes his own discoveries will very often find that his views have already been recorded by the scholars of previous generations. But, unlike other spheres of knowledge, talmudic study does not insist that interpretations be original and innovative. To a certain extent every scholar tries to prove that his own revelations are not totally new but are implied in the remarks of his predecessors. There is no greater glory for a scholar than to find that the thought he has developed independently has already been formulated by others before him, since this constitutes sound proof that his methods of study have not exceeded the bounds of true knowledge and are a continuation of talmudic thought itself. The talmudic saying that "Everything that the distinguished scholar creates anew has already been said to Moses on Sinai" was not aimed at discouraging the scholar but rather at stressing that all true innovations are inherent in the Torah itself and merely need to be uncovered. Here too the analogy of Torah study with scientific methods is valid. The man who studies the nature of the material world feels that he is not seeking new facts, but rather unveiling existing reality. This is also true of the talmudic scholar who strives to uncover, develop, and emphasize aspects already present in the Talmud. The predilection of the great scholars throughout the centuries for seeking similarities between their theories and those of other scholars is expressed in the saying: "Blessed is He that I have expressed the same view as the great scholars." Innovation and substantiation are therefore complementary rather than conflicting, and each scholar tries, in his own way, to arrive at "Torah from Sinai."

34

The Talmud's Importance for the People

HISTORICALLY SPEAKING, the Talmud is the central pillar of Jewish culture. This culture is many faceted, but each of its numerous aspects is connected in some way with the Talmud. This is true not only of the literature that deals directly with the interpretation or continuation of the Talmud, but also of all other types of Jewish creativity. Halakhic literature is, of course, based entirely on the Talmud, but most original Jewish philosophy has also drawn inspiration from it in one way or another. It is impossible to approach biblical exegesis or Jewish or esoteric philosophy without knowledge of the Talmud. Even works that have no ostensible connection with talmudic literature—like poetry or prayers—are inspired by it in various ways. The student who claims to understand the significance and intention of material will realize, after close perusal of this literature, how barren are the attempts to absorb Jewish knowledge while ignoring its basic sources.

Jewish culture was created throughout the centuries by

The Talmud's Importance for the People

scholars who were unable to step outside the talmudic sphere of influence. Most of them had no desire to do so. Even when they wrote seemingly independent works, their ideas, principles, and methods of expression were indebted to talmudic literature. A medieval scholar once stated: "When I studied Maimonides' halakhic work, it seemed to me that I was understanding it all equally. But I looked at it and saw that I had truly understood only those sections where I could apply my basic knowledge of Talmud, while elsewhere I had understood nothing." This fact, which is most evident in halakhic literature, can likewise be applied to other types of Jewish literature, where those who are not versed in the basic background material are unaware of the limitations on their understanding of the text.

The Talmud is not merely important on an intellectual and literary plane; it also has far-reaching socio-historical implications. It is reasonably certain that no Jewish community could survive for long without the ability to study Talmud. Some communities did not produce scholars from their midst because of material poverty, lack of suitable candidates (as the result of the decrees of the authorities), or indifference. Whatever the reason, however, the fact is they did not survive for long. In the course of Jewish history, various ethnic communities have tried to maintain their Judaism, sometimes even on a strictly traditional basis, without talmudic scholarship. The same process occurred in all of them; the components of their Judaism were weakened and began to disintegrate, the deeper significance of issues was no longer fully understood, and inappropriate interpretations were evolved, so that despite sincere efforts to maintain traditions, such communities lost their vitality and died out. Sometimes the process was protracted, with tradition gradually becoming more and more a matter of outward show for lack of sages capable of endowing it with new life, and assimilation inevitably followed. Sometimes the catastrophe came swiftly; strong external pressures were exerted on the Jews, and many were unable to withstand them and abandoned their Judaism.

The power of the Talmud derives from two elements. The first, already noted, is the fact that it constitutes the backbone of diverse Jewish knowledge, and, when it is removed—whether by malicious intent or by force of events—the other components are only mechanically linked to one another and gradual disintegration occurs, each individual choosing to retain only those aspects that appeal to him. The other facet of the Talmud's significance is related to the singular methods of study. As we have already noted, study of the Talmud cannot be confined to mere mechanical memorization and entails constant renewal and innovation, requiring the active participation and emotional and intellectual involvement of the students. A man may observe all the laws of the *halakhah* mechanically, by rote, without detrimental effect on the observance of the *mitzvot;* he may study many other spheres of Judaism in completely passive fashion. But this passive study transfers the center of gravity of experience to other spheres and makes it possible to offer any desired interpretation. A man may study the Bible or Kabbalah intensively, wittingly or unwittingly inserting concepts relevant to his own time and place. But after a time it will become apparent that although the external appearance has been maintained the inner content has changed beyond recognition. This is not true of the Talmud. Although it appears to demand immeasurably less inner faith or reverence, it calls for a much higher degree of active participation. There is no real possibility of studying the Talmud in externalized and alienated fashion, since the sincere student becomes part of the essence of the Talmud, and thus an active participant in Jewish creative life.

In certain generations the sages warned against excessive study of the Bible in itself, just as they warned against the study of philosophy (even Jewish philosophy) or feared unsupervised study of Kabbalah. In all these spheres they insisted that before a student plumbed their depths, "he [should] fill his belly with Talmud and codifiers." This basic grounding enables him to study other areas later without being lured aside by various partialities or deviant

[268]

views. And since the Talmud is of such fundamental importance for the Jewish people, extensively studied by every Jewish scholar, it is evident that not only was it created by the Jewish people, but later, in turn, molded the people.

There is no effective way of pinpointing the Talmud's influence on the Jewish people and separating it from other influences, but it is possible to point to several basic facts. Talmudic scholarship is to a certain extent self-contradictory, a type of "sacred intellectualism." It places unparallelled emphasis on the theoretical, analytical, and critical aspects of human thought. No individual can study Talmud without being or becoming an eternal skeptic; the form of study itself is based on series of questions, and the student himself is expected to submit his own questions and voice his own doubts and problems. At the same time, talmudic study is not regarded merely as a secular exercise in developing the mind or abstract capacity for thought, but as a subject of intrinsic sanctity. The questioning, searching, and skeptical man is not excluded from the circle of believers; he becomes, rather, the spokesman of the central work of the Jewish religion, the prime source for *halakhah* and daily conduct. This very process creates the unique blend of profound faith and questioning skepticism that has characterized the Jewish people throughout the ages. Incessant self-criticism, together with the constant awareness that beyond it lies a reality to which one must adhere, is a central theme of Jewish existence. An interesting anecdote relates that as the result of a series of personal catastrophes a certain scholar felt his faith weakening and asked the guidance of one of the great scholars of the age. The sage posed a difficult question from the *tosafot* and the man answered correctly. The sage then posed another problem, and again the man provided the solution. They continued in this fashion for some time until the sage said: "You see, despite the problems they raise, the *tosafot* are truth, and the Holy One, Blessed be He, is also truth, despite all our queries and problems." Such a conclusion is more than mere casuistry, since it reflects the humanitarian education the Talmud extends to those who study it—a blend of the ability and right to question with the ability to create harmony and accord between different elements.

Thus talmudic study has guided its students—all Jews who showed any talent for study—in the search for truth, into paths of thought that refuse to be hampered by any obstacle, into the incessant attempt to find better methods of solving existing problems. The search for truth is undoubtedly reflected not only in the Talmud itself but in all the spheres of life with which its students dealt.

This attitude also explains the untiring search for the alternate dimension of things. The refusal to remain content with simplistic solutions generates the desire to see matters in a different light. The talmudic phrases *ve-dilma ipkha?* (and perhaps the opposite is true) and *ipkha mistbra* (the opposite holds) also influence the general approach. The critical sense is later levelled at social, scientific, and economic problems and sometimes creates the spark of genius that can reveal the "other possibility," the opposite of the existing order.

The Talmud is also a powerful weapon for disseminating levelheadedness. The Jewish spiritual world was always exposed to a high degree of social, economic, and intellectual tension, and such pressures inevitably encourage extremism—from concentration on the material aspects of life to the attempt to escape into a sphere of mysticism remote from the everyday world. The Talmud constituted a stabilizing factor, the voice of sanity in a discordant and disunified world. Its objects, the models according to which it operates, are always borrowed from this world, and points of consideration are always real and never take flight from the prosaic and mundane sphere. At the same time, however, they never exist solely within pragmatic reality, and in the background we always sense the great mystery of the Torah and the urge to act and think in ways that are unrelated to daily experience and common sense. This combination saved the Jewish people and the Jewish individual from the twofold danger of materialism on the one hand and alienated mysticism on the other. This force of restraint was not because the Talmud is the happy medium between the two, but because it is, to a certain extent, their synthesis, combining both elements in unique fashion.

35

The Talmud Has Never Been Completed

FROM the strictly historical point of view, the Talmud was never completed, never officially declared finished, without need for additional material. The Bible, by comparison, underwent various stages of compilation and redaction, but was eventually completed, and it was categorically stated that no additions could be introduced. The same was true of the Mishnah in its day. But although a certain edition of the Talmud was regarded as definitive, this fact was not heralded by an official and public declaration that the work had reached its end and a new era had commenced.

The final edition of the Talmud may be compared to the stages of maturity of a living organism; like a tree, it has reached a certain form that is not likely to change substantially, although it continues to live, grow, and proliferate. Although the organism has taken on this final form, it still produces new shoots that draw

The Talmud Has Never Been Completed

sustenance from the roots and continue to grow. This fact is more important to our approach to the Talmud than it is to history. The principle that the Talmud is unfinished holds out a constant challenge to continue the work of creation. It is incumbent on every scholar to add to the Talmud and to contribute to the work, although it can never be finally completed.

The Talmud was edited by R. Ashi, yet it is not his work; rather, it is the collective endeavor of the entire Jewish people. Just as it has no one protagonist, no central figure who sums up all the discussions and subjects, so it has continued throughout the centuries to be part of a constant creative process. One of the great talmudic commentators, the Maharsha, often ended his commentaries with the word *vedok* (continue to examine the matter). This exhortation is an explicit admission that the subject has not been exhausted and that there is still room for additions and arguments on the question. To a certain extent the whole Talmud is rounded off by this *vedok*, the injunction to continue the search, to ask, to seek new aspects of familiar problems.

In a way this trait is also the source of the difficulties entailed in study, which can never be entirely passive. But it is also the source of the Talmud's great fascination and ability to captivate the student and make him an integral part of it. It demands of the student, above all, a sense of inner resonance, the ability to identify, yet it does not insist on ardent faith. There are very few sacred works that do not demand of the student prior acceptance of certain principles. The talmudic scholar, however, is not forced to accept everything he encounters, and if he chooses to ask or appeal, he is permitted—and in fact obliged—to do so.

On the other hand, no other work demands such quantitative erudition on the part of the student. The sages assume that the student is already extremely knowledgeable, for they quote extensively from other sources without taking into consideration the fact that the student may not yet be acquainted with them. It has already been said that the Talmud is not a schematic textbook, but essentially a slice of life. As such, it commences for no man at

[273]

the beginning. When a man begins to study Talmud, he always finds himself right in the middle of things, no matter where he starts. Only through study and the combination of facts can he arrive at the ability to understand, and, in general, the more he studies the better he understands what he has already studied; his comprehension grows constantly deeper as he peruses the material over and over again. A pair of scholars who studied a certain complicated tractate a generation ago perused it forty times and stated that only the forty-first time did they feel that they were beginning to understand it. This conviction is not a reflection of excessive humility, nor is it related to the complexity of the issue, but is based on the belief that every time a subject is studied it takes on new dimensions for the student. After the first few perusals of the material, the student will have solved most of the central problems, but new problems will always emerge. Generally speaking, talmudic study is not restricted to one aspect of a subject, nor is it a closed circle; rather, it should be seen as a spiral that continues to rise and develop from time to time. Each time the same point is passed and a slightly higher point is reached.

During the two millennia of the Talmud's existence, many thousands of sages have occupied themselves with talmudic literature, and the finest intellectual forces of the Jewish people have dedicated their lives with great perseverance to talmudic scholarship. It is not surprising therefore that the student sometimes feels that he can add nothing new, since every subject, every issue, every sentence has been pored over by great scholars and sages and discussed from every possible viewpoint. Nevertheless, the Talmud has not yet been completed. Every day, every hour, scholars find new subjects of study and new points of view. Not every student is capable of constructing his own systems, but the individual, from his own peculiar and personal point of view, is still capable of seeing some detail, however small, in a new light.

The Talmud Has Never Been Completed

The work that is a compilation of the endeavors of many generations, is edited with excessive precision, and has been studied by tens of thousands of scholars still remains a challenge. Of the verse "I have seen an end of every purpose," the sages said: "Everything has its boundaries, even Heaven and earth have their boundaries. Only Torah has no bounds."

Appendix

APPENDIX

Orders and Tractates of the Mishnah and Talmud

	MISHNAH CHAPTERS	BABY-LONIAN TALMUD PAGES	JERU-SALEM TALMUD PAGES	CONTENT
ZERAIM ORDER				
Berakhot	9	64	68	Prayers, benedictions
Pe'ah	8		37	Laws of gleanings and charity
Demai	7		34	Doubtfully tithed produce
Kilayim	9		44	Various kinds of seeds, trees, and animals
Shevi'it	10		31	Laws of the sabbatical year
Terumot	11		59	Contributions to the priests
Ma'aserot	5		26	Tithes for the Levites and the poor
Ma'aser Sheni	5		33	The second tithe and bringing it to Jerusalem
Halah	4		28	The dough offering to the priests
Orlah	3		20	Prohibition against harvesting trees for four years
Bikurin	3		13	Offering of the first fruits at the Temple
MOED ORDER				
Sabbath	24	157	92	Sabbath laws
Iruvin	10	105	65	The laws of permissible limits on the Sabbath
Pesahim	10	121	71	Laws of *hametz* and *matzah* and the paschal sacrifice
Shekalim	8		33	The shekel dues for the Temple and Temple ceremonies

Appendix

	MISHNAH CHAPTERS	BABY-LONIAN TALMUD PAGES	JERU-SALEM TALMUD PAGES	CONTENT
Yoma	8	88	42	Sacrifices and the fast on Yom Kippur
Sukkah	5	56	26	The building of a *sukkah*, the four species, and the festival in the Temple
Betza	5	40	22	General festival laws
Rosh Hashanah	4	35	22	Fixing the months and years, blowing the *shofar*, and the Rosh Hashanah prayers
Taanit	4	31	26	The regular fast days
Megillah	4	32	34	Laws of Purim
Moed Katan	3	29	19	Laws of the intermediate festival days
Hagigah	3	27	22	*Halakhot* for pilgrimage festivals

NASHIM ORDER

	MISHNAH CHAPTERS	BABY-LONIAN TALMUD PAGES	JERU-SALEM TALMUD PAGES	CONTENT
Yebamot	16	122	85	Levirate marriage, prohibitions on marriage, testimony on the death of the husband
Ketubot	13	112	72	The marriage contract and special agreements
Nedarim	11	91	40	Various types of vows
Nazir	9	66	47	The *nazirite* laws
Sotah	9	49	47	Laws concerning an adulteress, murder in which the perpetrator is unknown, and war

Appendix

	MISHNAH CHAPTERS	BABY-LONIAN TALMUD PAGES	JERU-SALEM TALMUD PAGES	CONTENT
Gittin	9	90	54	Divorce, writing and sending the *get*
Kiddushin	4	82	48	The marriage act, laws of genealogy

NEZIKIN ORDER

Baba Kama	10	119	44	Direct and indirect damages
Baba Metzia	10	119	37	Losses, loans, work, and wage contracts
Baba Batra	10	176	34	Partnership, sales, promissory notes, and inheritance
Sanhedrin	11	113	57	Various types of courts, criminal law, principles of faith
Makot	3	24	9	Punishment by flagellation
Shevuot	8	49	44	Oaths
Eduyot	8			A collection of testimonies on various subjects
Avodah Zarah	5	76	37	Keeping one's distance from idolatry and idolators
Avot	5			Ethics and *derekh eretz*
Horayot	3	14	19	Erroneous rulings of the courts and their rectification

KODASHIM ORDER

Zevahim	14	120		Laws of sacrifice
Menahot	13	110		Meal offerings, *tzit-zit, tefilin*
Hulin	12	142		Laws of ritual slaughter and dietary laws

Appendix

	MISHNAH CHAPTERS	BABY-LONIAN TALMUD PAGES	JERU-SALEM TALMUD PAGES	CONTENT
Bekhorot	9	61		The first-born child and animal, defective animals
Arakhin	9	34		Valuation of Temple offerings and soil
Temurah	7	34		Substituting an animal offering
Keritot	6	28		Sins requiring extirpation and sacrifices for them
Me'ilah	6	22		Sins of sacrilege against Temple property and atonement for them
Tamid	6	8		Daily sacrifices in the Temple
Midot	5			Measurements of the Temple
Kinim	3			What to do when various sacrifices have been mixed

TOHAROT ORDER

	MISHNAH CHAPTERS	BABY-LONIAN TALMUD PAGES	JERU-SALEM TALMUD PAGES	CONTENT
Kelim	30			Various types of utensils and their sensitivity to pollution
Oholot	18			Laws of the uncleanliness of the dead
Negaim	14			Laws regarding leprosy
Parah	12			Preparation of the ashes of the red heifer and purification after contact with the dead
Tohorot	10			Various laws of purification

Appendix

	MISHNAH CHAPTERS	BABY-LONIAN TALMUD PAGES	JERU-SALEM TALMUD PAGES	CONTENT
Mikvaot	10			Laws of the *mikvaot* for purification
Nidah	10	73	13	Ritual impurity of the woman
Makhshirin	6			Ways in which foods become ritually unclean
Zavim	5			Gonorrhea and purification from it
Tevul Yom	4			Discussion of various kinds of ritual uncleanliness
Yadaim	4			Ritual uncleanliness of the hands
Uktzkin	3			Categorization of things that are susceptible to ritual uncleanliness

INDEX

Index

Index

Index

Index

Index

Index

Midrash aggadah (aggadic exegesis), 54, 55, 222, 252, 256–258
Midrash halakhah (halakhic exegesis), 15, 41, 221–229
Mikveh (water for purification purposes), 195–196
Milk, dietary laws on mixing meat and, 189
Minim (heretics), 24
Minyan (quorum of ten), 103, 137
Mishnah, 4, 31–39, 81, 200; compilation and codification of, 33–40; interpreters and translators of, *see* Amoraim; orders of, *see* Orders; tractates of, *see* Tractates
Mishnah (plural: *mishnayot*), 37, 92, 93; Babylonian academies' method of studying, 59–62
Mishnat hassidim, 200–201
Mitnagdim, 78
Mnemonic aids, biblical texts used as, 33–34
Models, talmudic use of, 228–229, 237
Moed (Holidays) order, 90, 116, 279–280
Moed Katan tractate, 62, 120
Monetary law *(dinei memonot)*, 145–147. *See also* Civil law
Moral responsibility, 201
Moriah, Mount, 181
Moshe Ben Nahman, R. (Ramban), 67, 82
Moslem Empire, 65–66
Murder, 172–173
Musaf prayer, 175, 177
Mutzeh (excluded or out of bounds) objects, 112
Mysticism, 211–218. *See also* Esotericism

Nahman, R., 44, 143
Nahman Bar Isaac, R., 46
Nahmani Ben Kaylil (Abbaye), 45, 248, 252

Names of God, 213–214
Nashim order, 136, 280–281
Nasi (president of Sanhedrin), 22, 48–49. *See also* Zugot
Nedarim (Vows) tractate, 90
Nehemiah, R., 41
Nehutei (those who go down), 52
Netherlands, the, 77
New Year (Rosh Hashanah), 119–121
Nezikin (Damages) order, 90–91, 281
Nezikin tractate, 90, 146–147
Nidah tractate, 91, 93, 193, 198
Ninth of Av, 128
Nissan, month of, 120, 121
Nissim Gaon, R., 67
North African Jewry, 66–67
Notes, civil law of, 160–161
Numbers and Deuteronomy *(Sifrei)*, 31

Oaths, laws pertaining to, 153–154
Oneg Shabbat (Sabbath delight), 112–113
Oness (coercion), 152, 178
Oral law or tradition *(Torah she-be-al-peh)*: basic tasks of, 11–13; era of *zugot* (pairs) and, 18–23; Great Assembly era and, 14–17; origins and early development of, 10–17; Sadducees and, 21. *See also* Mishnah; Talmud
Orders *(sedarim)* of Mishnah, 36–37, 89–94, 279–283
Ordination *(semikhah)*, 164
Oshaya, R., 40
Ownership (possession), civil law on, 150–151, 154–156

Pairs *(zugot)*, era of, 18–23
Palestine (Palestinian Jews), 19, 20, 66, 126–127; *amoraim* in, 48–55; decline of, as center of learning, 42; fixing of festival dates in, 117–119

Index

Index

Index

Index

Index